Linux DevOps Tools Engineer (701) Practice Tests: 400 Questions to Ace Your Certification

Q1: You are a DevOps engineer at a mid-sized software company. Your team uses Vagrant to spin up development environments for testing a new application. Recently, developers reported issues accessing the Vagrant virtual machines from their local systems. You need to ensure that everyone on the team can SSH into the Vagrant VMs using a shared public key. You've decided to implement a solution that involves modifying the Vagrantfile. What is the most efficient way to update the Vagrantfile to ensure all developers can access the VMs using SSH?

A) Add a configuration to copy each developer's public key into the Vagrant VM's ~/.ssh/authorizedkeys file.

B) Use a shell provisioner in the Vagrantfile to install and configure an SSH server on the VM.

C) Configure Vagrant to use a shared, global insecure key and distribute this key to all developers.

D) Modify the Vagrantfile to create user-specific SSH keys for each developer.

E) Use Vagrant's vagrant ssh-config command to generate SSH configurations for each developer.

F) Implement network port forwarding in the Vagrantfile to expose SSH on a different port.

Answer: C

Explanation: The best approach is to configure Vagrant to use a shared, global insecure key. By default, Vagrant uses a standard insecure key pair to access VMs. Distributing this global insecure private key to all developers allows them to SSH into any Vagrant VM without needing individual keys. While adding each developer's public key to authorizedkeys could work, it requires manual updates and is prone to error. Creating user-specific keys or configuring individual SSH servers adds unnecessary complexity. Using the global insecure key is efficient and leverages Vagrant's default behavior, simplifying access management.

Q2: To enable port forwarding for a Vagrant virtual machine, what configuration should be added to the Vagrantfile to forward the guest machine's port 80 to the host machine's port 8080?

A) config.vm.network "forwardedport", guest: 8080, host: 80

B) config.vm.network "forwardedport", guest: 80, host: 8080

C) config.vm.network "publicnetwork", guest: 80, host: 8080

D) config.vm.network "forwardedport", guest: 80, host: 80

E) config.vm.network "privatenetwork", type: "dhcp"

F) config.vm.network "forwardedport", guest: 8080, host: 8080

Answer: B

Explanation: In Vagrant, to forward a port from the guest machine to the host machine, you use the forwardedport configuration. The syntax requires specifying the guest port first, followed by the host port. Therefore, to forward the guest's port 80 to the host's port 8080, you use the configuration config.vm.network "forwardedport", guest: 80, host: 8080. This configuration tells Vagrant to listen on the host's port 8080 and forward any traffic to the guest's port 80, allowing access to services like a web server running on the VM.

Q3: A DevOps engineer needs to access a Vagrant virtual machine using the SSH protocol. Which command will establish an SSH connection to the running Vagrant VM using the default settings?

A) ssh vagrant@127.0.0.1

B) vagrant ssh

C) ssh root@localhost

D) vagrant connect ssh

E) ssh vagrant@vagrant.local

F) ssh user@192.168.33.10

Answer: B

Explanation: The vagrant ssh command is specifically designed to SSH into a running Vagrant VM using the default settings specified in the Vagrantfile. This command abstracts away the need to know the specific IP address or private key details, as Vagrant manages these internally. The other options require manual specification of the user, IP, or key, which Vagrant handles automatically when using vagrant ssh. This command simplifies access and is the standard method for accessing Vagrant-managed VMs.

Q4: True or False: You can configure Vagrant to use a custom SSH key pair instead of the default insecure key pair.
A) True

B) False

Answer: A

Explanation: It is indeed possible to configure Vagrant to use a custom SSH key pair instead of the default insecure key pair. This is done by specifying the config.ssh.privatekeypath in the Vagrantfile to point to the location of the custom private key on the host machine. This customization allows for enhanced security by using a key pair unique to your environment, which is particularly useful in production or sensitive environments where the default insecure key might pose a security risk. By default, Vagrant uses a global insecure key, but this behavior can be overridden with custom configurations.

Q5: Fill in the gap: To customize the username used for SSH connections in a Vagrantfile, you should use the configuration option config.ssh.. (multiple correct answers)
A) host

B) user

C) username

D) username

E) sshuser

F) login

Answer: C, D

Explanation: The correct configuration option to customize the SSH username in a Vagrantfile is config.ssh.username. This setting allows you to specify the username that Vagrant will use when establishing SSH connections to the VM. By default, Vagrant uses the username 'vagrant', but this can be changed to a different user if your VM configuration requires it. This flexibility is crucial for scenarios where the default user setup does not align with custom VM configurations or security policies.

Q6: In a mid-sized e-commerce company, the DevOps team is tasked with deploying a scalable web application using containers. They have decided to use Ansible to manage containerized services across their environments. The team is particularly interested in using Ansible Container to build, deploy, and orchestrate their application. The company has strict guidelines requiring that all configuration management tools should directly support integration with their existing continuous integration/continuous deployment (CI/CD) pipelines. Considering these requirements, which command would the DevOps team use to initialize a new Ansible Container project that aligns with their CI/CD integration needs?

A) ansible-container init --ci

B) ansible-container new-project

C) ansible-container create

D) ansible-container init

E) ansible-container start-new

F) ansible-container bootstrap

Answer: D

Explanation: The ansible-container init command is used to initialize a new Ansible Container project. This command sets up the necessary directory structure and default configuration files required for managing containers with Ansible. It supports integration with CI/CD pipelines by providing a structured approach to container orchestration and deployment. The other options do not initiate an Ansible Container project in the same way. The command is designed to be the first step in setting up a containerized environment using Ansible, making it the correct choice for teams looking to integrate container management with their CI/CD processes.

Q7: True or False: Ansible Container natively supports the orchestration of multi-container applications using Docker Compose files.
A) True

B) False

Answer: B

Explanation: Ansible Container does not natively orchestrate multi-container applications using Docker Compose files. Instead, it uses its own configuration format, defined in an ansible-container.yml file, to describe the services, their dependencies, and the orchestration logic. This format is designed to integrate with Ansible's playbook and role structures, providing a more flexible and powerful way to manage containerized services. Docker Compose is a separate tool with its own syntax and capabilities, and while there may be some overlap in functionality, Ansible Container is not directly compatible with Docker Compose files out of the box.

Q8: When managing a multi-container environment with Ansible Container, which tool or command should be used to build the defined container images from an ansible-container.yml file?
A) ansible-container build

B) ansible-playbook build

C) docker build

D) ansible-container images

E) ansible-container run

F) ansible-container compile

Answer: A

Explanation: The ansible-container build command is used to build container images as defined in the ansible-container.yml file. This command processes the configuration specified in the file, executing the build steps for each service defined therein. It leverages Ansible's playbooks to automate the building process, ensuring that all images are built according to the specified configurations and dependencies. The other options either do not relate to the building process or are incorrect commands within the context of Ansible Container.

Q9: In a scenario where you need to push built container images to a remote Docker registry from your Ansible Container project, which Ansible command would you use to achieve this task?

A) ansible-container push

B) ansible-container deploy

C) ansible-container publish

D) ansible-container register

E) ansible-container release

F) ansible-container upload

Answer: A

Explanation: The ansible-container push command is used to push built container images to a remote Docker registry. This command is part of the Ansible Container suite, allowing developers to distribute their container images to a wider audience or deploy them to production environments. The process involves tagging the images appropriately and then using Docker's push capabilities to upload them to the specified registry. The other options are either non-existent within the Ansible Container context or do not pertain to pushing images to a registry.

Q10: You are tasked with ensuring that your Ansible Container project is correctly set up to run in a production environment. Which command would you use to verify that all the defined services in your ansible-container.yml file can be successfully started without errors?

A) ansible-container validate

B) ansible-container run

C) ansible-container test

D) ansible-container start

E) ansible-container verify

F) ansible-container deploy

Answer: B

Explanation: The ansible-container run command is used to start all services defined in the ansible-container.yml file. This command is critical for verifying that the containerized services can be initiated without errors, which is an important step before deploying to production. Running the services locally helps identify configuration issues, dependency problems, or other potential errors that might occur in the production environment. While other options may sound relevant, they either do not exist or are not applicable for this specific verification task in the Ansible Container context.

Q11: A medium-sized enterprise runs a diverse IT infrastructure with Windows servers and macOS workstations alongside their Linux environment. They are considering using Ansible to manage configurations across all these platforms. The IT manager is particularly interested in using Ansible's features to automate tasks like software installation and configuration management on non-Linux systems. Given this context, which feature of Ansible would be most beneficial for managing Windows systems?   ---

A) Ansible Tower

B) Playbooks

C) Windows Subsystem for Linux (WSL)

D) PowerShell execution via WinRM

E) Ansible Galaxy

F) Ansible Modules

Answer: D

Explanation: Ansible is a powerful automation tool primarily used for configuration management and application deployment. Its capabilities extend to non-Linux systems such as Windows through the use of WinRM (Windows Remote Management) and PowerShell. Ansible can manage Windows systems by executing PowerShell commands and scripts via WinRM. This feature allows administrators to automate tasks like software installation or configuration changes on Windows servers. Ansible's flexibility in using PowerShell makes it suitable for managing a Windows environment without needing Linux-specific solutions like WSL. Ansible Tower and Galaxy are additional tools and repositories that enhance Ansible's functionality, but they are not specific to managing Windows. Playbooks and modules are general Ansible functionalities applicable to all systems but do not specifically facilitate Windows management.

Q12: Ansible can be used to manage macOS systems. Which of the following Ansible modules is specifically designed for managing macOS system settings?   ---

A) homebrewcask

B) winfeature

C) macdefaults

D) apt

E) yum

F) macosxdefaults

Answer: F

Explanation: Ansible provides a variety of modules to manage different system types. For macOS systems, the macosxdefaults module is specifically designed to manage macOS system settings. This module allows administrators to read and write macOS default values, which are part of the macOS preference system. It is similar to the defaults command in macOS and provides a way to automate configuration changes on macOS machines. The homebrewcask module is also used for macOS but is focused on managing applications via the Homebrew package manager. Other options like winfeature, apt, and yum are related to Windows and Linux package management and are not applicable to macOS.

Q13: To effectively manage Windows machines with Ansible, certain prerequisites must be met. Which of the following is NOT a prerequisite for using Ansible to manage Windows systems?   ---

A) Python must be installed on Windows machines.

B) WinRM service must be enabled on Windows machines.

C) Ansible must be installed on a control node.

D) PowerShell must be available on Windows machines.

E) The WinRM listener must be properly configured.

F) Network connectivity between the control node and Windows machines.

Answer: A

Explanation: When managing Windows systems with Ansible, there are several prerequisites to ensure successful communication and task execution. Ansible requires the WinRM service to be enabled and properly configured on Windows machines, as it is the protocol used for communication. PowerShell must be available because Ansible uses it to execute commands on Windows. Ansible must be installed on a control node, typically a Linux machine, to issue commands to the Windows hosts. Network connectivity is necessary to facilitate communication between the control node and Windows machines. Unlike Linux systems, Windows does not require Python to be installed, as Ansible does not rely on Python for Windows management.

Q14: Ansible supports macOS management. True or False: Ansible requires macOS systems to have a Python interpreter installed to perform automation tasks. ---

A) True

B) False

Answer: B

Explanation: Ansible can manage macOS systems without requiring a Python interpreter to be installed on the macOS client machines. Ansible is agentless, meaning it does not require any specific software to be installed on the managed nodes. Instead, Ansible uses SSH to communicate and execute commands on macOS systems. While Python is a common requirement for Ansible on Linux systems, macOS management can be achieved without it, leveraging native macOS tools and commands through SSH. This makes Ansible a flexible tool for managing diverse environments, including macOS, without additional dependencies.

Q15: A multinational organization uses Ansible to manage a mixed environment of Linux, Windows, and macOS systems. They want to ensure security by encrypting sensitive data, such as passwords, used in their playbooks. Which Ansible feature allows them to achieve this goal?

A) Ansible Vault

B) SSH keys

C) ControlPersist

D) Agent forwarding

E) Sudo password

F) Host key checking

Answer: A

Explanation: Ansible Vault is a feature that allows users to encrypt sensitive data within Ansible projects. This is particularly useful for protecting passwords, secret keys, and other confidential information that might be stored in playbooks or inventory files. By using Ansible Vault, organizations can ensure that sensitive information is not exposed, even if the playbooks are shared or stored in version control systems. SSH keys and host key checking are related to secure connections, while ControlPersist and agent forwarding are SSH configuration options that enhance connection management. The sudo password is used for privilege escalation on managed nodes and does not pertain to encrypting data in playbooks.

Q16: A company named TechSolutions has recently adopted a cloud-based infrastructure to host its applications. The operations team needs to maintain the configuration of numerous virtual machines spread across different regions and cloud providers. They have decided to use Ansible for configuration management and automation. However, the dynamic nature of their infrastructure poses a challenge for inventory management because new instances are frequently launched and terminated based on demand. The team is exploring dynamic inventory scripts to automatically reflect the current state of their infrastructure. Which of the following statements correctly describes the benefit of using dynamic inventory in this scenario?

A) Dynamic inventory requires manual updates whenever a new instance is added or removed.

B) Dynamic inventory allows Ansible to automatically detect changes in the infrastructure and update the inventory without manual intervention.

C) Dynamic inventory is used only for managing static virtual machines with fixed IP addresses.

D) Dynamic inventory provides a GUI interface to manage hosts and groups.

E) Dynamic inventory scripts are only compatible with AWS.

F) Dynamic inventory scripts are built into Ansible and require no additional configuration.

Answer: B

Explanation: Dynamic inventory in Ansible is crucial for environments where the infrastructure is constantly changing, such as in cloud-based environments where instances are frequently added or removed. By using dynamic inventory, Ansible can automatically query the infrastructure to discover the current state of resources and update the inventory accordingly, without requiring manual intervention. This is particularly beneficial for companies like TechSolutions that use multiple cloud providers and need to keep their inventories up-to-date. Dynamic inventory scripts can be custom-written or provided by plugins for various cloud providers, such as AWS, Google Cloud, and Azure, allowing Ansible to fetch the current list of hosts dynamically.

Q17: Ansible's dynamic inventory can be used to manage cloud instances. Which of the following technologies is NOT typically associated with providing dynamic inventory capabilities for Ansible?

A) Amazon EC2

B) Docker

C) Google Compute Engine

D) Vagrant

E) Microsoft Azure

F) VirtualBox

Answer: F

Explanation: VirtualBox is a virtualization software that is typically used for running virtual machines on local hardware rather than cloud-based instances. It does not inherently provide dynamic inventory capabilities for Ansible. On the other hand, cloud services like Amazon EC2, Google Compute Engine, and Microsoft Azure are designed to manage and scale virtual instances dynamically, allowing Ansible to query these services for up-to-date inventory information. Docker and Vagrant also offer environments where dynamic inventory can be used, as they often involve orchestrating multiple containers or virtual environments.

Q18: A small tech startup is using Docker to containerize its microservices, and they want to use Ansible for orchestration and configuration management. The development team is considering using Ansible's dynamic inventory capabilities to manage the Docker containers. However, they are unsure about which prerequisites are necessary. Which of the following is NOT a prerequisite for using dynamic inventory with Docker containers in Ansible?

A) Ansible must be installed on the control node.

B) A Python interpreter must be available inside each Docker container.

C) The Docker SDK for Python must be installed on the Ansible control node.

D) The dynamic inventory script for Docker must be configured.

E) Docker must be running on the host machine where Ansible is executed.

F) A static inventory file is required to initialize the dynamic inventory.

Answer: F

Explanation: When using Ansible's dynamic inventory with Docker, there is no requirement to have a static inventory file to initialize the dynamic inventory. Instead, dynamic inventory scripts or plugins can be used to query the Docker environment directly, fetching information about running containers. Ansible needs to be installed on the control node, and the Docker SDK for Python must be installed to allow Ansible to interact with Docker. The dynamic inventory script must be correctly configured to gather data about the Docker containers. A Python interpreter inside each container is not a prerequisite for dynamic inventory but may be necessary for running Ansible playbooks within the containers.

Q19: True or False: Ansible's dynamic inventory can only be used with resources from a single cloud provider at a time.

A) True

B) False

Answer: B

Explanation: Ansible's dynamic inventory is flexible and can be configured to work with multiple cloud providers simultaneously. This is achieved by using multiple dynamic inventory scripts or plugins tailored to each cloud provider. As a result, Ansible can manage a diverse infrastructure that includes resources from AWS, Google Cloud, Microsoft Azure, and other providers, all within the same inventory. This capability makes Ansible a powerful tool for organizations leveraging multi-cloud strategies.

Q20: A global e-commerce company is implementing Ansible to automate its server configurations across multiple regions and cloud platforms. The company wants to ensure that their Ansible playbooks always target the correct and most recent set of servers. Which configuration step is essential to achieve this using Ansible's dynamic inventory?

A) Use a cron job to regularly update a static inventory file.

B) Configure environment variables for each cloud provider.

C) Enable and configure the appropriate dynamic inventory plugins or scripts.

D) Manually input the server list into Ansible before each run.

E) Install the latest version of Ansible for built-in dynamic inventory support.

F) Use a combination of SSH keys and passwords to authenticate servers.

Answer: C

Explanation: To utilize Ansible's dynamic inventory effectively, it is essential to enable and configure the appropriate dynamic inventory plugins or scripts that correspond to the cloud providers in use. This configuration allows Ansible to query the cloud platforms directly, retrieving up-to-date information about the servers and ensuring that playbooks target the correct resources. While installing the latest version of Ansible and using authentication methods are important for general operation, they do not specifically address the need for dynamic inventory updates. Similarly, relying on cron jobs or manual input defeats the purpose of dynamic inventory management.

Q21: A mid-sized e-commerce company wants to streamline its infrastructure management using Chef. They have a mixed environment with several Linux distributions and want to ensure that all their web servers have a specific version of Nginx installed, configured with custom settings. Additionally, they wish to automate the deployment of security patches to these servers. Which Chef component or feature would best help the company achieve these objectives?

A) Chef Server

B) Chef Workstation

C) Chef Solo

D) Chef Client

E) Chef InSpec

F) Chef Habitat

Answer: A

Explanation: Chef Server is the central component of the Chef ecosystem, responsible for storing and managing all the configuration policies, cookbooks, and node configurations. In this scenario, the e-commerce company needs to maintain consistent configurations across a range of Linux servers, which involves storing and managing the recipes for Nginx installation and configuration, as well as automating security patch deployments. Chef Server enables centralized management and distribution of these configurations. Chef Workstation is used for developing and testing recipes, while Chef Solo is for standalone use without a server. Chef Client is the agent that runs on nodes to apply policies. Chef InSpec is for compliance and security testing, and Chef Habitat is for application automation, which does not directly address the needs of managing server configurations and security patches in this context.

Q22: Which command is used to bootstrap a new node so that it can communicate with the Chef server and receive its configurations?

A) knife bootstrap

B) chef-client -z

C) chef-server-ctl install

D) chef-run

E) chef-repo-init

F) knife configure

Answer: A

Explanation: The "knife bootstrap" command is used to install the Chef client on a node and register it with the Chef server. This command helps in configuring the node so it can communicate with the Chef server and download its necessary configurations and cookbooks. The bootstrap process involves installing the Chef client software and setting up the initial configuration, enabling nodes to be managed through Chef. Other options like "chef-client -z" are used for zero configuration without a server, "chef-server-ctl install" is for server installation, "chef-run" is a targeted execution tool, "chef-repo-init" is for setting up a new Chef repository, and "knife configure" is for setting up knife configuration on a workstation.

Q23: The concept of idempotency is crucial in configuration management tools like Chef. What does idempotency mean in the context of Chef, and why is it important?

A) Ensuring that a resource is only updated if it has changed

B) Running recipes in parallel to reduce execution time

C) Allowing multiple configurations to be applied to the same node

D) Storing node information in a version-controlled repository

E) Loading cookbooks dynamically at runtime

F) Scheduling periodic execution of recipes on nodes

Answer: A

Explanation: Idempotency in Chef refers to the ability of Chef recipes to apply configurations repeatedly without altering the system state beyond the intended outcome. This means if a resource is already in the desired state, no action is taken, ensuring that running a recipe multiple times leads to the same result. This is crucial for maintaining consistent environments, preventing unnecessary changes, and reducing the risk of configuration drift. Parallel execution, multiple configurations, version control, dynamic loading, and periodic execution are important in their own right but do not directly address the concept of idempotency.

Q24: True/False: Chef uses a master-agent architecture where the Chef server acts as the central point for storing configurations, and the nodes communicate with the server to pull these configurations.

A) True

B) False

Answer: A

Explanation: Chef indeed uses a master-agent architecture, where the Chef server acts as the master that stores all the configuration data, including cookbooks, recipes, and policies. Nodes, which are the agents in this scenario, communicate with the Chef server to pull their respective configurations and apply them. This architecture allows for centralized management of configurations, ensuring that nodes are consistently configured according to the policies defined on the Chef server. This setup contrasts with other architectures like peer-to-peer or standalone systems.

Q25: A company is using Chef to manage its infrastructure and has encountered an issue where certain nodes fail to apply updates due to network connectivity problems. They want to ensure that these updates are automatically retried once connectivity is restored. Which Chef feature or strategy would best address this requirement?

A) Chef Push Jobs

B) Chef Reporting

C) Chef Automate

D) Chef Supermarket

E) Retry Logic in Recipes

F) Chef Analytics

Answer: E

Explanation: Implementing retry logic within Chef recipes is the most effective strategy for handling transient network connectivity issues. By leveraging Ruby's "retry" functionality, or using Chef's built-in retry mechanisms, recipes can be designed to automatically attempt resource actions again after a failure. This ensures that once network connectivity is restored, the updates that initially failed will be retried without manual intervention. Chef Push Jobs, Reporting, Automate, Supermarket, and Analytics do not directly provide a mechanism for retrying failed recipe executions due to network issues. Chef Push Jobs is more about executing jobs on nodes, Automate provides workflow and compliance features, Supermarket is a community repository for sharing cookbooks, and Analytics is for tracking changes and activities within Chef.

Q26: An enterprise-level company has recently adopted Puppet to manage its fleet of Linux servers. The DevOps team is responsible for maintaining consistent configurations across all servers to ensure compliance with security policies and streamline software deployments. The team is particularly interested in leveraging Puppet's capabilities for automation and reducing manual errors. They have a specific requirement to ensure that the application server package httpd is always installed and running on all their web servers. They also want the configuration file, /etc/httpd/conf/httpd.conf, to be managed with specific settings. Which resource type in Puppet should the team use to achieve this?

A) Exec

B) File

C) Package

D) Service

E) Notify

F) Class

Answer: F

Explanation: In Puppet, defining a comprehensive configuration that includes package installation, service management, and file configuration is best encapsulated within a Puppet class. A class allows you to group and manage these resources together, ensuring that all necessary configurations are applied consistently to the target nodes. Using a class, you can ensure the httpd package is installed, the service is enabled and running, and the configuration file has the desired settings. This approach not only simplifies management but also enhances reusability and scalability, as the class can be included across multiple nodes or environments as needed.

Q27: Puppet's architecture involves a centralized server-client model. Identify the component that acts as the configuration language interpreter and compiles configurations into catalogs that are then applied to managed nodes.

A) PuppetDB

B) Puppet Agent

C) Puppet Master

D) Puppet Node Manager

E) Puppet Dashboard

F) Puppet Console

Answer: C

Explanation: The Puppet Master is the central component that interprets the Puppet configuration language and compiles the configurations into catalogs. These catalogs are then sent to Puppet Agents, which apply the configurations to the managed nodes. The Puppet Master acts as the brain of the Puppet infrastructure, managing the distribution and application of configuration across all nodes. It ensures that the desired state specified in the Puppet manifests is consistently enforced on the client systems.

Q28: Determine whether the following statement is true or false: "In Puppet, a resource is used to describe the desired state of a system component, such as a package, service, or file."

A) True

B) False

Answer: A

Explanation: In Puppet, a resource is indeed used to describe the desired state of a system component. Resources are the fundamental building blocks in Puppet's configuration language, and they represent the state that should be enforced on the system. A resource can describe various elements of a system, such as packages, services, files, users, and more. By defining resources, Puppet ensures that each component is maintained in the specified state, aiding in achieving and maintaining system consistency.

Q29: While managing a Puppet infrastructure, a DevOps engineer wants to ensure that certain tasks are executed only when a specific file changes. Which built-in Puppet resource attribute should be utilized to achieve this conditional execution?

A) before

B) require

C) notify

D) subscribe

E) refreshonly

F) schedule

Answer: D

Explanation: The subscribe attribute in Puppet is used to establish a relationship between resources, enabling conditional execution. When a resource subscribes to another resource, it will trigger a refresh of the subscribing resource whenever the subscribed-to resource changes. This is particularly useful for scenarios where you need to execute or re-execute an action, such as restarting a service, whenever a configuration file changes. The subscribe attribute helps in maintaining dynamic dependencies and ensuring that the system state is updated appropriately in response to changes.

Q30: A company uses Puppet to manage its infrastructure and has defined a module that includes multiple manifests. They need to ensure that a specific manifest within the module is applied only once, regardless of how many times it is declared in node definitions. Which Puppet feature should they use to achieve this?

A) Anchor

B) Define

C) Include

D) Import

E) Require

F) Contain

Answer: C

Explanation: The include function in Puppet ensures that a class is evaluated only once per catalog, regardless of how many times it is declared. This is particularly important when dealing with modules that contain multiple manifests or classes, as it helps prevent duplicate resource declarations and ensures idempotency. By using include, you can guarantee that the manifest logic is applied only once, maintaining consistency and avoiding potential conflicts or redundant executions within the Puppet infrastructure.

Q31: A mid-sized company is in the process of migrating its legacy monolithic application to a microservices architecture. The current setup runs on several physical Linux servers, and the company plans to move to a cloud-based Kubernetes environment. During this migration, maintaining consistent API responses and minimizing downtime are critical. The legacy system also relies heavily on a custom-built logging service that is not compatible with the new architecture. Which of the following strategies would best address these concerns while integrating the legacy logging system with the new architecture?

A) Rewrite the logging service to be compatible with Kubernetes and deploy it as a microservice.

B) Use a sidecar container pattern to integrate the legacy logging service without modification.

C) Implement a middleware API gateway to handle requests and route them to the appropriate logging service.

D) Utilize a hybrid model, keeping the legacy system operational while gradually migrating services.

E) Deploy the legacy logging service on a dedicated VM within the cloud environment.

F) Use a message broker to queue log messages, processing them asynchronously in the legacy system.

Answer: B

Explanation: The sidecar container pattern is an effective way to integrate legacy services into a modern microservices architecture without requiring extensive modifications. By deploying the legacy logging service as a sidecar container alongside each microservice, the existing logging functionality can be retained while taking advantage of the scalability and orchestration features provided by Kubernetes. This approach minimizes downtime by maintaining logging consistency across both systems, and it does not require a complete rewrite of the logging service, which would be time-consuming and risky. Additionally, this strategy allows the company to maintain consistent API responses, as the logging service can be accessed seamlessly by all microservices.

Q32: During the migration of a monolithic application to a containerized environment, which factor poses the greatest risk of data inconsistency in a distributed system?

A) Using persistent storage volumes without proper configuration.

B) Implementing a rolling update strategy for continuous deployment.

C) Employing a single network interface for all microservices.

D) Utilizing stateless services across the entire architecture.

E) Deploying multiple replicas of a database without synchronization.

F) Running all containers on a single host node to simplify networking.

Answer: E

Explanation: Deploying multiple replicas of a database without proper synchronization mechanisms can lead to data inconsistency, which is a critical risk in distributed systems. In a microservices architecture, data consistency is often more challenging due to the distributed nature of the components. Without proper synchronization, such as consensus algorithms or distributed transaction support, database replicas may serve stale or conflicting data, leading to application errors and integrity issues. Ensuring that all database instances are synchronized is essential to maintaining data consistency, particularly when scaling services or during failover scenarios.

Q33: A company is considering migrating its legacy monolithic application to a containerized microservices model. One significant concern is the integration of its existing user authentication system, which was designed for single-instance operation. Which method is most suitable for addressing this concern without rewriting the authentication logic?

A) Implement a reverse proxy with session affinity to direct all requests from the same user to the same instance.

B) Use a centralized authentication service and update all microservices to support it.

C) Containerize the existing authentication system and use an external load balancer.

D) Deploy a token-based authentication system across all microservices.

E) Create a microservices-based authentication service and gradually replace the old system.

F) Integrate the existing authentication system into a service mesh for consistent communication.

Answer: A

Explanation: Implementing a reverse proxy with session affinity, also known as sticky sessions, is a practical approach to integrating a legacy authentication system designed for single-instance operation. This method ensures that all requests from the same user session are directed to the same instance, maintaining session consistency without requiring significant changes to the existing authentication logic. Session affinity is particularly useful when dealing with stateful applications in a load-balanced environment, allowing the legacy system to function as expected while transitioning to a microservices architecture.

Q34: True/False: Migrating a legacy monolithic application to a microservices architecture inherently reduces complexity and eliminates the need for robust monitoring and logging solutions.
A) True

B) False

Answer: B

Explanation: False. Migrating to a microservices architecture does not inherently reduce complexity; in fact, it often introduces new challenges that require robust solutions. Unlike monolithic applications, microservices architectures are composed of many independent services that communicate over a network, increasing the complexity of monitoring, logging, and troubleshooting. Each microservice can have its own logging and monitoring requirements, necessitating a comprehensive strategy to ensure system visibility and reliability. Effective monitoring and logging are crucial to identify issues, track performance, and maintain the health of the entire system.

Q35: An enterprise organization is planning to integrate its monolithic enterprise resource planning (ERP) system into a new microservices architecture. One of the critical components of this system is a batch processing module that handles large volumes of data nightly. What is the most effective strategy to handle this batch processing in the new architecture?

A) Convert the batch processing module into a set of microservices and schedule them using a job scheduler.

B) Keep the batch processing module as a monolithic component and integrate it using a service mesh.

C) Use a cloud-based batch processing service to offload the workload from the new architecture.

D) Containerize the batch processing module and deploy it as a standalone service.

E) Replace batch processing with real-time data streams across all microservices.

F) Implement a serverless architecture for the batch processing functions.

Answer: A

Explanation: To handle batch processing in a microservices architecture, converting the batch processing module into a set of microservices and scheduling them using a job scheduler is an effective strategy. This approach allows the organization to break down the batch processing tasks into smaller, manageable services that can be independently scaled and maintained. A job scheduler can orchestrate these tasks, ensuring they run in the correct sequence and handle large data volumes efficiently. This method also aligns with the principles of microservices by promoting modularity and scalability while leveraging existing cloud-native tools and frameworks for job scheduling and execution.

Q36: A financial services company is tasked with deploying a highly secure microservices application. The infrastructure team decides to use Packer to create and manage the custom images for their application. They need to build images that can run on multiple cloud providers such as AWS, Azure, and Google Cloud. The company also requires the images to have specific security configurations and application dependencies pre-installed. Which Packer feature should the team leverage to ensure they can easily maintain a single source of truth for these configurations across different cloud platforms?

A) Using different provisioners for each cloud provider

B) Writing separate template files for each provider

C) Leveraging Packer's multi-builder functionality

D) Using shell scripts to customize each image post-build

E) Manually configuring each image after build completion

F) Utilizing environment variables for shared configurations

Answer: C

Explanation: The correct approach is to leverage Packer's multi-builder functionality. Packer allows you to define multiple builders within a single template file, enabling you to create images for different platforms from one source configuration. This ensures consistency and reduces the overhead of maintaining separate templates for each provider. Using multi-builders, the team can specify different builders for AWS, Azure, and Google Cloud, while sharing common configurations such as security settings and application dependencies. This approach aligns with best practices in maintaining infrastructure as code and ensures that all images are built with the same baseline configuration, enhancing security and operational efficiency.

Q37: You are tasked with optimizing the build process for a Linux-based Docker image using Packer. The current build process involves several steps, including installing packages, configuring services, and setting up application dependencies. Which strategy can minimize the size of the final Docker image while ensuring all dependencies are included?

A) Use a minimal base image and run a single shell script for all configurations

B) Install packages, then remove unnecessary package caches and temporary files

C) Create a Dockerfile with multiple stages and use a multi-stage build

D) Use a larger base image with most dependencies pre-installed

E) Build the image using a different containerization tool instead of Docker

F) Include only essential services in the image and configure others post-deployment

Answer: C

Explanation: The best strategy to minimize the size of a Docker image while ensuring all dependencies are included is to use a multi-stage build within a Dockerfile. Multi-stage builds allow you to use different stages to compile, build, and finally package your application into a smaller, production-ready image. By using a minimal base image in the final stage and copying only necessary files and dependencies from previous stages, you significantly reduce the image size. This method is efficient as it eliminates the need for intermediate build artifacts and reduces attack surfaces by including only essential components in the final image.

Q38: Building immutable infrastructure is a key practice in DevOps. True or False: One of the benefits of using Packer to create machine images is that it inherently enforces immutability by allowing post-build modifications to the created images.

A) True

B) False

Answer: B

Explanation: The statement is false. Packer enforces immutability by creating images that are meant to be static and not modified post-build. The benefit of using Packer is that it allows you to create machine images with all necessary configurations and dependencies baked in, which means that the images are ready to be deployed as-is without further modification. This immutability ensures consistency and reliability across environments, as each deployment uses the same pre-configured image. If changes are required, a new image should be built, maintaining the integrity and consistency of your infrastructure.

Q39: A development team needs to automate the creation of virtual machine images for their application using Packer. They want to ensure that the images are built with the latest security patches and software updates. Which Packer provisioner should they use to achieve this during the image build process?

A) Ansible

B) PowerShell

C) Chef

D) Shell

E) Puppet

F) Salt

Answer: D

Explanation: To ensure that virtual machine images are built with the latest security patches and software updates, the team should use the Shell provisioner. The Shell provisioner is versatile and can execute shell commands or scripts during the image build process. By scripting the package manager to update all installed packages, the team can apply the latest updates and patches, ensuring that the images are secure and up-to-date. This approach is straightforward and can be easily integrated into Packer's build process, providing a reliable method for maintaining security compliance within the images.

Q40: In a scenario where a company is using Packer to build images that are deployed on both on-premises VMware infrastructure and AWS, they encounter difficulties managing different network configurations for each environment. What is a recommended approach to handle these variations in network settings within Packer?

A) Hardcode network settings into the image

B) Use conditional logic within the Packer template

C) Create separate Packer templates for each environment

D) Use user variables to parameterize network configurations

E) Manually configure network settings after image deployment

F) Use different builders with shared network configurations

Answer: D

Explanation: The recommended approach to manage different network configurations within Packer is to use user variables to parameterize these settings. By defining user variables in your Packer template, you can customize network configurations for each environment without altering the core template. This method allows you to pass different values for network settings at build time, depending on whether you're building for VMware or AWS. This parameterization enhances flexibility and reduces the complexity of maintaining separate templates for each platform, promoting a more efficient and streamlined image-building process.

Q41: Your company, which operates a large-scale e-commerce platform, is transitioning from a monolithic architecture to a microservices-based architecture. As part of this transition, the operations team is required to maintain an inventory file that lists all servers, their roles, and configurations. This inventory file will be used by Ansible for configuration management. The DevOps team has decided to use a dynamic inventory script that queries AWS to fetch the latest server details automatically. Which of the following steps is crucial to ensure that the dynamic inventory script can successfully retrieve the necessary server information?

A) Ensure that the AWS CLI is installed and configured with the correct IAM credentials.

B) Use a cron job to manually update the inventory file every hour.

C) Write a custom Python script to parse the AWS console output.

D) Use a static inventory file and update it manually.

E) Configure AWS S3 to store the inventory file.

F) Use Terraform to provision the servers and generate the inventory file.

Answer: A

Explanation: To use a dynamic inventory script with Ansible, especially when querying AWS for details, the AWS CLI must be installed and properly configured with the correct IAM credentials that have permissions to describe the necessary AWS resources. This setup allows the script to use the AWS API to retrieve information about the EC2 instances, such as their IP addresses, tags, and roles, which are essential for managing them with Ansible. Without the AWS CLI configured correctly, the dynamic inventory script would fail to query AWS, resulting in an incomplete or outdated inventory. Other options like manually updating the inventory or using static files would not leverage the dynamic capabilities of a script and would likely lead to manual errors and outdated data.

Q42: Fill in the gap to complete the command that creates an Ansible inventory file with a single group named "webservers" and two hosts with IPs 192.168.1.10 and 192.168.1.11: echo -e "[webservers]\n192.168.1.10\n192.168.1.11" >

A) /etc/ansible/hosts

B) /etc/ansible/inventory/hosts

C) /var/lib/ansible/hosts

D) /etc/ansible/inventory.ini

E) /home/user/ansibleinventory

F) /etc/ansible/inventory/groupvars

Answer: A

Explanation: The default location for Ansible's inventory file is /etc/ansible/hosts. An inventory file in Ansible is crucial as it contains the list of hosts that Ansible will manage. By echoing the group name and IP addresses into this file, Ansible recognizes the "webservers" group and the two hosts as part of that group. Using the default location ensures that Ansible commands and playbooks will automatically reference this inventory file unless explicitly instructed otherwise. Other paths listed, such as /etc/ansible/inventory/hosts, are non-standard and would require additional configuration to be recognized by Ansible as the inventory file location.

Q43: In maintaining an inventory file, which Ansible command would you use to verify the syntax and the reachability of all hosts listed in your inventory file without executing any tasks?
A) ansible-playbook --check

B) ansible-inventory --list

C) ansible all -m ping

D) ansible-playbook --syntax-check

E) ansible all --list-hosts

F) ansible-vault view

Answer: C

Explanation: The command ansible all -m ping is used to verify the reachability of all hosts listed in the inventory file by checking if Ansible can connect to them using the specified connection details (like SSH). The -m ping module sends a simple ping command to each host, which is useful for testing connectivity and ensuring that Ansible can execute commands on the remote machines. This command does not execute any tasks beyond checking connectivity. Other commands like ansible-playbook --check or ansible-playbook --syntax-check are used for different purposes, such as checking playbook syntax or simulating a playbook run, and do not test host reachability.

Q44: A company uses Ansible for configuration management across multiple environments (development, testing, and production). Each environment has different host configurations. What is the best practice for organizing inventory files to manage these environments effectively?

A) Use a single inventory file with all hosts listed under environment-specific groups.

B) Create separate inventory files for each environment and use the -i option to specify the file.

C) Use an environment variable to switch between environments in a single inventory file.

D) Maintain a single inventory file and use tags to differentiate environments.

E) Use a YAML-based inventory file to manage all environments in one file.

F) Store inventory files in a version control system and manually switch them as needed.

Answer: B

Explanation: The best practice for managing multiple environments with Ansible is to create separate inventory files for each environment and specify the appropriate file using the -i option when running Ansible commands. This approach provides clear separation between environments, reducing the risk of accidental changes being applied to the wrong environment. It also makes it easier to manage environment-specific variables and configurations. While using a single inventory file with environment-specific groups is possible, it can become cumbersome and error-prone with large inventories. Using separate files also aligns well with version control practices, allowing for clear tracking of changes in each environment's configuration.

Q45: True or False: In Ansible, an inventory file can only be written in the INI format.
A) True

B) False

Answer: B

Explanation: False. Ansible supports multiple formats for inventory files, including INI, YAML, and JSON. The INI format is the traditional and most commonly used format, but YAML is increasingly popular due to its readability and ease of use in complex configurations. JSON can also be used, especially in dynamic inventory scripts where JSON output is common. Ansible's flexibility in supporting different formats allows users to choose the format that best suits their needs and preferences. This adaptability makes Ansible a powerful tool for configuration management across diverse environments and systems.

Q46: A medium-sized software company is transitioning its infrastructure to a DevOps model and has decided to use Ansible for configuration management. The team needs to create a template file to configure their web servers. The template must dynamically include the server's hostname and IP address in the configuration file. Additionally, they want to ensure that the same template can be used across different environments (development, testing, and production) with minimal changes. Which templating language should they use for creating these Ansible templates to achieve maximum flexibility and maintainability?
A) Jinja2

B) Smarty

C) Mako

D) Velocity

E) Freemarker

F) Mustache

Answer: A

Explanation: Ansible uses Jinja2 as its default templating language, which is a powerful tool that allows for dynamic content generation in configuration files. Jinja2 supports variable substitution, loops, conditionals, and more, making it ideal for creating templates that need to adapt based on different variables such as server hostname and IP address. This flexibility is crucial in a DevOps environment where configurations might need to change based on the environment or specific server attributes. By using Jinja2, the team can leverage Ansible's inventory variables and facts to fill in the template dynamically, ensuring that the same template can be reused across development, testing, and production environments with minimal changes. This promotes maintainability and reduces the potential for errors that could arise from manually configuring each environment.

Q47: When using the envsubst command in a Bash script to substitute environment variables in a template file, which command would correctly substitute all environment variables present in the file config.template and output the result to config.conf?

A) envsubst < config.template > config.conf

B) envsubst config.template config.conf

C) envsubst -f config.template > config.conf

D) cat config.template | envsubst > config.conf

E) envsubst -i config.template -o config.conf

F) envsubst -t config.template -d config.conf

Answer: A

Explanation: The envsubst command is used in shell scripting to substitute environment variables into a template file. The correct syntax to achieve this involves redirecting the input and output using < and > operators. The command envsubst < config.template > config.conf reads config.template, substitutes any present environment variables using the current shell's environment, and writes the output to config.conf. This technique is simple and effective for generating configuration files with dynamic content based on the environment the script is executed in. It is important to ensure that the environment variables expected in the template are set in the shell where the script runs for envsubst to replace them correctly.

Q48: True or False: Configuring a Linux system to automatically substitute template variables in configuration files on boot using systemd requires the use of a systemd service unit file with the EnvironmentFile directive.
A) True

B) False

Answer: B

Explanation: The EnvironmentFile directive in a systemd service unit file is used to specify a file that contains environment variables for the service. However, it does not automatically substitute template variables within configuration files. To achieve automatic substitution at boot, a custom script or service would need to be created that reads a template file and performs the substitution using a tool like envsubst or a configuration management tool like Ansible or Puppet. This script can then be executed via a systemd service unit on boot. The EnvironmentFile directive alone does not have the capability to parse and replace template variables in arbitrary files.

Q49: A server administrator needs to ensure that the template file /etc/myapp/config.template is transformed into a final configuration file at /etc/myapp/config.conf with the correct variable substitutions for each deployment. The template includes placeholders for the database URL, username, and password. Which of the following tools or methods is most suitable for securely handling sensitive information like database credentials during this process?

A) Storing credentials in plain text in a shell script

B) Using Ansible Vault to encrypt sensitive data

C) Including credentials directly in the template file

D) Using a version control system to track the credentials

E) Writing a custom Python script to manage credentials

F) Using a cloud-based secret management service

Answer: B

Explanation: Ansible Vault is a feature of Ansible that allows users to encrypt sensitive data such as passwords and keys. When using Ansible to handle template files, Ansible Vault provides an effective way to ensure that sensitive information, such as database credentials, remains secure. By encrypting the variables file containing the credentials, the administrator can safely include it in the Ansible playbook without exposing the information. During the execution of the playbook, Ansible will decrypt the necessary variables to perform the substitutions in the template file. This approach is preferable to storing credentials in plain text or embedding them directly in templates, which could lead to potential security breaches.

Q50: Consider a DevOps team tasked with managing configuration templates for a fleet of Linux servers. They decide to use Puppet for configuration management. The team needs to create a template that will populate the configuration based on node-specific facts such as the operating system and memory size. Which Puppet feature should the team use to dynamically generate these templates based on the node's facts?

A) Custom Ruby scripts

B) ERB templates

C) Bash scripts

D) Docker containers

E) JSON data files

F) YAML configuration

Answer: B

Explanation: Puppet uses ERB (Embedded Ruby) templates to dynamically generate configuration files. ERB templates allow for the embedding of Ruby code within a configuration file, enabling the template to access Puppet's facts and variables related to each node. This allows the configuration file to be tailored to the specific attributes of the node, such as its operating system and memory size. By using ERB templates, the DevOps team can ensure that each server's configuration is appropriate for its environment and hardware specifications, leveraging Puppet's facter tool to gather node-specific data. This method is efficient and maintains the flexibility required for managing configurations across a diverse set of servers.

Q51: A company is looking to streamline its development environment setup by using Vagrant. The development team requires a consistent Ubuntu 20.04 environment with a specific version of Node.js and MongoDB installed. The environment should be provisioned automatically upon 'vagrant up'. You have been tasked with creating the Vagrantfile. How should the Vagrantfile be configured to meet these requirements?

A) Use the 'ubuntu/focal64' box and a shell provisioner to install Node.js and MongoDB.

B) Use the 'ubuntu/bionic64' box and a Puppet provisioner to install Node.js and MongoDB.

C) Use the 'ubuntu/focal64' box and a Docker provisioner to install Node.js and MongoDB.

D) Use the 'ubuntu/xenial64' box with inline shell commands in the Vagrantfile to install Node.js and MongoDB.

E) Use the 'ubuntu/focal64' box and a Chef provisioner to install Node.js and MongoDB.

F) Use the 'ubuntu/focal64' box with configuration management tools baked into a custom box.

Answer: A

Explanation: The 'ubuntu/focal64' box corresponds to Ubuntu 20.04, which is required by the development team. The shell provisioner is a straightforward method to install software like Node.js and MongoDB, making it suitable for simple provisioning needs. Inline shell scripts can execute commands directly on the guest machine during 'vagrant up', ensuring that the environment is provisioned automatically. This approach allows quick modifications to the provisioning script without needing to maintain separate provisioning files, making it efficient for iterative development needs.

Q52: When configuring a Vagrantfile to automatically run a database setup script every time the virtual machine starts, which Vagrant command should be used to ensure the script is executed repeatedly regardless of the VM's state?

A) Vagrant::Config.runonce

B) Vagrant::Provisioner::always

C) Vagrant::Provisioners::onboot

D) Vagrant::Triggers::beforeup

E) Vagrant.configure("2") do |config| config.vm.provision "shell"

F) Vagrant.configure("2") do |config| config.vm.provision "file"

Answer: E

Explanation: Vagrant's provisioning system allows you to define scripts that run during specific lifecycle events, such as 'vagrant up'. The "shell" provisioner can be configured to run scripts every time the machine is booted using the 'config.vm.provision "shell"' configuration. This ensures that any setup scripts are applied consistently, maintaining the desired state of the environment. Using this method, scripts can be rerun without having to destroy or recreate the virtual machine, which is particularly useful for development environments that require frequent updates or changes.

Q53: You are tasked with creating a Vagrant environment that uses a specific network configuration. The VM must be accessible from the host machine using a static IP address, and it should not conflict with any existing network devices. Which network configuration should you include in the Vagrantfile?
A) config.vm.network "forwardedport", guest: 80, host: 8080

B) config.vm.network "privatenetwork", type: "dhcp"

C) config.vm.network "publicnetwork", ip: "192.168.1.10"

D) config.vm.network "privatenetwork", ip: "192.168.50.4"

E) config.vm.network "publicnetwork", bridge: "en0: Wi-Fi (AirPort)"

F) config.vm.network "privatenetwork", ip: "10.0.2.15"

Answer: D

Explanation: A private network with a static IP address allows the VM to be accessed from the host machine without affecting other network devices. In this configuration, the IP address '192.168.50.4' is typically used for private networks and does not interfere with public IP ranges. Vagrant's private networking ensures that the VM is isolated from the external network, preventing IP conflicts with other devices. This setup is particularly useful for development and testing environments where consistent access to the VM is required.

Q54: True or False: Vagrant can be used to manage and configure both Linux and Windows virtual machines using the same Vagrantfile syntax.
A) True

B) False

Answer: A

Explanation: Vagrant is designed to be a multi-platform tool, capable of managing and provisioning both Linux and Windows environments with the same Vagrantfile syntax. The key to this flexibility lies in Vagrant's use of provider plugins, which allow it to interface with different virtualization technologies, such as VirtualBox, VMware, and Hyper-V. While the provisioning scripts and tools (e.g., shell scripts, PowerShell, etc.) might differ between operating systems, the overarching Vagrantfile remains consistent, enabling cross-platform development and testing workflows.

Q55: You need to ensure that a Vagrant-managed virtual machine uses a specific version of a base box and does not automatically update to a newer version. Which configuration should be used in the Vagrantfile?
A) config.vm.boxversion = ">= 1.0"

B) config.vm.box = "hashicorp/bionic64"

C) config.vm.boxversion = "= 1.0.0"

D) config.vm.boxcheckupdate = true

E) config.vm.boxcheckupdate = false

F) config.vm.boxversion = "<= 1.0"

Answer: C

Explanation: Specifying an exact box version using 'config.vm.boxversion = "= 1.0.0"' ensures that Vagrant will use a specific version of a base box and will not automatically update it to a newer version. This is crucial in environments where stability and consistency are required, such as production or development environments that rely on specific software dependencies. By locking the box version, teams can avoid unexpected changes in their virtual environments, which can lead to compatibility issues or unforeseen bugs.

Q56: Your organization, a large e-commerce company, is implementing Ansible to automate the configuration of its server infrastructure. The IT team is tasked with creating a playbook to deploy a web server environment that includes Nginx, a custom configuration file, and a service restart handler. Additionally, the deployment needs to check the server's OS version and apply specific tasks only if the server is running Ubuntu 20.04. Finally, the playbook should log the status of the deployment in a centralized log file. Given these requirements, which task sequence best fulfills this scenario within an Ansible playbook?

A) Use a 'when' statement to check the OS version, copy the configuration file, and include a handler to restart Nginx.

B) Use a 'block' with a 'when' condition to apply tasks conditionally, set a 'register' to capture task output, and call a handler to log results.

C) Employ a 'loop' to iterate over tasks, use 'ignoreerrors' for error handling, and use a 'notify' statement for the handler.

D) Leverage 'tags' to selectively run tasks, use 'until' for retries, and include a 'notify' for the service restart.

E) Utilize a 'withitems' loop for configuration deployment, conditionally run tasks with 'when', and log deployment status using a handler.

F) Implement an 'includetasks' to modularize the playbook, use 'when' for conditions, and employ a 'notify' statement for conditional logging.

Answer: B

Explanation: The key requirement here is to conditionally execute tasks based on the server's OS version and ensure proper logging. Using a 'block' with a 'when' condition allows you to group tasks that should be executed only if the server is running Ubuntu 20.04. This approach ensures that all tasks within the block are subject to the same condition. By setting a 'register', you can capture the output of a task, which is crucial for logging the deployment status. The 'notify' statement is used to call a handler that can restart the Nginx service and log deployment results. This method satisfies all the requirements: conditional execution, configuration deployment, service restart, and comprehensive logging.

Q57: When writing an Ansible playbook, which of the following statements about using 'handlers' is false?

A) Handlers are used to execute certain actions only when notified.

B) Handlers can be triggered multiple times within a single playbook run.

C) Handlers should be defined at the same level as tasks.

D) Handlers are typically used to restart services after configuration changes.

E) Handlers run at the end of a playbook by default.

F) Handlers can be overridden by using a 'forcehandlers' directive.

Answer: B

Explanation: Handlers in Ansible are designed to be idempotent, meaning they only run once if they are notified, regardless of how many times the notification occurs during a playbook run. This behavior ensures that actions like service restarts or other changes are applied only once per execution, which is crucial for maintaining system stability and avoiding unnecessary disruptions. Handlers are indeed defined at the same level as tasks, and they are typically used for actions like restarting services after a configuration change. While they run at the end of a playbook by default, they can be forced to run earlier using the 'forcehandlers' directive.

Q58: Consider the following Ansible task: yaml - name: Install necessary packages package: name: "{{ item }}" state: present loop: - git - curl - wget register: packageinstallation Which subsequent task should be included to handle the situation where package installation fails and you need to notify a handler to roll back the changes?

A) Use a 'rescue' block to notify the handler on failure.

B) Add a 'notify' statement immediately after the 'register'.

C) Implement a 'when' condition to check for failure and notify.

D) Use 'ignoreerrors' and a handler to manage failures.

E) Set a 'failedwhen' condition and notify the handler.

F) Directly notify the handler within the 'loop' block.

Answer: E

Explanation: The correct approach to handle failures in an Ansible task and notify a handler is by using a 'failedwhen' condition. This condition allows you to define custom criteria for a task failure, which can then trigger a notification to a handler designed to address the failure, such as rolling back changes. In this context, checking the result of the 'register' variable for failure and specifying those conditions under 'failedwhen' ensures that appropriate actions, like rollback via a handler, are taken when package installation does not succeed. This method provides a controlled and reliable way to manage task failures.

Q59: In an Ansible playbook, which directive allows you to repeat a task a specified number of times or until a particular condition is met?
A) withitems

B) retry

C) until

D) loop

E) repeat

F) retryuntil

Answer: C

Explanation: In Ansible, the 'until' directive is used to repeat a task until a specified condition is met or a certain number of retries is exhausted. This directive is particularly useful for tasks that might fail initially but are expected to succeed eventually, such as waiting for a service to become available or a system to reach a desired state. By specifying an 'until' condition, you ensure that the task will keep attempting execution, providing a level of resilience to potential transient failures. The 'until' directive works in conjunction with the 'retries' and 'delay' parameters, allowing you to control the number of attempts and the wait time between attempts.

Q60: True or False: In Ansible, a task using a 'register' statement to capture output can directly notify a handler based on the registered variable's value.
A) True

B) False

Answer: B

Explanation: In Ansible, a task using a 'register' statement captures the output into a variable, but it cannot directly notify a handler based on the value of that variable. Instead, the playbook must include a subsequent task that evaluates the registered variable and then uses a 'when' condition to determine whether to notify a handler. This separation of capturing output and notifying handlers ensures clarity and modularity in playbook design, allowing for more sophisticated and controlled logic in response to task results. Therefore, while a 'register' can inform decision-making, it cannot directly trigger a handler without an additional conditional task.

Q61: Smith & Co. is a software development company that uses Jenkins for continuous integration and delivery. They have a Jenkins job set up to build their application, which requires different configurations for development and production environments. The team needs to pass a parameter to the Jenkins job to specify the target environment. This parameter will determine which configuration file should be used during the build process. The Jenkins job should be able to validate the input parameter and use it to execute the correct configuration script. Which built-in Jenkins feature can be used to achieve this functionality?

A) Build triggers

B) Post-build actions

C) Parameterized build

D) Environment variables

E) Build wrappers

F) Jenkins plugins

Answer: C

Explanation: Jenkins provides the option to configure jobs with parameters, known as "Parameterized Builds." This feature allows users to pass parameters to a build job, which can include environment-specific variables such as configuration files. The parameterized build enables the Jenkins job to prompt the user for input before the build starts, ensuring that the correct configuration is used based on the provided parameter. This functionality is crucial for managing different environments, as it allows for flexible and dynamic execution of build tasks without modifying the job configuration manually for each environment.

Q62: You are tasked with configuring a Jenkins job that requires interaction with a Linux-based system to execute a series of shell scripts. To ensure proper execution, you need to set up environment-specific variables before running the shell scripts. Which Jenkins feature or plugin allows you to manage environment variables effectively within a Jenkins job?

A) Build steps

B) Jenkins CLI

C) Node properties

D) Global Tool Configuration

E) Environment Injector Plugin

F) Build Pipeline Plugin

Answer: E

Explanation: The Environment Injector Plugin in Jenkins is designed to manage environment variables effectively within a Jenkins job. This plugin allows injecting environment variables at different stages of the build process. It supports loading variables from properties files, injecting variables based on job parameters, and setting them manually. This flexibility is particularly useful when dealing with complex build environments and ensures that the necessary variables are available for the shell scripts to execute correctly. This approach also helps in maintaining a clean and modular build configuration by separating environment settings from the build logic.

Q63: A Jenkins job is configured to run a shell script that requires user input for parameters like the build version and deployment region. The script needs to validate these inputs to ensure they meet the required format and constraints (e.g., version should be numeric, region should be one of the predefined options). What is the best way to handle parameter validation within Jenkins?

A) Use Jenkinsfile with Groovy

B) Use a pre-build shell script

C) Leverage Jenkins' input step

D) Implement Active Choices Plugin

E) Configure a post-build action

F) Use Jenkins' Job DSL Plugin

Answer: D

Explanation: The Active Choices Plugin in Jenkins is designed for parameter validation and dynamic input options. It allows the creation of dynamic parameters that can be validated and changed based on the selections made in the build parameter screen. With this plugin, you can define Groovy scripts that generate parameter options, verify input formats, and enforce constraints. This ensures that only valid inputs are accepted, thus reducing errors during the build process. By using this plugin, Jenkins can provide real-time feedback and validation to users, ensuring that parameters like build version and deployment region are correctly formatted and within specified constraints.

Q64: Consider the scenario where you are managing a Jenkins job for a web application deployment. The deployment process requires different parameters for database connection strings depending on whether it is a staging or production environment. This parameter needs to be dynamically selected during the job execution. True or False: The "Choice Parameter" in Jenkins is suitable for this requirement, as it allows users to select from a predefined list of options.
A) True

B) False

Answer: A

Explanation: The "Choice Parameter" feature in Jenkins is suitable for situations where users need to select from a predefined list of options. It allows you to define a parameter with multiple choice options, which can be selected during the build. This is especially useful for environment-specific configurations, such as selecting the correct database connection string for staging or production environments. By using the Choice Parameter, you ensure that users can only select valid options, minimizing the risk of errors during deployment. This feature is integrated into Jenkins and provides a straightforward way to handle dynamic parameter selection without requiring additional plugins or complex scripts.

Q65: An organization uses Jenkins to automate their build process, which includes compiling code, running tests, and deploying applications. They want to enhance their Jenkins job by allowing users to input a Git branch name as a parameter, which will be validated before the build starts. The validation should ensure the branch exists in the repository. What is the most efficient way to implement this in Jenkins?

A) Add a shell script validation step in the build

B) Use the Git Parameter Plugin

C) Configure a Jenkinsfile with custom validation logic

D) Implement a webhook to check branch existence

E) Use the Extended Choice Parameter Plugin

F) Set up a post-build action for validation

Answer: B

Explanation: The Git Parameter Plugin in Jenkins is specifically designed to handle parameters related to Git operations, such as selecting branches, tags, or revisions. This plugin provides a dynamic list of Git branches, which can be used as input parameters for a Jenkins job. By using this plugin, you can automatically fetch and display a list of existing branches from the repository, ensuring that users can only select valid branches. This approach eliminates the need for manual validation steps or custom scripts, streamlining the build process and reducing the risk of errors caused by incorrect branch names.

Q66: Your company, TechCloud Solutions, is transitioning its core application to a cloud-native architecture to improve scalability and reliability. The application consists of several microservices that need to communicate securely and efficiently. As the DevOps engineer, you are tasked with designing the deployment process using Infrastructure as Code (IaC) on a Linux-based system. It is crucial to ensure that the deployment is repeatable and consistent, and that it adheres to best practices for security and maintainability. You are considering using tools like Terraform and Ansible to manage the infrastructure and configurations. Which approach should you take to ensure that the application is deployed consistently across different environments while maintaining security best practices?

A) Use Terraform to provision infrastructure and manage configuration changes, focusing on storing all secrets in the code repository.

B) Use Ansible to deploy all services and manage infrastructure, storing credentials in Ansible Vault.

C) Use Terraform for infrastructure provisioning and Ansible for configuration management, ensuring secrets are managed with HashiCorp Vault.

D) Use Kubernetes to manage infrastructure and configurations, storing secrets in Kubernetes Secrets.

E) Use a combination of Docker Compose and shell scripts to manage the application deployment, with secrets stored in environment variables.

F) Use Terraform to manage the entire stack, including application configurations and secrets, storing everything in a private Git repository.

Answer: C

Explanation: In this scenario, using Terraform for infrastructure provisioning and Ansible for configuration management is a robust approach. Terraform excels at managing infrastructure as code, providing a declarative way to define cloud resources, which ensures repeatability and consistency across different environments. For configuration management and application deployment, Ansible is a suitable choice due to its agentless nature and ease of use. Managing secrets with HashiCorp Vault is a best practice for maintaining security, as it provides dynamic secrets, access control, and audit capabilities. This approach separates concerns effectively, using each tool's strengths, while ensuring that sensitive data is not hardcoded in scripts or stored insecurely.

Q67: When deploying a Linux-based application to cloud services, which of the following practices helps ensure application scalability and fault tolerance?

A) Deploy the application on a single large instance with a load balancer in front.

B) Use container orchestration tools like Kubernetes to manage multiple instances.

C) Deploy the application on multiple small instances without any orchestration.

D) Use a managed database service to reduce instance count.

E) Deploy the application using serverless architecture exclusively.

F) Store application logs on the same instances as the application.

Answer: B

Explanation: Using container orchestration tools like Kubernetes is a well-recognized practice for ensuring application scalability and fault tolerance. Kubernetes automates the deployment, scaling, and management of containerized applications, allowing for efficient scaling of services based on demand. It also provides mechanisms for load balancing and failover, ensuring that the application remains available even if individual instances fail. By abstracting the underlying infrastructure, Kubernetes enables efficient resource utilization and simplifies operations, making it an ideal choice for cloud-native applications.

Q68: In a Linux-based cloud environment, ensuring that application deployments are consistent and reliable is crucial. Which method is most effective for validating the application configuration before deploying to production?

A) Manually review configuration files before each deployment.

B) Implement CI/CD pipelines with automated tests and configuration checks.

C) Use configuration management tools to trigger manual validations.

D) Deploy to production first and rollback if issues are detected.

E) Use a dedicated staging environment but skip automated tests.

F) Rely on developer workstation tests before code merges.

Answer: B

Explanation: Implementing CI/CD pipelines with automated tests and configuration checks is the most effective method for validating application configurations before deploying to production. CI/CD pipelines automate the build, test, and deployment processes, ensuring that configurations are tested in a consistent manner. Automated tests can include unit tests, integration tests, and configuration linting to catch errors early in the development cycle. This approach not only helps in identifying issues before they reach production but also speeds up the deployment process by reducing manual intervention. It ensures that every change is validated under controlled conditions, providing a high level of confidence in the deployment's reliability.

Q69: When designing software for deployment to cloud services, it is essential to consider cost optimization. Which deployment strategy is typically most cost-effective for a Linux-based application with variable workloads?

A) Deploying on dedicated instances with fixed capacity.

B) Using cloud provider's auto-scaling groups with spot instances.

C) Deploying on-premises and using VPN to extend to cloud services.

D) Utilizing a hybrid cloud approach with reserved instances.

E) Deploying on the largest available instance type to minimize scaling.

F) Using a multi-cloud strategy to avoid vendor lock-in.

Answer: B

Explanation: Using cloud provider's auto-scaling groups with spot instances is a cost-effective strategy for applications with variable workloads. Auto-scaling allows the application to scale resources up or down based on demand, ensuring optimal resource utilization. Spot instances, offered at a significant discount compared to on-demand instances, can further reduce costs, especially for transient workloads that can tolerate interruptions. By leveraging both auto-scaling and spot instances, organizations can effectively manage costs while maintaining the flexibility to handle varying workloads, thus achieving a balance between performance and budget constraints.

Q70: True or False: When configuring a Linux-based application for deployment in a cloud environment, it is advisable to hardcode environment-specific variables directly into the application's source code to simplify deployment.
A) True

B) False

Answer: B

Explanation: Hardcoding environment-specific variables directly into the application's source code is not advisable. This practice can lead to several issues, such as difficulties in managing different configurations for various environments (e.g., development, staging, production), challenges in maintaining and updating these variables across multiple deployments, and potential security risks if sensitive information is exposed in the source code. Instead, environment variables should be managed using configuration management tools or environment-specific configuration files. This approach provides the flexibility to change configurations without altering the source code, enhances security by keeping sensitive data separate, and simplifies the deployment process by allowing the same codebase to be used across different environments with minimal changes.

Q71: Your company, Tech Innovators, is transitioning its applications to a microservices architecture to improve scalability and deployment flexibility. You have been tasked with designing a containerized environment for a new application. The application requires access to a configuration file that stores sensitive information, such as API keys and database credentials. Additionally, the application needs to be able to scale horizontally according to demand. What is the best practice for managing the configuration file to ensure security and scalability?

A) Embed the configuration file within the container image.

B) Store the configuration file in a shared network drive accessible by all containers.

C) Use environment variables to pass configuration details at runtime.

D) Utilize a secrets management tool to inject configuration data at startup.

E) Include the configuration file in a mounted volume.

F) Hardcode the configuration file contents in the application code.

Answer: D

Explanation: When designing containerized applications, especially those that handle sensitive information, security and scalability are critical considerations. Embedding configuration files within the container image or hardcoding them in the application code can expose sensitive data and require rebuilding the image for any configuration change, which is not scalable. Storing the configuration file on a shared network drive or including it in a mounted volume could lead to security vulnerabilities if not managed properly. Using environment variables to pass configuration details is a common practice, but it can expose sensitive information in logs or process listings. The best practice is to use a secrets management tool, such as HashiCorp Vault or AWS Secrets Manager, which securely injects configuration data at runtime. This approach keeps sensitive data out of the image and allows for dynamic configuration changes without redeploying the containers, thus ensuring both security and scalability.

Q72: A developer needs to build a Docker image for a Python application and wants to ensure that the image is as small as possible to reduce deployment time and resource usage. Which of the following strategies would help achieve the smallest image size?

A) Use a base image that includes all possible Python libraries.

B) Start with a minimal base image and install only the necessary dependencies.

C) Include development tools and compilers in the Docker image.

D) Use a virtual machine as the base for the Docker image.

E) Add a package manager to the Docker image for future installations.

F) Use a multi-stage build to separate build-time and runtime dependencies.

Answer: F

Explanation: When aiming to reduce the size of a Docker image, it's crucial to minimize unnecessary components. Starting with a minimal base image and installing only necessary dependencies is a good practice, but the most effective strategy is to use multi-stage builds. Multi-stage builds allow you to separate the build environment from the runtime environment, including only the necessary runtime dependencies in the final image. This technique significantly reduces the image size by keeping development tools, compilers, and any build-time dependencies out of the final image. Using a base image with all possible libraries or including development tools increases the image size unnecessarily. Similarly, using a virtual machine as the base for a Docker image is counterproductive, as it contradicts Docker's lightweight nature. Adding a package manager might be useful for development, but it can lead to larger image sizes when included in production images.

Q73: Which of the following commands should be used to list all running containers on a Linux system using Docker?

A) docker ps -a

B) docker container ls -a

C) docker ps

D) docker container list

E) docker images

F) docker container inspect

Answer: C

Explanation: The command docker ps is used to list all currently running Docker containers on a system. This command shows details such as container ID, image name, command, creation time, status, ports, and names of the running containers. The docker ps -a command lists all containers, including those that are stopped, which is not what is asked in this question. The docker container ls -a command is a variation that also lists all containers, including stopped ones, similar to docker ps -a. The docker container list is not a valid command. The docker images command lists available images, not containers. Lastly, docker container inspect provides detailed information about specific containers, but does not list them.

Q74: True or False: When deploying applications in Kubernetes, it is recommended to run containers as root for ease of management and access.

A) True

B) False

Answer: B

Explanation: Running containers as root is generally discouraged in Kubernetes deployments due to security concerns. Containers running as root have elevated privileges, which can pose a significant security risk if the container is compromised. Kubernetes provides mechanisms to enforce security contexts and restrict the capabilities granted to containers, promoting the principle of least privilege. Running processes with the minimal necessary privileges reduces the potential attack surface and limits the damage that can be done if a container is exploited. Best practices include running containers as a non-root user and using tools like PodSecurityPolicies or Open Policy Agent (OPA) to enforce security policies across your Kubernetes cluster.

Q75: You are tasked with designing a CI/CD pipeline for deploying a Node.js application using Docker containers. The pipeline should automatically build, test, and deploy the application whenever changes are pushed to the main branch. Which of the following tools is specifically designed to help automate the building and testing of Docker containers in this scenario?

A) Jenkins

B) GitLab CI/CD

C) Ansible

D) Vagrant

E) Terraform

F) Docker Compose

Answer: B

Explanation: GitLab CI/CD is a powerful tool that integrates seamlessly with GitLab repositories to automate the process of building, testing, and deploying applications. It is specifically designed to work with Docker containers, offering built-in support for Docker-based pipelines. Jenkins is also a popular CI/CD tool and can be configured to work with Docker, but GitLab CI/CD offers a more integrated experience for projects hosted on GitLab. Ansible and Terraform are primarily configuration management and infrastructure as code tools, respectively, and are not specifically designed for CI/CD pipelines. Docker Compose is used for defining and running multi-container Docker applications, but it is not a CI/CD tool. Vagrant is a tool for building and managing virtualized development environments, not for CI/CD.

Q76: A large e-commerce company is experiencing issues with their web servers, which are running on Linux. To analyze and resolve the issues, the DevOps team decides to examine the log files generated by the Apache HTTP Server. They need to ensure that the logs are stored in a standardized format for easy integration with their centralized logging system, which utilizes Elasticsearch and Kibana for log analysis and visualization. The team considers using the Common Log Format (CLF) or the Combined Log Format for Apache logs. Which configuration directive should they use in their Apache configuration file to ensure logs are in the Combined Log Format? ---

A) LogFormat "%h %l %u %t \"%r\" %>s %b" common

B) CustomLog "/var/log/apache2/access.log" common

C) LogFormat "%h %l %u %t \"%r\" %>s %b \"%{Referer}i\" \"%{User-Agent}i\"" combined

D) CustomLog "/var/log/apache2/access.log" combined

E) LogFormat "%v:%p %a %l %u %t \"%r\" %>s %b \"%{Referer}i\" \"%{User-Agent}i\"" common

F) CustomLog "/var/log/apache2/error.log" combined

Answer: D

Explanation: Apache HTTP Server supports different log formats through the LogFormat and CustomLog directives. The Common Log Format (CLF) is a standardized text file format used by web servers for producing log files, defined by the first option. However, the Combined Log Format extends CLF by adding two more fields: the Referer and User-Agent HTTP request headers. To configure Apache to use the Combined Log Format, you need both a LogFormat directive defining the format and a CustomLog directive that specifies the file location and the format to use. Option D correctly pairs the Combined Log Format with the file path in a CustomLog directive, which is necessary for the logs to be generated in that format and stored in the specified location. This setup is crucial for seamless integration with tools like Elasticsearch and Kibana, which can parse these standardized logs for analysis.

Q77: Which of the following statements is true regarding the syslog standard for logging on Linux systems? ---

A) Syslog provides a mechanism for log message filtering and forwarding, allowing centralized logging from multiple sources.

B) Syslog is only used for logging kernel messages and cannot be used for user-space applications.

Answer: A

Explanation: Syslog is a widely used standard for message logging on Unix-like systems, including Linux. It provides a way to collect logs from different applications and services in a centralized fashion, which can then be filtered, stored, and forwarded to a central server. This capability makes syslog an essential tool in environments where logs need to be aggregated from multiple systems for analysis or auditing. Although syslog can handle kernel messages, it is not limited to them; it can also manage logs from user-space applications, making option B incorrect. The flexibility and scalability of syslog make it a preferred choice for centralized logging solutions.

Q78: Identify the logging format that includes detailed information about the client browser and referer URL, and is commonly used in web server log configuration for enhanced analytics. ---

A) Common Log Format (CLF)

B) Extended Log Format (ELF)

C) Combined Log Format

D) JSON Log Format

E) Syslog Format

F) XML Log Format

Answer: C

Explanation: The Combined Log Format is an extension of the Common Log Format, adding two additional fields: the Referer and the User-Agent. These fields provide more detailed information about the client browser and the source of the request, which are crucial for web analytics and understanding user behavior. While the Common Log Format provides basic details such as the IP address, client identity, timestamp, and request details, the Combined Log Format's inclusion of referer and user-agent information enables more comprehensive analysis, which is vital for understanding traffic sources and client software.

Q79: In a Linux environment, which command allows you to view live log entries from the system log in a real-time manner?   ---

A) cat /var/log/syslog

B) head /var/log/syslog

C) tail -f /var/log/syslog

D) grep syslog

E) less /var/log/syslog

F) dmesg --follow

Answer: C

Explanation: The tail command with the -f (follow) option is used to monitor log files in real-time on a Linux system. By specifying tail -f /var/log/syslog, the command continuously reads new lines as they are appended to the log file, providing a dynamic view of the log entries. This is particularly useful for monitoring ongoing system activity, troubleshooting issues, and examining log entries as they occur. Other commands like cat, head, and less do not provide real-time updates and are static views of the file's current state. The dmesg --follow command is used for kernel messages, not general system logs.

Q80: A financial services firm needs to ensure that their application logs are compliant with industry standards for security and privacy. They decide to implement a structured logging format that can be easily parsed and analyzed by their security information and event management (SIEM) system. Which logging format should they choose to achieve this goal?

A) Common Log Format (CLF)

B) JSON Log Format

C) Combined Log Format

D) Plain Text Log Format

E) Syslog Format

F) Binary Log Format

Answer: B

Explanation: The JSON Log Format is a structured logging format that encapsulates log entries as JSON objects. This structure allows logs to be easily parsed and analyzed by automated systems, making it ideal for integration with SIEM systems that require detailed and structured data for security analysis. JSON's flexibility and readability make it suitable for including extensive metadata about each log event, such as timestamps, severity levels, and additional contextual information. This capability aligns with industry standards for security and privacy by enabling precise data extraction and correlation, ensuring compliance with stringent regulatory requirements. Other formats like the Common Log Format and Combined Log Format are less structured and don't provide the same level of detail or integration ease for modern security systems.

Q81: Your company is in the process of transitioning its infrastructure management from manual processes to a more automated, configuration-managed approach. You've been tasked with evaluating Puppet and Chef as potential tools for this transition. Part of the evaluation involves setting up a simple configuration to manage NTP services across your Linux servers. The goal is to ensure all servers are using the same NTP server. Consider the task of configuring a Puppet manifest and a Chef recipe for this purpose. Which of the following best describes the initial step in preparing your Linux environment to execute Puppet and Chef commands effectively?

A) Install Puppet and Chef server software on all target nodes.

B) Set up a central Git repository to store all configuration files.

C) Ensure all target nodes have the Puppet agent and Chef client installed.

D) Configure SSH access between the central management server and all target nodes.

E) Install a package manager like yum or apt-get on the central management server.

F) Establish a VPN connection between all target nodes and the central management server.

Answer: C

Explanation: To effectively use Puppet and Chef for configuration management, it's crucial that the Puppet agent and Chef client are installed on all target nodes. This is because Puppet operates using a client-server model where the Puppet agent communicates with the Puppet master to apply configurations. Similarly, Chef uses a client-server model where the Chef client pulls configurations from the Chef server. Installing the necessary client software ensures that each node can be managed remotely and consistently. While other steps like setting up version control or ensuring network access are important, the presence of the Puppet agent and Chef client is fundamental for the configuration management process.

Q82: When utilizing Puppet for configuration management, which command would you use to apply a manifest on a target node manually?
A) puppet apply

B) puppet execute

C) puppet run

D) puppet manifest

E) puppet enact

F) puppet deploy

Answer: A

Explanation: The puppet apply command is used to apply Puppet manifests locally on a target node, without requiring communication with a Puppet master. This command is particularly useful for testing or applying configurations on a single node or when a full client-server setup is not necessary. It reads a Puppet manifest file and directly applies the configurations described therein. Other options like puppet execute or puppet deploy are not valid Puppet commands.

Q83: A systems administrator needs to verify the version of Chef installed on a Linux server. Which command should they execute to obtain this information?
A) chef-server version

B) chef-client -v

C) chef-check version

D) chef-info -v

E) chef-status version

F) chef-node -v

Answer: B

Explanation: The chef-client -v command is used to display the version of the Chef client installed on a system. It's a straightforward way to verify the installed version, which is crucial for ensuring compatibility with recipes and cookbooks. The Chef client is responsible for pulling configurations from the Chef server and applying them on the node. Other commands listed are not valid for checking the version of Chef.

Q84: A company has multiple Linux servers managed by Puppet. They need to ensure that a specific configuration is only applied to servers in the "production" environment. Which Puppet feature allows you to target nodes based on their environment?

A) Puppet roles

B) Node definitions

C) Puppet classes

D) Environment-specific directories

E) Puppet facts

F) Site manifest

Answer: D

Explanation: Puppet environments are designed to allow different configurations to be applied based on the environment a node belongs to, such as "production" or "development". By organizing manifests and modules into environment-specific directories on the Puppet master, you can ensure that nodes only apply configurations intended for their environment. This approach helps maintain separation and control over configurations in different stages of deployment. Node definitions and Puppet classes are used to specify configurations, but environment-specific directories are what directly separate configurations by environment.

Q85: True/False: Chef and Puppet both require a central server to manage configurations across all nodes.

A) True

B) False

Answer: B

Explanation: While both Chef and Puppet can operate in a client-server model, they do not strictly require a central server to manage configurations. Puppet can use puppet apply to apply configurations locally without a Puppet master. Similarly, Chef can operate in a solo mode using the Chef Solo tool, which allows the execution of recipes without a Chef server. This flexibility is useful for smaller environments or testing purposes where a full client-server architecture may not be necessary.

Q86: A company is using Ansible to automate its infrastructure management. They need to securely store sensitive data such as API keys and passwords used in playbooks. The DevOps team has decided to use Ansible Vault for this purpose. The team wants to ensure that the playbooks can be executed without manually entering the vault password each time. They are considering using a script to automatically provide the vault password. How should they configure Ansible to achieve this? ---

A) Use the --ask-vault-pass option in the ansible-playbook command.

B) Store the vault password in a .vaultpass file in the home directory.

C) Specify the --vault-password-file option in the ansible-playbook command with a script that outputs the password.

D) Embed the vault password directly in the playbook file.

E) Use the VAULTPASSWORD environment variable to store the password.

F) Store the vault password in a .ansible.cfg file under the defaults section.

Answer: C

Explanation: Ansible Vault allows you to encrypt sensitive data in playbooks, and when running these playbooks, a vault password is required to decrypt the encrypted content. For automated environments where manual password entry isn't feasible, the --vault-password-file option is used. This option allows specifying a script or a file that automatically outputs the vault password. While embedding passwords directly in files or configurations might seem convenient, it's a security risk and should be avoided. Using environment variables like VAULTPASSWORD isn't supported in Ansible for vault passwords. Therefore, utilizing a script with the --vault-password-file option is the most secure and practical approach.

Q87: When using Ansible Vault, which command is used to initially encrypt a file containing sensitive information? ----

A) ansible-vault create

B) ansible-vault encrypt

C) ansible-vault lock

D) ansible-vault secure

E) ansible-vault protect

F) ansible-vault encode

Answer: B

Explanation: The ansible-vault encrypt command is specifically used to encrypt an existing file containing sensitive information. This command prompts the user to enter a vault password, which is then used to encrypt the file's contents. This is different from ansible-vault create, which is used to create a new encrypted file, prompting the user to both create the file and enter the data. There are no ansible-vault lock, ansible-vault secure, ansible-vault protect, or ansible-vault encode commands in Ansible Vault. Encrypting files with ansible-vault encrypt ensures that only users with the correct password can access the file, maintaining the confidentiality of the sensitive information.

Q88: A DevOps engineer is tasked with updating an encrypted variables file using Ansible Vault. The file is currently encrypted, and the engineer needs to modify its contents. Which command should they use to safely and correctly edit this encrypted file?   ---

A) ansible-vault update

B) ansible-vault modify

C) ansible-vault edit

D) ansible-vault change

E) ansible-vault rewrite

F) ansible-vault adjust

Answer: C

Explanation: The ansible-vault edit command is utilized to open an encrypted file in the default system editor, allowing the user to make modifications to the file's contents. When this command is executed, it temporarily decrypts the file in memory, enabling secure editing without exposing the decrypted content on disk. Once editing is complete, the file is automatically re-encrypted with the same vault password. This command is crucial for maintaining security while allowing necessary updates to encrypted files. Other options like ansible-vault update, modify, change, rewrite, and adjust do not exist in Ansible Vault for this purpose.

Q89: True or False: Ansible Vault allows the use of multiple passwords for different vault files within the same playbook execution.   ---

A) True

B) False

Answer: A

Explanation: Ansible Vault supports using different passwords for different vault files, even within the same playbook execution. This feature is particularly useful in scenarios where different teams or departments maintain separate sets of sensitive data, each protected by its own password. To facilitate this, Ansible provides the --vault-id option, which allows specifying multiple vault identifiers, each associated with a different password file or script. This flexibility enhances security and access control across various components of an infrastructure, as each vault file can be independently managed while still being used collectively in a single automation run.

Q90: Your organization has a policy that requires rotation of vault passwords every 90 days. As the DevOps engineer, you are responsible for updating the vault password in a way that minimizes downtime and disruption. Which procedure should you follow to ensure a smooth transition to a new vault password?

A) Create a new vault file with the new password and update all references in the playbooks.

B) Decrypt all vault files, change the password, then re-encrypt them with the new password.

C) Use ansible-vault change-password to update the password for all vault files.

D) Manually edit each encrypted file to update the password.

E) Synchronize password change across all vault files using rsync.

F) Create a new vault file with a temporary password, then change it to the new password.

Answer: C

Explanation: The ansible-vault change-password command is specifically designed to change the password of existing vault files. This command will prompt for the current password and the new password, then re-encrypt the files with the new password. This approach ensures a smooth transition with minimal disruption, as it systematically updates the password without needing to manually decrypt or re-create files. It is important to update any password scripts or files used in automation to reflect the new password. The other options, such as decrypting and re-encrypting files manually or using rsync, are either inefficient or inappropriate for a seamless password update.

Q91: A development team is working on a new feature for their application and is using a Git repository hosted on a Linux server. The team needs to ensure that all new files added to the repository are automatically checked for a specific code style guide compliance. They plan to implement a pre-commit hook to run a custom script that performs this check. The team wants the hook to be available for all developers in their local clones of the repository without requiring individual setup. Which approach should they take to achieve this?

A) Create a pre-commit hook script in the .git/hooks/ directory of the repository and commit it to the repository.

B) Use the git config command to set the core.hooksPath configuration variable to a shared directory containing the hook script.

C) Add the pre-commit hook script to the repository and include instructions in the README for developers to copy it to their .git/hooks/ directory.

D) Utilize a global Git template directory to store the pre-commit hook script and instruct developers to clone the repository using git init --template.

E) Implement a client-side Git alias that executes the pre-commit hook script before each commit.

F) Install a server-side Git hook on the repository hosting server that rejects commits not passing the style guide check.

Answer: B

Explanation: To ensure that the pre-commit hook is automatically available to all developers without individual setup, the most effective approach is to use a shared hooks directory. By configuring the core.hooksPath variable, you can specify a directory that contains all the hook scripts shared across the development team. This configuration makes the hooks available for all clones of the repository, as Git will look in the specified directory for hooks instead of the default .git/hooks/. While committing the hook script or including setup instructions could work, they require manual steps for each developer. A server-side hook would enforce checks only on the server level, not locally before commits.

Q92: A developer is trying to remove a file from the Git index but wants to keep the file in the working directory. Which Git command will accomplish this task?

A) git rm filename

B) git reset filename

C) git rm --cached filename

D) git stash filename

E) git checkout filename

F) git revert filename

Answer: C

Explanation: The git rm --cached filename command removes the file from the Git index (staging area) without deleting the file from the working directory. This operation is useful when you want to stop tracking a file but keep it in your local file system. The git rm command without the --cached option would also delete the file from the working directory, which is not the desired behavior in this scenario. Other options, like git reset or git stash, serve different purposes and do not specifically remove a file from the index while retaining it in the working directory.

Q93: A company has implemented a policy that all changes to the main branch must be reviewed and approved before merging. After the review, a developer should merge changes from a feature branch into the main branch while retaining the individual commit history of the feature branch. Which Git command should the developer use to achieve this?

A) git rebase

B) git merge --squash

C) git merge --no-ff

D) git merge --ff-only

E) git pull --rebase

F) git cherry-pick

Answer: C

Explanation: The git merge --no-ff command ensures that a merge commit is created even if the merge could be resolved with a fast-forward. This approach retains the individual commit history of the feature branch and creates a specific commit that represents the merge. Using --squash would combine all changes into a single commit, which is not desired when the commit history should be preserved. git rebase changes the commit history, which is not suitable for this scenario. The --ff-only option would perform a fast-forward merge and not create a merge commit if possible.

Q94: In a collaborative environment, developers frequently need to identify which files have been changed between two branches in the Git repository. They want a command that lists the files changed, ignoring any file mode changes, between branch feature and branch develop. Which command should be used for this purpose?

A) git diff feature develop --name-only

B) git diff feature develop --name-status

C) git log feature..develop --name-only

D) git diff-tree feature develop

E) git ls-files feature develop

F) git status feature develop

Answer: A

Explanation: The git diff feature develop --name-only command lists the names of files that differ between the two specified branches, feature and develop. This command output will exclude details about file mode changes and focus solely on file names, making it ideal for quickly identifying which files have been altered. The --name-status option would include the status of the files (e.g., added, modified, deleted), which is not requested here. The git log and git diff-tree commands provide different types of information and are not directly used for listing changed files between branches.

Q95: True/False: Using the git clean -f command will remove untracked files from the working directory in a Git repository.

A) True

B) False

Answer: A

Explanation: The git clean -f command is used to remove untracked files from the working directory in a Git repository. Untracked files are those that are not part of the Git index, meaning they have not been staged or committed. The -f flag is required to force the clean operation since the command is potentially destructive, removing files that are not under version control. This command is useful for cleaning up a working directory, especially before starting a new feature or release to ensure there are no lingering files that could affect the build or development process.

Q96: You are working as a DevOps engineer at a mid-sized company that has recently adopted Ansible for configuration management and automation. The security team has requested that all SSH connections used by Ansible for managing servers be made using unprivileged login accounts. However, these accounts should be able to perform administrative tasks without compromising security controls. You decide to use a combination of SSH key-based authentication and sudo privileges. Which configuration file would you modify to ensure that the Ansible user can execute commands as root without providing a password every time?

A) /etc/ssh/sshconfig

B) /etc/ansible/hosts

C) /etc/sudoers

D) /home/ansible/.ssh/config

E) /etc/passwd

F) /etc/ansible/ansible.cfg

Answer: C

Explanation: The file /etc/sudoers is used to define which users can execute commands as other users, and what commands they can run. By configuring the sudoers file, you can allow the Ansible user to execute specific commands as root without needing to enter a password each time. This is achieved by adding a line in the sudoers file, such as ansible ALL=(ALL) NOPASSWD: ALL, which allows the 'ansible' user to execute all commands as any user without a password prompt. This configuration supports security by ensuring that the Ansible user cannot log in as root directly, instead allowing privilege escalation only for specified tasks. It is crucial to use visudo to edit the sudoers file to prevent syntax errors that could lock you out of administrative privileges.

Q97: Which SSH option allows an Ansible playbook to connect to a managed host using a specific private key file for authentication?
A) StrictHostKeyChecking

B) UserKnownHostsFile

C) IdentityFile

D) ControlPath

E) LogLevel

F) ForwardAgent

Answer: C

Explanation: The IdentityFile option in SSH is used to specify the private key file that should be used for authentication when connecting to a host. In the context of Ansible, this can be set either in the Ansible configuration file or directly in the inventory file to ensure that the appropriate SSH key is used for each managed host. This is particularly important when managing multiple servers that require different credentials or when operating in a multi-environment setup. Using the correct private key ensures secure, password-less authentication, aligning with best practices for automated deployments and configurations.

Q98: While configuring Ansible to manage a fleet of Linux servers, you encounter a requirement to disable host key checking to avoid prompts during playbook execution. Which configuration adjustment is necessary to achieve this?

A) Set hostkeychecking = False in the /etc/ansible/ansible.cfg

B) Set PermitRootLogin no in /etc/ssh/sshdconfig

C) Add -o UserKnownHostsFile=/dev/null to the ansible-playbook command

D) Add -o StrictHostKeyChecking=no to the ansible-playbook command

E) Edit ~/.ssh/config to include StrictHostKeyChecking no

F) Set remoteuser = root in the playbook

Answer: A

Explanation: Disabling host key checking in Ansible can be achieved by setting the hostkeychecking parameter to False in the Ansible configuration file, typically located at /etc/ansible/ansible.cfg. This parameter, when set to false, prevents Ansible from prompting the user to verify the authenticity of the host key during SSH connections. While this can be useful in development or testing environments to streamline playbook execution, it poses a security risk in production environments as it can expose the system to man-in-the-middle attacks. Best practices suggest using this configuration sparingly and considering alternatives, such as properly managing known hosts entries.

Q99: Ansible requires SSH access to manage remote machines. True or False: SSH login using password authentication is more secure than using key-based authentication.

A) True

B) False

Answer: B

Explanation: Key-based authentication is generally more secure than password-based authentication for SSH connections. With key-based authentication, a unique cryptographic key pair is used, which eliminates the need to transmit passwords over the network. This reduces the risk of password interception or brute-force attacks. Furthermore, SSH keys can be protected with a passphrase, adding an additional layer of security. Key-based authentication also allows for more granular access control and can be easily managed and revoked. In contrast, password-based authentication relies on user-entered passwords, which can be weaker or reused across different systems, increasing security risks.

Q100: A new policy at your organization requires that all SSH connections initiated by Ansible use unprivileged accounts with key-based authentication. You need to ensure these accounts are able to execute necessary administrative tasks. Which command would you use to generate an SSH key pair for the Ansible user?

A) ssh-add -t rsa

B) ssh-keygen -b 4096

C) ssh-keyscan -t rsa

D) ssh-copy-id -i

E) ssh-agent bash

F) ssh -o

Answer: B

Explanation: The ssh-keygen command is used to generate SSH key pairs. The option -b 4096 specifies the bit length of the key, with 4096 being a common choice for strong security. By running ssh-keygen -b 4096, you create a new pair of public and private keys in the default location, usually ~/.ssh/idrsa and ~/.ssh/idrsa.pub. The public key can then be distributed to the remote servers you wish to manage with Ansible, allowing for secure, password-less authentication. This practice aligns with the organization's requirement for using unprivileged accounts while maintaining the ability to execute administrative tasks via sudo configurations.

Q101: A medium-sized tech company is transitioning its infrastructure to use Vagrant for managing development environments. The DevOps team is tasked with setting up consistent environments for developers across various teams. They decide to leverage pre-configured boxes from HashiCorp Atlas (now referred to as Vagrant Cloud) to speed up the process. The team needs to ensure that they are using the most suitable box for their Ubuntu-based application stack, which requires a specific version of Ubuntu with minimal setup overhead. How should the team retrieve and use the correct box from Atlas?

A) Use the command vagrant box add ubuntu/trusty64 and specify the version in the Vagrantfile.

B) Search on Atlas for an Ubuntu box and use the command vagrant init <box-name> to initialize.

C) Directly download the box file from Atlas and manually import it using vagrant box add.

D) Run vagrant box list to find available Ubuntu boxes on Atlas and select one.

E) Configure the Vagrantfile with config.vm.boxurl to point to the desired box on Atlas.

F) Use the vagrant search command to find the box and then vagrant box add with the appropriate version.

Answer: A

Explanation: To retrieve and use a box from Atlas (Vagrant Cloud), the team should first identify the desired box by searching on the platform. The command vagrant box add is used to add a box from Vagrant Cloud, and specifying the box name, such as ubuntu/trusty64, will fetch the latest version unless specified otherwise. In the Vagrantfile, the version can be explicitly set to ensure consistency across environments. This approach ensures that the team is using the correct version of Ubuntu with minimal setup overhead. Option A is correct because it streamlines the process by adding the box and managing versions directly through the Vagrantfile, which is essential for keeping development environments consistent.

Q102: In the context of using Vagrant boxes from Atlas, is it necessary to always specify the box version in the Vagrantfile to ensure consistency across different environments?

A) True

B) False

Answer: A

Explanation: Specifying the box version in the Vagrantfile is crucial for ensuring that every developer or environment is using the same base image. This practice prevents discrepancies that might arise from using different versions of a base box, which could lead to inconsistencies in the development environment. By locking the version, you ensure that even if newer versions of the box are released, the environments remain stable and predictable, mirroring production conditions more closely. Therefore, always specifying the box version is a best practice for maintaining consistency.

Q103: When managing Vagrant boxes from Atlas, which command allows you to update an already added box to its latest version available on Vagrant Cloud?

A) vagrant box update

B) vagrant box upgrade

C) vagrant box refresh

D) vagrant box sync

E) vagrant box reinstall

F) vagrant box patch

Answer: A

Explanation: The vagrant box update command is used to update an existing box to the latest version available on Vagrant Cloud. This command checks for updates to the box specified in the Vagrantfile or the added box list and downloads the latest version if it is available. This functionality is crucial for keeping environments up-to-date with the latest patches and improvements, enhancing security and performance. Using this command ensures that the most recent, stable, and secure version of the box is being used across all instances.

Q104: Which configuration in the Vagrantfile would you use to ensure that a Vagrant box is always reloaded from scratch rather than using an existing one from the cache, particularly useful in a continuous integration setup?
A) config.vm.boxcheckupdate = true

B) config.vm.boxversion = "latest"

C) config.vm.provision :reload

D) config.vm.boxreload = true

E) config.vm.boxcleancache = true

F) config.vm.destroyonreload = true

Answer: A

Explanation: The config.vm.boxcheckupdate = true setting in the Vagrantfile is used to ensure that Vagrant checks for updates to the box each time it is brought up. This setting is particularly useful in continuous integration (CI) setups where you want to ensure that the most recent box version is used, avoiding cached versions that might not include the latest updates or patches. This approach helps maintain an up-to-date and consistent environment across CI pipelines, crucial for testing and development reliability.

Q105: While setting up a new project, a DevOps engineer decides to utilize a custom Vagrant box hosted on Atlas. The engineer needs to share this environment with the team, ensuring everyone uses the same setup without manually installing the box. Which step should be taken to achieve this?

A) Share the Vagrantfile with the box URL specified using config.vm.boxurl.

B) Provide the team with access to the box file and instructions to manually add it.

C) Use the vagrant package command to create a reusable package.

D) Instruct the team to clone the repository and run vagrant box install.

E) Host the box on a local server and provide the link in the Vagrantfile.

F) Ensure the box is public on Atlas and reference it in the Vagrantfile.

Answer: F

Explanation: By hosting the custom Vagrant box on Vagrant Cloud (formerly Atlas) and ensuring it is set to public, the engineer can simply reference the box by name in the Vagrantfile. This method allows each team member to automatically download and use the exact same box configuration by running vagrant up, without requiring any manual installation. This practice ensures consistency across all development environments, as everyone pulls from the same source, reducing setup errors and environment drift.

Q106: You are working as a DevOps engineer for a company that has multiple environments for development, testing, and production. Each environment has a dedicated server with different configurations and paths to critical resources. The development team frequently needs to switch between these environments to deploy and test their applications. To streamline the process, you decide to use environment variables to manage different configurations. You want a solution that allows developers to easily switch between environments by exporting a single file that sets all necessary variables. Which of the following methods would best achieve this goal? ---

A) Use individual files for each environment and source the appropriate file.

B) Manually export variables in the shell for each session.

C) Use a centralized configuration management tool to set variables.

D) Use command-line arguments to pass necessary variables for each session.

E) Write a shell script that prompts for environment selection and sets variables accordingly.

F) Use a version control system to manage different configuration files.

Answer: A

Explanation: The most efficient way to manage different environment configurations in a Linux environment is by using individual files for each environment. Each file would contain the necessary export commands to set the environment variables specific to that environment. By sourcing the appropriate file (e.g., source devenv.sh), developers can quickly switch contexts without manually setting variables each time. This approach is both scalable and maintains separation of concerns, as it keeps configuration data organized and easily manageable. Alternative methods, such as using command-line arguments or manually exporting variables, can be error-prone and inefficient, especially as the number of variables grows and as more environments are added. A centralized configuration management tool could be overkill for this task and might introduce unnecessary complexity.

Q107: To ensure that a specific environment variable is set for every user session on a Linux server, where should the variable be defined? ---

A) ~/.bashprofile

B) /etc/environment

C) ~/.bashrc

D) /etc/profile

E) ~/.profile

F) /etc/bashrc

Answer: B

Explanation: The /etc/environment file is used to set environment variables that should be available to all users and all sessions on a Linux system. Unlike shell-specific configuration files like ~/.bashrc or /etc/bashrc, /etc/environment is a part of the PAM (Pluggable Authentication Modules) system and is used by the system to set variables for all users. This makes it ideal for defining environment variables that need to be globally available. Files like ~/.bashprofile and ~/.profile are user-specific and affect only the login sessions of the user for whom they are configured. While /etc/profile can be used for system-wide configuration, it is generally used for login shells and not for setting environment variables per se.

Q108: A company utilizes a build server which runs various CI/CD pipelines. These pipelines require the use of a secret API key, which should not be exposed in the codebase. To securely manage this API key as an environment variable, what is the most appropriate practice? ---

A) Store the API key in a version-controlled environment configuration file.

B) Hardcode the API key into the build scripts.

C) Use encrypted secrets management provided by the CI/CD tool.

D) Set the API key as a global environment variable on the build server.

E) Pass the API key as a command-line argument to each script.

F) Use a shared network drive to store the API key and read it during the build.

Answer: C

Explanation: Using encrypted secrets management provided by the CI/CD tool is the most secure and appropriate method for handling sensitive information like API keys. Most modern CI/CD tools offer built-in secrets management features, which allow you to store and access sensitive data in a secure and controlled manner. This approach ensures that the API key is not exposed in the codebase or logs and is only accessible to authorized pipelines. Hardcoding the API key or storing it in a version-controlled file would risk exposing the secret, while setting it as a global environment variable on the build server could lead to unintended access or leakage. Passing secrets as command-line arguments or storing them on a shared network drive are also insecure practices that could lead to exposure.

Q109: When working with a Bash script, you need to pass a variable from the parent shell to the script. Which command should you use in the parent shell to ensure the variable is accessible within the script?   ---
A) export VARIABLE=value

B) VARIABLE=value

C) set VARIABLE=value

D) declare VARIABLE=value

E) source VARIABLE=value

F) env VARIABLE=value

Answer: A

Explanation: To pass a variable from the parent shell to a script, you must use the export command. The export command marks an environment variable to be passed along to child processes. By exporting a variable, you make it part of the environment that is inherited by any subsequently executed commands, including scripts. Simply setting a variable without exporting it makes it available only within the current shell session and not to any child processes. Commands like set, declare, and env do not inherently make a variable available to child processes in the same way that exporting does. The source command is used to execute commands from a file in the current shell, not to set environment variables for scripts.

Q110: True or False: When a shell script is executed, it creates a new child process and inherits all environment variables from the parent shell.
A) True

B) False

Answer: A

Explanation: When a shell script is executed, it indeed creates a new child process, and this process inherits all the environment variables from the parent shell. This inheritance is a fundamental aspect of how processes work in Unix-like operating systems, including Linux. Environment variables set in the parent shell are passed to any child processes, allowing scripts to access configuration and state information needed for their execution. However, any changes made to environment variables within the script do not affect the parent shell's environment; they only affect the child process and any processes it spawns thereafter. This behavior allows for a controlled environment where scripts can operate with the necessary context without altering the state of the parent shell.

Q111: You are working as a DevOps engineer for a company that is transitioning its development environments to use Vagrant for increased consistency and ease of deployment. One of the requirements is to ensure that developers can seamlessly edit code on their local machines and have changes reflected immediately in the Vagrant virtual machine (VM). The development team uses a variety of Linux distributions as their host systems. You need to set up a shared folder between the host system and Vagrant VM that works reliably across these distributions without requiring additional software installations on the host. Which Vagrant sync folder type should you configure to meet these requirements?

A) NFS (Network File System)

B) VirtualBox shared folders

C) Rsync

D) SMB (Server Message Block)

E) Bindfs

F) SSHFS (SSH Filesystem)

Answer: C

Explanation: Rsync is the best choice here as it allows for synchronization between the host and the guest without requiring additional software installations on the host, which is a primary requirement in this scenario. While Rsync does not provide real-time syncing by default, it can be configured with the rsync-auto command to watch for changes and update the VM automatically. This method is highly platform-independent, which is crucial given the use of various Linux distributions. Other options like NFS, VirtualBox shared folders, and SMB might require specific configurations or software on the host, potentially violating the requirement for no additional installations.

Q112: When configuring a shared folder in Vagrant using the default provider VirtualBox, which command would you use in your Vagrantfile to define a shared directory between the host system and the virtual machine?
A) config.vm.sharefolder "/host/path", "/vm/path"

B) config.vm.syncedfolder "/host/path", "/vm/path"

C) config.vm.networkshare "/host/path", "/vm/path"

D) config.vm.mountfolder "/host/path", "/vm/path"

E) config.vm.nfsshare "/host/path", "/vm/path"

F) config.vm.bindfolder "/host/path", "/vm/path"

Answer: B

Explanation: The config.vm.syncedfolder directive in the Vagrantfile is used to define shared folders between the host system and the Vagrant virtual machine when using VirtualBox as the provider. This command ensures that the specified host directory is available inside the VM at the defined path, allowing for easy file synchronization. This is particularly useful for development environments where code changes need to be reflected immediately in the VM.

Q113: True or False: The Vagrant syncedfolder feature only works with VirtualBox as the provider.
A) True

B) False

Answer: B

Explanation: False. The syncedfolder feature in Vagrant is not limited to the VirtualBox provider. It is a general feature of Vagrant that supports multiple providers, including VMware, Hyper-V, and Docker, among others. Each provider might have different capabilities and requirements for setting up synced folders, but the basic functionality is supported across various providers. This flexibility allows Vagrant to be a versatile tool for development environments, regardless of the underlying virtualization technology.

Q114: You have set up a synced folder using NFS between your Linux host and a Vagrant VM. However, you notice that file permissions on the VM do not match those on the host. What configuration should you add to your Vagrantfile to ensure file permissions are preserved correctly?

A) config.vm.syncedfolder "/host/path", "/vm/path", type: "nfs", mountoptions: ["rw", "allsquash"]

B) config.vm.syncedfolder "/host/path", "/vm/path", type: "nfs", mountoptions: ["rw", "actimeo=2"]

C) config.vm.syncedfolder "/host/path", "/vm/path", type: "nfs", mountoptions: ["rw", "norootsquash"]

D) config.vm.syncedfolder "/host/path", "/vm/path", type: "nfs", mountoptions: ["rw", "anonuid=1000", "anongid=1000"]

E) config.vm.syncedfolder "/host/path", "/vm/path", type: "nfs", mountoptions: ["rw", "async"]

F) config.vm.syncedfolder "/host/path", "/vm/path", type: "nfs", mountoptions: ["rw", "sync"]

Answer: D

Explanation: To ensure that file permissions are preserved correctly when using NFS, you can use the anonuid and anongid options in the mountoptions array. These options map the anonymous user and group IDs that NFS uses to the desired user ID (uid) and group ID (gid) on the host. This setup is essential for maintaining correct file ownership and permissions, especially when working with development environments that require accurate permission settings for software builds and other processes.

Q115: A development team is using a Vagrant configuration with the rsync synced folder type. They have reported that files edited on the host are not immediately reflected in the VM. You need to address this issue without changing the synced folder type. What step should you take to ensure changes are synchronized automatically?

A) Modify the Vagrantfile to use config.vm.syncedfolder "/host/path", "/vm/path", type: "rsync", rsyncauto: true

B) Run vagrant rsync-auto in the terminal after starting the VM

C) Change the provider to VirtualBox to enable real-time synchronization

D) Install a file watcher tool on the VM to monitor changes and sync them

E) Use a cron job to periodically run vagrant rsync

F) Switch to using a different synced folder type that supports mirroring, like NFS or SMB

Answer: B

Explanation: To ensure that changes are synchronized automatically when using the rsync synced folder type, you should run vagrant rsync-auto in the terminal after starting the VM. This command enables a file watcher on the host machine that detects changes in the specified directories and automatically syncs them to the VM. This approach allows developers to continue using rsync while achieving near real-time synchronization without altering the Vagrantfile or the synced folder type.

Q116: Your company, TechSolutions, is deploying a new microservices-based application to improve its e-commerce platform. The application consists of several services, each running in its own container. You are tasked with setting up a reverse proxy to route requests to the appropriate service based on the URL path. The services are named users, orders, and inventory, with the following respective paths: /api/users, /api/orders, and /api/inventory. Which of the following configurations for the Nginx reverse proxy would correctly route the requests?

A) Using location /api/ to match all services, with proxypass for each path.

B) Using location / for a default route, with sub-locations for each service.

C) Using specific location blocks for each path /api/users, /api/orders, /api/inventory.

D) Using location ~ with regex for dynamic path matching.

E) Using a single location block with conditional statements to differentiate services.

F) Using location = for exact path matching.

Answer: C

Explanation: When configuring Nginx as a reverse proxy for a microservices architecture, it is crucial to define specific location blocks for each service path to ensure accurate routing. By using distinct location blocks for /api/users, /api/orders, and /api/inventory, you can direct traffic to the correct backend service based on the requested URL path. This approach is clear and maintainable, allowing each service to be configured independently, which is essential for managing changes and scaling services. Using a catch-all or regex-based approach can complicate configurations and lead to misrouting if paths overlap or aren't clearly defined.

Q117: In a service-based architecture, you need to ensure that your application services can communicate securely over the network using TLS. Which Linux command is most appropriate for generating a private key and a self-signed certificate for testing purposes?

A) openssl req -newkey rsa:2048 -nodes -keyout key.pem -x509 -days 365 -out certificate.pem

B) openssl genrsa -out key.pem 2048

C) ssh-keygen -t rsa -b 2048 -f key.pem

D) gpg --gen-key

E) certbot certonly --standalone

F) keytool -genkeypair -alias mycert -keyalg RSA -keystore keystore.jks

Answer: A

Explanation: The openssl req command with the -newkey, -x509, and -days options is used to generate a new private key and a self-signed certificate in one step. This is particularly useful for testing environments where a fully-fledged certificate isn't necessary. The rsa:2048 option specifies the key size, and the -nodes option indicates that the private key should not be encrypted with a passphrase. This command is a standard approach for creating self-signed certificates, ensuring secure communication for application services in development or testing phases.

Q118: True or False: In a Linux-based service architecture, using systemd unit files is an effective way to manage and automate the start-up of services across different environments.

A) True

B) False

Answer: A

Explanation: systemd is the init system used by many modern Linux distributions to bootstrap the user space and manage system processes. It provides a standardized way to define service unit files, which specify how services should be started, stopped, and managed. Utilizing systemd unit files allows services to be consistently managed across different environments, such as development, testing, and production. It also supports dependency management, parallel start-up, and log management, making it an effective tool for service management in complex Linux-based architecture setups.

Q119: You are tasked with optimizing the performance of a service-based application running on multiple Linux servers. Which command would you use to monitor and analyze CPU usage by each service to identify potential bottlenecks?

A) top

B) htop

C) vmstat

D) iostat

E) perf stat

F) netstat

Answer: B

Explanation: htop is an interactive process viewer for Unix systems, which is a more user-friendly and visually appealing alternative to top. It provides a comprehensive overview of system resource usage, including CPU and memory consumption by each process. htop makes it easier to identify which services are consuming the most CPU resources, allowing you to pinpoint bottlenecks more effectively. It displays processes in a tree view, highlights resource-intensive processes, and offers filtering and sorting options, making it ideal for detailed performance analysis in a service-oriented architecture.

Q120: During the deployment of a new service on your Linux server, you need to ensure that the service starts automatically after a system reboot. Which command should you use to accomplish this in a systemd-managed environment?

A) systemctl enable <service>

B) systemctl start <service>

C) systemctl reload <service>

D) systemctl daemon-reload

E) systemctl is-enabled <service>

F) systemctl status <service>

Answer: A

Explanation: In a systemd-managed environment, the systemctl enable command is used to configure a service to start automatically at boot time. This command creates the necessary symbolic links in the system's multi-user.target or graphical.target directories, depending on the service type, ensuring that the service is activated during system initialization. It is important to distinguish between enable and start; enable configures the service for future boots, while start only affects the current session. This distinction is crucial for maintaining service availability and reliability across reboots in production environments.

Q121: You are working as a DevOps engineer for a mid-sized technology firm that is transitioning to Infrastructure as Code (IaC) using Ansible. The company has a mix of applications that need standardized configurations across various environments, such as development, testing, and production. Your team has decided to use Ansible roles to streamline this process. The company wants to leverage community roles from Ansible Galaxy to expedite development but is concerned about security and compatibility with existing infrastructure. To address these concerns, you must ensure that the roles are properly vetted and compatible with your current Ansible version (2.9) before implementation. What is your first step in acquiring and using a role from Ansible Galaxy?   ---

A) Run the command ansible-galaxy install <rolename> without checks.

B) Review the role's documentation and dependencies on its Ansible Galaxy page.

C) Directly clone the role's GitHub repository to your Ansible roles directory.

D) Use the ansible-galaxy search command to find roles compatible with Ansible 2.9.

E) Install the role in a testing environment and execute a playbook to verify functionality.

F) Check the role's ratings and reviews to determine its reliability.

Answer: B

Explanation: The correct first step in acquiring and using a role from Ansible Galaxy is to review the role's documentation and dependencies on its Ansible Galaxy page. This ensures that you understand the role's purpose, the variables it requires, and any dependencies or compatibility issues with your current Ansible version. This step is critical to avoid potential conflicts and ensure that the role aligns with your organization's infrastructure needs. While other steps, such as testing the role in a safe environment, are important, starting with a thorough review of documentation is essential to inform your next actions.

Q122: Which command would you use to list all installed roles on your local system using Ansible Galaxy?   ---

A) ansible-galaxy list

B) ansible-galaxy show

C) ansible-galaxy info

D) ansible-galaxy roles

E) ansible-galaxy collection list

F) ansible-galaxy display

Answer: A

Explanation: The ansible-galaxy list command is used to display all the roles that are currently installed on your local system. This command helps you quickly verify which roles are available for use in your playbooks and can be an essential tool for managing role dependencies and updates. While other commands might provide specific information about roles or collections, they do not list all installed roles succinctly.

Q123: You have downloaded a role from Ansible Galaxy and included it in your project's directory. You want to verify if the role has been properly installed and available for use in your Ansible playbooks. Which Ansible command would you use to accomplish this?   ---

A) ansible-galaxy install -r requirements.yml

B) ansible-playbook check-role.yml

C) ansible-galaxy list

D) ansible-role check <rolename>

E) ansible-galaxy verify <rolename>

F) ansible-role list

Answer: C

Explanation: The ansible-galaxy list command is used to verify that a role has been properly installed on your system. This command will display all roles that are available, including any that have been recently added, confirming their availability for use in your playbooks. It's a straightforward method to ensure the presence and correct installation of roles without executing a playbook or manually searching through directories.

Q124: A company is concerned about security vulnerabilities when using roles from Ansible Galaxy. They have asked you to ensure that all roles are from trusted sources before being implemented. How would you verify the source of an Ansible Galaxy role?   ---

A) Check the role's source code for any security issues.

B) Verify the role's maintainer and source repository against trusted lists.

C) Use the ansible-galaxy verify command to check for trusted sources.

D) Only use roles with a high number of downloads and positive reviews.

E) Review the role's version history and update notes for security patches.

F) Install roles only if they have been tagged as "secure" by Ansible Galaxy.

Answer: B

Explanation: The most effective way to verify the source of an Ansible Galaxy role is to check the role's maintainer and source repository against trusted lists. This involves researching the role's author, ensuring they have a reputable standing in the community, and confirming that the repository used to develop the role is recognized as a trusted source. While reviews and download counts can provide some insight into a role's reliability, they do not guarantee the authenticity or security of the source. Security is paramount, and verifying the source helps mitigate the risk of incorporating malicious or vulnerable code into your environment.

Q125: True or False: Ansible roles on Ansible Galaxy can be directly installed on any version of Ansible without compatibility concerns.
A) True

B) False

Answer: B

Explanation: False. Ansible roles on Ansible Galaxy are not universally compatible with all versions of Ansible. Each role may have specific version requirements or dependencies that need to be met to function correctly. It is crucial to check the compatibility of a role with your specific version of Ansible before installation. This often involves reviewing the role's metadata or documentation, which usually specifies the versions of Ansible that the role supports. Failure to ensure compatibility can lead to errors or unexpected behavior when executing playbooks.

Q126: A tech company is transitioning to an Infrastructure as Code model using Ansible. The DevOps team needs to automate user account creation across multiple servers. They must ensure that all users are added to a specific group and that their home directories are created with the correct permissions. Which Ansible module should the team use to achieve this task efficiently? ---
A) service

B) user

C) group

D) copy

E) shell

F) template

Answer: B

Explanation: The user module in Ansible is specifically designed to handle user account management tasks, such as creating, modifying, and deleting users. This module allows the specification of parameters such as the user's name, UID, group, home directory, and shell. In this scenario, the team can use the user module to automate the creation of user accounts, ensuring they are added to the correct group and that their home directories are set up with the correct permissions. This is much more efficient and error-proof than manually configuring each account across multiple servers.

Q127: A financial services company is using Ansible to manage configurations across their Linux servers. They need to ensure that specific lines exist in a configuration file without completely replacing the file. Which Ansible module should they use to insert or update lines in a file?   ---

A) copy

B) template

C) lineinfile

D) inifile

E) replace

F) patch

Answer: C

Explanation: The lineinfile module is designed for ensuring that a specific line is present in a file or replacing an existing line with a new value. This is particularly useful when you want to modify configuration files without overwriting the entire file, allowing for precise updates or insertions. The module provides options to specify the line to be inserted, whether it should be inserted before or after a particular line, and whether changes should be made only if a particular line is found. This is ideal for the scenario where a company wants to ensure specific configurations without disrupting the entire file content.

Q128: A multinational corporation is planning to deploy a web application on multiple Linux servers using Ansible. As part of their deployment, they need to ensure that the web service is enabled and running on all servers. Which Ansible module will allow them to control the service state effectively? ---
A) shell

B) systemd

C) debug

D) cron

E) command

F) apt

Answer: B

Explanation: The systemd module in Ansible is used to manage services on systems that use systemd as their init system. This module can start, stop, restart, reload, and enable services, making it ideal for managing service states. In this scenario, enabling and ensuring that the web service is running across multiple servers can be efficiently handled by the systemd module. It allows administrators to manage services across different servers consistently and reliably, ensuring that the application is always available and properly configured.

Q129: A software development company needs to manage its application configuration files, which are often updated and templated with environment-specific variables. They want to use Ansible to deploy these configuration files with variables dynamically replaced based on the environment. Which module is best suited for this task? ---
A) copy

B) template

C) lineinfile

D) inifile

E) replace

F) patch

Answer: B

Explanation: The template module in Ansible is used to manage Jinja2 templates, allowing dynamic configuration file creation. This module enables the substitution of variables at runtime, making it ideal for deploying configuration files that need environment-specific customization. Templates in Ansible can include conditional logic and filters, providing a powerful mechanism for generating configuration files. This is particularly useful for the software development company, which needs to ensure that their application configurations are correctly set up for each environment, reducing the risk of configuration errors and simplifying the deployment process.

Q130: True/False: The replace module in Ansible is used to replace specific sequences in a file, and it can be used to substitute text across multiple files in a directory.

A) True

B) False

Answer: B

Explanation: The replace module in Ansible is indeed used to replace specific text sequences in a file. However, it operates on a single file at a time as specified in the module's parameters. To replace text across multiple files in a directory, you would need to use a loop or a task that iterates over the files in the directory, applying the replace module to each file individually. This design ensures precise control over text replacement operations, minimizing the risk of unintended changes across multiple files.

Q131: A company is using a combination of traditional and cloud-based infrastructure to store and manage their data. They have been experiencing issues with inconsistent session management across their distributed systems, leading to user sessions being lost during high traffic periods. They are considering implementing a centralized session handling mechanism. The DevOps team is tasked with evaluating tools that can facilitate distributed session management and ensure data consistency across their infrastructure. Which tool or technology would best fit their needs for handling session data consistently across both traditional and cloud environments?

A) Redis

B) PostgreSQL

C) NFS (Network File System)

D) Apache Kafka

E) MySQL

F) MongoDB

Answer: A

Explanation: Redis is an in-memory data structure store that can be used as a distributed, highly available session store. It supports replication, persistence, and is designed for high performance, making it suitable for handling session data across distributed systems. Redis can store session data in-memory, which allows for quick read and write operations, essential during high traffic periods. Its ability to operate in a distributed manner with clustering and replication ensures data consistency and availability, which are critical for maintaining user sessions across both traditional and cloud-based infrastructure.

Q132: You are responsible for managing service statuses on a Linux server and need to check whether a critical service, nginx, is currently active. Which command should you use to check the status of the nginx service?

A) systemctl is-active nginx

B) service nginx check

C) systemctl status nginx

D) service status nginx

E) nginx status

F) systemctl check nginx

Answer: C

Explanation: The systemctl status nginx command provides detailed information about the status of the nginx service, including whether it is active, any recent logs, and configuration details. This command is part of the systemd system and service manager, which is widely used in modern Linux distributions to manage services. While systemctl is-active nginx can tell you if the service is active, it does not provide the verbose output that systemctl status nginx does, which can be useful for diagnosing issues or confirming the service's operational state.

Q133: To ensure reliability and performance, a company needs to set up a shared storage solution that multiple Linux servers can access simultaneously to store large volumes of data. Which solution would best meet these requirements?
A) Local SSDs

B) NFS (Network File System)

C) AWS S3

D) FTP (File Transfer Protocol)

E) SMB (Server Message Block)

F) ZFS (Zettabyte File System)

Answer: B

Explanation: NFS (Network File System) is designed for sharing files between multiple Linux systems over a network. It allows multiple clients to access and write data simultaneously, making it ideal for environments that require a shared storage solution. NFS is both scalable and reliable, supporting a large number of clients with the ability to handle substantial data volumes. Unlike local SSDs, which are limited to a single machine, NFS provides a centralized storage system that can be accessed concurrently, ensuring data consistency and high availability across different servers.

Q134: A Linux system administrator is tasked with ensuring that a service automatically restarts if it fails. They need to configure this for a critical application service. Which systemd directive in the service unit file is used to ensure that a service automatically restarts upon failure?

A) Restart=on-failure

B) Restart=always

C) Restart=never

D) Restart=on-abort

E) Restart=on-success

F) Restart=on-watchdog

Answer: A

Explanation: The Restart=on-failure directive in a systemd service unit file ensures that the service is automatically restarted only when it exits with a non-zero status, indicating a failure. This is useful for maintaining service availability, as it allows the service to recover automatically without manual intervention. The Restart=always directive would restart the service in all situations, including normal exits, which may not be desirable. By using Restart=on-failure, the system administrator ensures that the service restarts only in the event of a failure, thus maintaining stability and reliability.

Q135: True/False: In Linux, using the lsof command, you can list open files and network connections for a specific process by specifying its process ID (PID).
A) True

B) False

Answer: A

Explanation: The lsof (list open files) command in Linux is a powerful utility that displays information about files that are currently open by processes. By specifying the process ID (PID) with the -p option, you can filter the output to show only the files and network connections associated with that specific process. This functionality is particularly useful for debugging and monitoring system activities, as it provides insights into which files are being accessed by a process and any related network activity. The ability to target a specific process makes lsof a valuable tool for system administrators managing Linux environments.

Q136: A tech company is developing a microservices architecture for an e-commerce platform, which will require multiple services to communicate over APIs. The development team is considering using RESTful APIs for internal service communication. However, they are debating how to structure their API endpoints and responses to ensure consistency and scalability. As part of this process, they need to decide on a standard format for their API responses that will be easy to parse and consistent with industry practices. They are evaluating various serialization formats. Which serialization format is most commonly used in RESTful APIs to ensure lightweight data interchange and ease of use in a Linux environment?
A) XML

B) YAML

C) JSON

D) CSV

E) Protocol Buffers

F) INI

Answer: C

Explanation: JSON (JavaScript Object Notation) is the most commonly used serialization format in RESTful APIs. It is lightweight, easy to read and write, and language-independent, making it an ideal choice for data interchange between services. JSON's syntax is simple and can be easily parsed by most programming languages, which is crucial in a microservices architecture where different services may be written in different languages. In a Linux environment, tools like jq can be used to manipulate JSON data efficiently, further supporting its use in API communications. XML is more verbose and complex, YAML is more human-readable but less standard for APIs, CSV is limited to tabular data, Protocol Buffers require compilation and are not as human-readable, and INI is unsuitable for complex data structures.

Q137: When deciding on an API authentication mechanism for a Linux-based service, which method is considered most secure and appropriate for use with RESTful APIs?

A) Basic Authentication

B) API Key

C) OAuth 2.0

D) Digest Authentication

E) JWT (JSON Web Tokens)

F) HMAC (Hash-based Message Authentication Code)

Answer: C

Explanation: OAuth 2.0 is considered the most secure and appropriate authentication mechanism for RESTful APIs. It is an industry-standard protocol for authorization and provides secure delegated access to resources without sharing credentials. OAuth 2.0 handles authorization through access tokens, which can be limited in scope and duration, making it a robust choice for securing API endpoints. Basic Authentication and API Key are simpler but less secure, as they rely on transmitting credentials or keys with each request, which can be intercepted. Digest Authentication, while more secure than Basic, is still less robust than OAuth 2.0. JWTs are often used in conjunction with OAuth 2.0 for token management, and HMAC is a method for message integrity but not a complete authentication strategy.

Q138: True or False: In RESTful API design, it is recommended to use HTTP GET requests to perform operations that modify server-side resources (such as creating or deleting data).
A) True

B) False

Answer: B

Explanation: The statement is false. In RESTful API design, HTTP GET requests should not be used to perform operations that modify server-side resources. GET requests are intended for retrieving data without causing any side effects on the server. Modifying operations should use HTTP methods such as POST, PUT, DELETE, or PATCH, which are designed to create, update, delete, or partially update resources, respectively. Using GET for modifying actions violates the principles of REST and can lead to unintended consequences, such as caching issues and accidental data modification through harmless-looking URLs.

Q139: In a Linux environment, you are tasked with testing a RESTful API service. Which command-line tool would you use to send HTTP requests and interact with the API directly from the terminal?
A) ssh

B) scp

C) curl

D) grep

E) awk

F) sed

Answer: C

Explanation: curl is the command-line tool most suited for sending HTTP requests and interacting with RESTful APIs directly from a Linux terminal. It supports various protocols, including HTTP and HTTPS, and allows users to perform operations such as GET, POST, PUT, DELETE, among others, making it versatile for testing and interacting with APIs. curl provides options to customize headers, body, and other request parameters, making it an essential tool for developers and testers working with APIs. ssh and scp are used for secure shell access and file transfer, respectively, while grep, awk, and sed are text processing utilities and not suited for HTTP requests.

Q140: A company is implementing API rate limiting to prevent abuse of their RESTful service. Which HTTP header is commonly used to communicate rate limit information to clients, indicating how many requests they have remaining within a given time frame?

A) Content-Type

B) Authorization

C) Retry-After

D) X-RateLimit-Remaining

E) Accept

F) X-Powered-By

Answer: D

Explanation: The X-RateLimit-Remaining HTTP header is commonly used to communicate API rate limit information to clients, specifically indicating how many requests a client can still make within a given time window. This header is part of a set of rate-limiting headers, which typically also include X-RateLimit-Limit (the request limit) and X-RateLimit-Reset (the time at which the limit resets). By providing this information, clients can better manage their request rates and avoid exceeding limits, which could result in throttling or blocking. The other headers, such as Content-Type and Authorization, serve different purposes related to content negotiation and authentication, respectively. Retry-After is used in scenarios like 503 Service Unavailable to indicate when to try the request again, Accept specifies the desired media type, and X-Powered-By is a server-side header that reveals server information.

Q141: A medium-sized e-commerce company is experiencing frequent security incidents related to unauthorized access and data breaches. The DevOps team is tasked with improving application security. After conducting a security audit, they identify that a significant number of vulnerabilities are due to improper configuration management and lack of regular updates. The team decides to implement a strategy to automate security updates and configuration hardening. What is the most effective approach to achieve this using Linux-based tools?

A) Manually update each server using SSH and apply security patches bi-weekly.

B) Implement a cron job on each server to automatically download and install security updates.

C) Use a configuration management tool like Ansible to automate the application of security patches and configuration changes across all servers.

D) Schedule regular security audits and manually fix issues as they are identified.

E) Deploy a centralized logging system to monitor security incidents and respond reactively.

F) Use a version control system to track configuration changes and manually apply updates.

Answer: C

Explanation: Automating security updates and configuration management is crucial for maintaining a secure infrastructure. Configuration management tools like Ansible allow you to define the desired state of your systems and ensure that they are consistently maintained. Ansible can automate the application of security patches and configuration changes across a large number of servers, reducing the risk of human error and ensuring that all systems are kept up-to-date with the latest security standards. This approach is more efficient and reliable than manual updates or reactive monitoring, as it proactively mitigates vulnerabilities.

Q142: Which Linux command can be used to identify open ports and services running on a system, which could potentially be exploited by attackers if not properly secured?

A) netstat

B) ps

C) top

D) df

E) chmod

F) ls

Answer: A

Explanation: The netstat command is used to display network connections, routing tables, interface statistics, masquerade connections, and multicast memberships. It is particularly useful for identifying open ports and services running on a system, which can be a vector for attackers if not properly secured. By analyzing the output of netstat, administrators can identify which services are listening on which ports and take appropriate actions to secure or limit access, such as using firewall rules or disabling unnecessary services.

Q143: True/False: Implementing a Web Application Firewall (WAF) is sufficient to protect a Linux-based application from all types of application security risks.

A) True

B) False

Answer: B

Explanation: While a Web Application Firewall (WAF) is an important security measure that can help protect against common web application attacks such as SQL injection and cross-site scripting, it is not sufficient on its own to protect against all application security risks. Security is a multi-layered approach, and a WAF should be part of a broader security strategy that includes secure coding practices, regular security audits, patch management, access controls, and monitoring. Other vulnerabilities, such as those related to application logic errors or insecure configurations, require additional measures beyond what a WAF can provide.

Q144: During a security review, it is discovered that an application is vulnerable to SQL injection attacks. Which of the following practices is the most effective immediate step to mitigate this vulnerability?
A) Implement input validation on the client-side.

B) Use prepared statements with parameterized queries.

C) Encrypt the database to protect sensitive data.

D) Increase the complexity of database user passwords.

E) Regularly backup the database to ensure data integrity.

F) Restrict database access to specific IP addresses.

Answer: B

Explanation: SQL injection attacks occur when untrusted data is sent to an interpreter as part of a command or query. The best immediate step to mitigate SQL injection vulnerabilities is to use prepared statements with parameterized queries. This practice ensures that user input is treated as data rather than executable code, effectively neutralizing the risk of SQL injection. Client-side input validation, while helpful for user experience, does not provide security as it can be bypassed. Other measures, such as database encryption and access restrictions, are important for overall security but do not directly address the SQL injection vulnerability.

Q145: A development team is integrating a new third-party API service into their Linux-based application. To minimize security risks associated with this integration, what is the most critical step they should take?

A) Enable verbose logging to monitor all interactions with the API.

B) Use API keys for authentication without additional security measures.

C) Implement rate limiting to control the volume of requests to the API.

D) Conduct a thorough security assessment of the API documentation and its endpoints.

E) Ensure that all data sent to and from the API is encrypted using HTTPS.

F) Store API credentials in plain text within the application code for easy access.

Answer: E

Explanation: Ensuring that all data exchanged with a third-party API is encrypted using HTTPS is critical to protect sensitive information from being intercepted by attackers. While other measures, such as conducting security assessments or implementing rate limiting, are important for comprehensive security, they do not address the fundamental risk of data exposure during transmission. Using HTTPS ensures that the data is encrypted in transit, protecting it from man-in-the-middle attacks. Storing API credentials securely, such as in environment variables or secret management tools, is also essential but not the focus of this specific question.

Q146: You are a DevOps engineer at a tech company that is transitioning its monolithic application into a microservices architecture. The project requires deploying multiple containers that need to communicate with each other and scale based on load. The infrastructure team has decided to use Kubernetes for orchestration and deployment. Your task is to ensure that the containers can discover each other dynamically and that their communication is secure. Which component of Kubernetes would you primarily use to handle service discovery and load balancing between these containers?

A) ConfigMap

B) Pod

C) ReplicaSet

D) Service

E) PersistentVolume

F) Namespace

Answer: D

Explanation: In Kubernetes, a "Service" is a key abstraction that defines a logical set of Pods and a policy by which to access them. The service discovery mechanism is crucial for microservices as it allows containers to find each other without hardcoding IP addresses, which are often ephemeral in a containerized environment. Services enable automatic load balancing and routing of traffic to the appropriate Pods, ensuring that communication within the microservices architecture is both efficient and secure. This is particularly important in a dynamic environment where Pods can be killed, restarted, or scaled up and down automatically.

Q147: True or False: In a Docker environment, it is possible to run multiple containers on the same host using the same network port.
A) True

B) False

Answer: B

Explanation: In Docker, each container runs in its own isolated environment, but they share the host's network interface by default. This means that two containers cannot bind to the same port on the host interface. If multiple containers need to run services on the same port, you must either assign them different ports on the host or use network namespaces to isolate them further. Docker's port mapping feature allows you to map a container's internal port to a different port on the host, thus avoiding conflicts.

Q148: Which command can be used to update a running container's configuration in a Kubernetes cluster without deleting and recreating the container?

A) kubectl update pod

B) kubectl apply -f

C) kubectl set image

D) kubectl edit deployment

E) kubectl replace -f

F) kubectl patch

Answer: F

Explanation: The kubectl patch command allows you to update specific fields of a resource configuration in a Kubernetes cluster without the need to delete and recreate resources like Pods or Deployments. This is particularly useful for making incremental changes to configurations, such as updating environment variables or changing resource limits. Unlike kubectl edit, which opens a text editor for manual edits, kubectl patch applies changes directly through command-line arguments, making it more efficient for automated scripts and CI/CD pipelines.

Q149: Consider a scenario where your organization has a strict data retention policy and needs to ensure that logs from containerized applications running on Kubernetes are kept for a minimum of one year. Which Kubernetes component or feature should you utilize to meet this requirement?

A) Pod

B) DaemonSet

C) ConfigMap

D) StatefulSet

E) PersistentVolume

F) CronJob

Answer: E

Explanation: To ensure logs are retained for an extended period, such as one year, you should utilize Kubernetes PersistentVolumes. PersistentVolumes provide storage that can persist beyond the lifecycle of individual Pods. By configuring your logging system to write logs to a PersistentVolume, you can ensure that logs are not lost when Pods are recreated or scaled. Additionally, this allows logs to be retained according to organizational policies, even if the underlying container infrastructure changes. This approach is crucial for compliance with data retention policies and audits.

Q150: Your company is deploying a high-traffic web application using containers, and you are tasked with ensuring that the application can handle traffic spikes without downtime. You decide to use Kubernetes to manage the deployment. Which Kubernetes feature would you configure to automatically adjust the number of running Pods based on the current load on the application?

A) ReplicaSet

B) Horizontal Pod Autoscaler

C) Ingress

D) ServiceAccount

E) NetworkPolicy

F) Job

Answer: B

Explanation: The Horizontal Pod Autoscaler (HPA) in Kubernetes is designed to automatically adjust the number of Pods in a deployment based on observed CPU utilization or other custom metrics. This feature is vital for applications that experience fluctuating traffic patterns, as it can scale the application out or in, ensuring resources are efficiently used and the application remains responsive during high-load periods. The HPA dynamically maintains the desired performance levels by monitoring the metrics and adjusting the number of replicas accordingly. This automated scaling is essential for maintaining application availability and performance without manual intervention.

Q151: Your company, Tech Innovations Inc., has recently adopted containerization for its application deployments to improve scalability and manageability. The IT team has been tasked with setting up a container infrastructure on a Linux server. The primary requirement is to ensure that the applications can run in isolated environments while maintaining efficient resource utilization. Your team is considering different container runtimes and orchestration tools to best fit the company's needs. Which of the following container runtimes would be most appropriate to use, considering the need for native integration with Linux kernel features and a focus on security and high performance?   ---

A) Docker

B) runc

C) containerd

D) LXC

E) Kubernetes

F) Podman

Answer: D

Explanation: LXC (Linux Containers) is the most appropriate choice when considering native integration with Linux kernel features. LXC containers are lightweight and provide a high level of security and performance by leveraging the kernel's cgroups and namespaces. Unlike Docker, which uses a daemon and an additional layer of abstraction, LXC runs containers as lightweight processes directly on the host system, allowing for efficient resource utilization. While Kubernetes and Docker are popular choices, they introduce additional layers that may not be necessary if the primary focus is on leveraging Linux kernel features for containerization. Runc and containerd are components used by Docker and are not standalone runtime environments. Podman is an alternative to Docker that provides daemonless container management but does not focus on native Linux kernel integration.

Q152: Which of the following commands would you use to list all running containers on a Linux server using Docker?   ---

A) docker run

B) docker ps

C) docker images

D) docker start

E) docker exec

F) docker inspect

Answer: B

Explanation: The docker ps command is used to list all running containers on a Docker-managed Linux server. This command displays a list of active containers, including their IDs, names, statuses, and other relevant information. The docker run command is used to start a new container, while docker images lists available images. The docker start command is used to start stopped containers, and docker exec is for executing commands within running containers. docker inspect provides detailed information about a specific container or image but does not list running containers.

Q153: Which of the following is true regarding the use of Linux namespaces in container technology?   ---

A) Namespaces allow for centralized logging of container activities.

B) Namespaces provide isolation for the network stack of containers.

Answer: B

Explanation: Linux namespaces are a fundamental feature used in container technologies to provide isolation across various system resources. Specifically, network namespaces allow each container to have its own network stack, including IP addresses, routing tables, and network devices. This isolation ensures that network activities in one container do not interfere with those in another. Namespaces do not directly handle centralized logging, which is typically managed through logging drivers or external tools. They focus on isolating resources such as processes, users, mounts, and IPC.

Q154: To ensure that a containerized application can communicate with services outside of its host network, which of the following configurations should be considered when setting up the container's networking?   ---

A) Use host networking mode.

B) Assign a static IP address to the container.

C) Expose the necessary ports on the host.

D) Use a bridge network and configure port forwarding.

E) Enable NAT traversal for the container.

F) Use a custom DNS resolver.

Answer: D

Explanation: Using a bridge network and configuring port forwarding is a standard method to enable containerized applications to communicate with external services. The bridge network provides a private internal network for containers, and port forwarding allows specific ports on the host to be mapped to the container, facilitating external communication. Using host networking can lead to port conflicts and reduced isolation. Assigning a static IP can result in address conflicts and is not scalable. NAT traversal is not typically required for container communication, and while a custom DNS resolver can aid in name resolution, it does not inherently solve the problem of external communication.

Q155: When setting up a container orchestration system on Linux, such as Kubernetes, what is the purpose of configuring a CNI (Container Network Interface) plugin?

A) To provide a web interface for managing containers.

B) To manage the lifecycle of container images.

C) To enable the network connectivity between containers.

D) To handle persistent storage for containers.

E) To ensure container security through isolation.

F) To monitor container resource usage.

Answer: C

Explanation: CNI (Container Network Interface) plugins are used in container orchestration systems like Kubernetes to enable and manage network connectivity between containers. These plugins provide the necessary networking capabilities, such as IP address management, routing, and connectivity across nodes. CNI plugins are essential for ensuring that containers can communicate both within a host and across a cluster. They do not provide web interfaces, manage container images, handle persistent storage, ensure security, or monitor resource usage, although these are critical aspects of container orchestration that are managed by other components or tools.

Q156: A medium-sized tech company has recently adopted containerization to improve their application deployment processes. They have chosen Docker as their container platform. The DevOps team has been tasked with creating a multi-container application that consists of a web server, a database, and a cache service. They want to ensure that all containers are networked together correctly to allow seamless communication while being isolated from other applications on the same host. What Docker networking feature should the team use to achieve this goal?

A) Bridge network

B) Host network

C) Overlay network

D) None network

E) MACVLAN network

F) Container network

Answer: A

Explanation: Docker uses a networking feature called the 'bridge network' to allow containers to communicate with each other when they are on the same host. This type of network creates an internal network on the host that containers can join, thus allowing them to communicate with each other using container names. In this scenario, using a bridge network ensures that the web server, database, and cache service can interact with each other seamlessly while keeping them isolated from other applications running on the same host. The bridge network is the default network type for containers on a single host, making it suitable for this multi-container application setup. Unlike the host network, which exposes containers directly to the host's network stack, the bridge network provides a layer of isolation, which is crucial for maintaining security and stability.

Q157: To troubleshoot a containerized application, a developer needs to enter the running container and perform some diagnostic commands. What Docker command should they use to open an interactive shell session inside a running container?

A) docker start -i <containerid>

B) docker attach <containerid>

C) docker exec -it <containerid> /bin/bash

D) docker run -d <containerid>

E) docker inspect <containerid>

F) docker connect <containerid>

Answer: C

Explanation: The docker exec -it <containerid> /bin/bash command is used to run an interactive shell session inside a running container. The exec command allows you to execute a command directly within a container, and the -it flags make the session interactive, providing a terminal interface that can take input from a user. This command is particularly useful for troubleshooting and performing diagnostics, as it gives the developer direct access to the container's environment. The attach command, while allowing interaction with the container, attaches to the main process running in the container and is not typically used for opening a separate shell session.

Q158: True or False: Using Docker's 'host' network mode provides better isolation between containers compared to the 'bridge' network mode.
A) True

B) False

Answer: B

Explanation: When Docker containers are run with 'host' network mode, they share the host's network stack, meaning there is no network isolation between the container and the host. This can lead to potential security issues because the container is exposed directly to the host's network interfaces. In contrast, 'bridge' network mode provides an isolated network environment for containers, allowing them to communicate with each other while remaining isolated from the host network and other containers. This isolation is a key aspect of container security, making 'bridge' network mode better suited for applications that require network separation.

Q159: A company is deploying a new microservices architecture using Kubernetes. They need to manage container images efficiently. Which of the following tools is most appropriate for securely storing and managing Docker container images?

A) Docker Registry

B) Kubernetes Dashboard

C) etcd

D) Prometheus

E) Grafana

F) Helm

Answer: A

Explanation: Docker Registry is a service specifically designed for storing and distributing Docker images. It allows teams to manage their container images securely, providing functionalities such as image versioning, access control, and integration with CI/CD pipelines. This makes it an ideal choice for managing container images in a Kubernetes environment, where efficient image distribution and management are critical. Kubernetes Dashboard, etcd, Prometheus, Grafana, and Helm serve other purposes such as cluster management, monitoring, and application deployment, but are not designed for managing Docker images.

Q160: A DevOps engineer is tasked with optimizing the storage usage of their Docker containers. They want to remove all unused data, including dangling images and stopped containers, to free up space on the server. Which Docker command should they use?

A) docker system prune

B) docker image prune

C) docker container prune

D) docker volume prune

E) docker network prune

F) docker prune all

Answer: A

Explanation: The docker system prune command is used to remove all unused data in Docker. This includes stopped containers, unused networks, dangling images (images that are not tagged and are not used by any container), and build cache. This command is particularly useful for freeing up disk space by cleaning up resources that are no longer in use. While docker image prune, docker container prune, docker volume prune, and docker network prune target specific types of unused resources, docker system prune is comprehensive and removes all types of unused resources, which is what the engineer needs to optimize storage usage effectively.

Q161: A technology company is deploying a microservices architecture using Docker. The team is tasked with ensuring secure and efficient communication between services that are running across multiple hosts in a multi-cloud environment. They have decided to utilize Docker's overlay networks to facilitate this communication. The team needs to create an overlay network named secureoverlay and ensure that it is encrypted to meet internal security policies. Which command should the team use to create this overlay network?

A) docker network create -d overlay secureoverlay

B) docker network create -d overlay --subnet=10.0.0.0/24 secureoverlay

C) docker network create -d overlay --attachable secureoverlay

D) docker network create -d overlay --opt encrypted secureoverlay

E) docker network create -d bridge secureoverlay

F) docker network create --driver=overlay secureoverlay

Answer: D

Explanation: Docker's overlay networks are designed to span multiple Docker daemon hosts, allowing containers connected to the same network to communicate securely across host boundaries. To enhance security, encryption can be enabled by using the --opt encrypted option when creating the network. This ensures that traffic is encrypted when traversing the network. The command docker network create -d overlay --opt encrypted secureoverlay creates an overlay network named secureoverlay with encryption enabled. This is critical for environments where data security is a priority, especially in multi-cloud or multi-host scenarios.

Q162: When configuring Docker networking, which type of network allows containers on different hosts to communicate securely without requiring a specific IP address configuration?
A) Bridge Network

B) Host Network

C) Overlay Network

D) Macvlan Network

E) None Network

F) Custom Bridge Network

Answer: C

Explanation: Overlay networks in Docker allow containers running on different Docker hosts to communicate as if they were on the same host. This is particularly useful in a Docker Swarm or Kubernetes environment where services might be spread across multiple hosts. Overlay networks abstract away the need for explicit IP address configuration by creating a virtual network that spans across multiple hosts. This network type also supports secure communication, which is essential for applications that require data protection across nodes.

Q163: In a Docker Swarm environment, you want to configure a service to use a specific overlay network for communication. Which option correctly associates the service with the overlay network during service creation?

A) docker service create --network=bridge myservice

B) docker service create --network=host myservice

C) docker service create --network=overlay myservice

D) docker service create --network=myoverlay myservice

E) docker service create --network=none myservice

F) docker service create --network=myoverlay --driver=overlay myservice

Answer: D

Explanation: In a Docker Swarm setup, services need to be explicitly associated with a network to enable communication. When creating a service, the --network option is used to specify the network name. If you have an overlay network named myoverlay, you should use docker service create --network=myoverlay myservice to connect the service to this network. This allows the service's containers to communicate over the specified overlay network, facilitating secure and efficient inter-container communication across the swarm.

Q164: Consider a scenario where a company needs to ensure that communication between Docker containers is isolated and secure, even when containers are running on different hosts. They decide to use Docker's overlay network feature for this purpose. True or False: Docker's overlay networks are inherently encrypted by default.

A) True

B) False

Answer: B

Explanation: While Docker's overlay networks allow for cross-host container communication, they are not encrypted by default. To enable encryption for overlay networks, the --opt encrypted option must be explicitly specified when creating the network. This feature is crucial for maintaining secure communication, especially when dealing with sensitive data or operating in environments where security compliance is a concern. By default, overlay networks provide connectivity but do not automatically encrypt traffic.

Q165: A DevOps team is tasked with setting up a Docker environment that supports service discovery and load balancing. They decide to use Docker's overlay networks for this purpose. Which of the following statements correctly describes a feature of Docker overlay networks in this context?

A) Overlay networks are limited to a single host only.

B) Overlay networks automatically provide built-in service discovery and load balancing.

C) Overlay networks require manual IP management for service discovery.

D) Overlay networks are designed to work only with Docker Compose.

E) Overlay networks do not support container-to-container communication.

F) Overlay networks require an external DNS server for service discovery.

Answer: B

Explanation: Docker's overlay networks are specifically designed to facilitate multi-host container communication in a Docker Swarm. One of the key features of overlay networks is their ability to provide built-in service discovery and load balancing. This is achieved through Docker's internal DNS server, which automatically resolves service names to the appropriate service tasks. As a result, containers can communicate with services using service names rather than IP addresses, simplifying network management in large-scale deployments. This feature is integral to the operation of a Docker Swarm, where services need to be dynamically discovered and balanced across different nodes.

Q166: A mid-sized company is migrating its traditional monolithic application to a microservices architecture. The development team is tasked with setting up a container orchestration platform to manage the deployment and scaling of their services. The IT manager is particularly concerned about the non-functional properties, such as scalability, availability, and performance, and wants to ensure that the platform chosen can support these requirements effectively. Which of the following tools or technologies should they prioritize to meet these non-functional requirements?

A) Docker Compose

B) Kubernetes

C) Ansible

D) Vagrant

E) GitLab CI/CD

F) Jenkins

Answer: B

Explanation: Kubernetes is a powerful container orchestration system that is specifically designed to manage containerized applications in a clustered environment. It focuses heavily on non-functional properties such as scalability, availability, and performance. Kubernetes enables horizontal scaling of applications, which allows for the seamless addition of more instances of a service to handle increased load. It supports high availability through its self-healing capabilities, automatically replacing failed containers and optimizing resource utilization across the cluster. Additionally, Kubernetes provides features like load balancing, service discovery, and automated rollouts and rollbacks, which contribute to maintaining the performance and reliability of services. In contrast, Docker Compose is limited to single-node deployments, Ansible and Vagrant are more suited for configuration management and virtual machine provisioning respectively, and GitLab CI/CD and Jenkins are primarily focused on continuous integration and delivery processes rather than orchestration.

Q167: In the context of IT services, non-functional properties are more concerned with the 'how' than the 'what.' Which of the following best describes a non-functional property?

A) The specific business logic implemented by a service.

B) The speed at which a service processes requests under load.

C) The type of data returned by an API endpoint.

D) The sequence of operations a service performs.

E) The user interface design of a web application.

F) The specific algorithms used for data processing.

Answer: B

Explanation: Non-functional properties pertain to how a service behaves and performs rather than what it does. These properties include attributes such as performance, scalability, availability, reliability, and security. The speed at which a service processes requests under load is a classic example of a performance-related non-functional property. It addresses concerns about how efficiently a service can handle traffic and maintain responsiveness, which is critical for user satisfaction and operational success. In contrast, options related to business logic, data types, operation sequences, UI design, and specific algorithms are more related to the functional aspects of a service, focusing on what the service does and the specific tasks it performs.

Q168: True or False: Functional properties of IT services are typically easier to measure and quantify than non-functional properties.
A) True

B) False

Answer: A

Explanation: Functional properties refer to what a system or service is supposed to do, including specific behaviors, tasks, or functions it must perform. These properties are usually easier to measure and quantify because they often have clear, defined criteria and can be validated through testing various inputs and verifying the outputs. Non-functional properties, on the other hand, deal with how a system performs these functions, including aspects like performance, security, and usability. These can be more subjective and variable, making them harder to measure precisely. For instance, while you can easily test if an API returns the correct data (functional), determining the exact threshold for acceptable latency under all conditions (non-functional) can be more complex and context-dependent.

Q169: Which of the following Linux commands can be used to assess the performance and load of a server, thus providing insights into non-functional properties such as system load and resource usage?
A) ls

B) cat

C) grep

D) top

E) mkdir

F) echo

Answer: D

Explanation: The 'top' command in Linux is a performance monitoring tool that provides real-time insights into system resource usage, including CPU and memory utilization, process management, and system load. It is particularly useful for assessing non-functional properties related to performance and load because it allows administrators to see how resources are being consumed over time, identify resource-intensive processes, and understand the overall health of the system. This information is crucial for making informed decisions about scaling, resource allocation, and identifying performance bottlenecks. In contrast, commands like 'ls', 'cat', 'grep', 'mkdir', and 'echo' are used for file management, text manipulation, and basic output operations, and do not provide the performance metrics necessary for assessing system load and resource usage.

Q170: A company is implementing a web service that must remain operational 99.999% of the time. The IT team is debating which non-functional properties to focus on to meet this availability requirement. Which property should they prioritize to ensure the highest level of service availability?

A) Scalability

B) Data Consistency

C) Fault Tolerance

D) Response Time

E) Usability

F) Modularity

Answer: C

Explanation: Fault tolerance is a critical non-functional property for ensuring high availability of services. It refers to the ability of a system to continue operating properly in the event of the failure of some of its components. By designing systems that can withstand hardware failures, software bugs, and other disruptions, the IT team can significantly reduce downtime and maintain the required level of operational availability. This is especially crucial for achieving a high level of availability such as 99.999%, often referred to as "five nines" availability. While scalability and response time are important for handling load and maintaining performance, and data consistency ensures data integrity, they do not directly address the continuity of service in the face of component failures. Usability and modularity, while beneficial for other aspects, are not directly related to maintaining continuous service availability.

Q171: A medium-sized technology firm has recently adopted Git for its version control needs. The development team is required to maintain a clean and efficient repository structure to manage collaborative efforts effectively. The team lead has mandated that before any new feature branch is merged into the main branch, it must be rebased on top of the latest main branch to ensure a linear commit history. This process should be managed using Git commands on a Linux platform. Which of the following commands should be used to rebase a feature branch named "feature-x" onto the latest "main" branch, assuming you are currently on "feature-x"?

A) git merge main

B) git rebase origin/main

C) git rebase main

D) git reset --hard main

E) git checkout main && git rebase feature-x

F) git pull --rebase main

Answer: C

Explanation: In Git, rebasing is used to apply your changes over a different base commit. When you are on the "feature-x" branch and want to rebase it onto the latest "main" branch, the correct command is "git rebase main". This command takes the commits from the current branch (feature-x), temporarily removes them, updates the branch pointer to the latest commit of "main", and then re-applies the changes. This ensures a linear history, which is often more straightforward for understanding project history and reviewing changes. The other options either merge the branches, reset the branch state, or incorrectly attempt to rebase from the main branch.

Q172: In the context of Git repository management, which of the following commands will initialize a bare repository on a Linux system, suitable for collaboration without a working directory?

A) git init --bare

B) git init

C) git clone --bare

D) git init --shared

E) git remote add origin

F) git init --mirror

Answer: A

Explanation: A bare repository in Git is one that lacks a working directory. This type of repository is typically used as a central repository to which all developers push their changes. The command "git init --bare" initializes a new Git repository without a working directory. This is often used on a server where developers will push their changes, and it is crucial for collaborative environments. The other options either create a regular repository with a working directory, clone a repository in a specific way, or perform unrelated actions like adding a remote.

Q173: Identify the correct Git command used to create a new branch named "bugfix" from the current branch and check it out immediately.

A) git checkout bugfix

B) git branch bugfix && git checkout bugfix

C) git checkout -b bugfix

D) git branch -m bugfix

E) git checkout -b bugfix origin/master

F) git checkout --orphan bugfix

Answer: C

Explanation: The command "git checkout -b bugfix" is used to create a new branch named "bugfix" and switch to it immediately. This combines the steps of creating a branch and checking it out into a single command, streamlining the workflow for developers. This is particularly useful for addressing issues or adding features without affecting the main branch. The other options either perform unnecessary steps, rename branches, or create orphan branches, which are not part of the typical branching workflow.

Q174: True/False: In Git, the command "git fetch" will automatically merge the fetched changes into the current branch.

A) True

B) False

Answer: B

Explanation: The command "git fetch" is used to download commits, files, and references from a remote repository into your local repository. However, it does not automatically merge these changes into your current branch; it only updates the remote tracking branches. To incorporate these changes into your current branch, you would need to execute a separate command, such as "git merge". This separation allows developers to review changes before integrating them into their current work, providing better control over the codebase.

Q175: A development team uses a Linux server as their Git server. They want to enforce that all developers pushing changes to the repository must have a clean working directory and no uncommitted changes. Which Git configuration setting should be set on the server to ensure this policy is enforced?

A) core.autocrlf

B) receive.denyCurrentBranch

C) receive.denyNonFastForwards

D) core.bare

E) fetch.prune

F) push.default

Answer: C

Explanation: The configuration setting "receive.denyNonFastForwards" is used to prevent anyone from pushing changes that would result in a non-fast-forward merge, which typically means that the pushed changes do not have a direct lineage from the current state of the branch. While this setting does not directly enforce a clean working directory, it ensures that developers do not force push without aligning with the current branch history, indirectly promoting best practices of maintaining a clean working state. The other settings are unrelated to enforcing a policy on the state of the working directory when pushing changes.

Q176: A medium-sized tech firm is transitioning from a manual server configuration process to an automated one using Ansible. The company has a mix of Linux distributions, including Ubuntu, CentOS, and Debian, across its infrastructure. The DevOps team needs to ensure that Ansible can seamlessly interact with all these systems for tasks like package installation, service management, and configuration file editing. They are particularly concerned about potential issues with SSH connectivity and Python dependencies on remote systems. What is the first step the team should take to ensure Ansible can manage these systems effectively?

A) Ensure all remote systems have the same version of Python installed.

B) Configure passwordless SSH access for Ansible on all remote systems.

C) Install Ansible's dependencies on the Ansible control node.

D) Write a single playbook that works for all distributions.

E) Use Ansible's raw module to install Python on remote systems.

F) Create a separate inventory file for each Linux distribution.

Answer: B

Explanation: The most crucial step to ensure Ansible can manage remote systems effectively is to configure passwordless SSH access for Ansible on all remote systems. Ansible primarily communicates with remote machines using SSH, so ensuring smooth and secure SSH connectivity is paramount. While having the correct Python version is important since many Ansible modules require Python, SSH access takes precedence as it is the foundation of Ansible's communication with remote nodes. Moreover, Ansible's raw module can be used to install Python if needed, but the ability to connect over SSH is a prerequisite for using any module. Configuring SSH keys allows Ansible to connect and execute playbooks without manual intervention, which is essential for automation.

Q177: Which Ansible module can be used to execute commands on remote systems that do not have Python installed?

A) shell

B) command

C) raw

D) script

E) setup

F) copy

Answer: C

Explanation: Ansible's raw module is designed to execute low-level commands on remote systems that do not have Python installed. This module sends the specified command as a raw SSH command, bypassing the need for Python, which is typically required by most other Ansible modules. This is particularly useful for initial setup tasks, such as installing Python itself on a newly provisioned server. The other modules, like shell, command, and script, generally require Python to be present on the managed node to function properly.

Q178: True/False: Ansible requires an agent to be installed on remote systems to manage them.

A) True

B) False

Answer: B

Explanation: Ansible is agentless, meaning it does not require an agent to be installed on remote systems to manage them. Instead, Ansible uses SSH to communicate with remote nodes, executing commands directly on them without needing any additional software beyond what is commonly available on most Unix-like systems. This agentless architecture simplifies deployment and management, as there is no need to maintain compatibility with agent versions or deal with agent-specific configuration issues.

Q179: A DevOps engineer is tasked with executing an Ansible playbook that installs and configures a web server on multiple remote nodes. However, the engineer notices that the playbook fails on certain nodes with an error indicating permission denied via SSH. Which of the following steps should the engineer take to resolve this issue?

A) Increase the Ansible verbosity level to debug the issue.

B) Reinstall Ansible on the control node.

C) Check and correct the SSH key permissions on the control node.

D) Update the Ansible configuration to use sudo for all tasks.

E) Reboot the remote nodes and retry the playbook.

F) Disable SELinux on the remote nodes.

Answer: C

Explanation: The issue of "permission denied via SSH" typically indicates a problem with SSH key authentication. The engineer should check and correct the SSH key permissions on the control node to resolve this. SSH requires specific permissions on key files (usually 600 for private keys) to function correctly. Ensuring these permissions are set correctly can resolve authentication issues. While increasing verbosity might help provide more information, it won't directly solve the permission problem. Using sudo, rebooting nodes, or disabling SELinux are unrelated to resolving SSH permission issues.

Q180: An e-commerce company uses Ansible to manage its fleet of web servers. A recent requirement is to ensure that all configuration changes made by Ansible are logged for auditing purposes. Which Ansible feature can the team enable to achieve this?

A) Enable Ansible's extra verbosity.

B) Use the -v option to log all commands executed.

C) Set up a centralized logging server.

D) Configure callback plugins to capture logs.

E) Utilize the debug module in Ansible playbooks.

F) Implement version control for playbooks.

Answer: D

Explanation: To ensure that all configuration changes made by Ansible are logged for auditing purposes, the team can configure callback plugins to capture logs. Callback plugins in Ansible allow custom actions to be executed at various stages of playbook execution, including logging. By configuring an appropriate callback plugin, logs of all tasks, changes, and results can be captured and sent to a centralized logging system or stored locally for auditing purposes. While version control is important for tracking changes to playbooks themselves, it does not log the execution details. Similarly, increasing verbosity or using the debug module provides more output but does not inherently capture logs for auditing in a structured manner.

Q181: A mid-sized e-commerce company is implementing a continuous integration/continuous deployment (CI/CD) pipeline to improve software delivery. The infrastructure team has decided to use Linux-based servers for hosting their applications. They need to ensure that the servers are scalable, highly available, and can be easily configured to handle traffic spikes during peak shopping seasons. The team is considering using infrastructure as code (IaC) to manage their configurations. What tool would be most appropriate for automating the provisioning and management of their Linux infrastructure in a cloud environment?

A) Puppet

B) Jenkins

C) Kubernetes

D) Terraform

E) Docker

F) Ansible

Answer: D

Explanation: Terraform is a tool that is particularly well-suited for provisioning and managing infrastructure in a cloud environment using infrastructure as code (IaC). It allows the team to describe their infrastructure as code, enabling them to version control their infrastructure configuration files and apply changes in a controlled and reproducible manner. Terraform supports multiple cloud providers, making it an excellent choice for managing infrastructure in a cloud-agnostic way. While Puppet and Ansible are also configuration management tools, Terraform is specifically designed for building, changing, and versioning infrastructure efficiently. Jenkins is primarily a CI/CD tool, Docker is used for containerization, and Kubernetes is for container orchestration, which do not directly address the need for provisioning cloud infrastructure.

Q182: An IT operations team needs to ensure that a Linux server hosting critical applications has high availability. They decide to implement a load balancer to distribute traffic across multiple instances of their application. Which Linux-based solution would best meet their needs for a software load balancer?

A) Nginx

B) Apache HTTP Server

C) HAProxy

D) Lighttpd

E) Varnish

F) Squid

Answer: C

Explanation: HAProxy is a reliable and high-performance software load balancer that is widely used in Linux environments to ensure high availability of applications. It can efficiently distribute incoming network or application traffic across multiple servers, thus ensuring resilience and high availability. HAProxy is known for its robust feature set, including SSL termination, connection persistence, and advanced health checks. Nginx can also be used as a load balancer, but HAProxy is specifically optimized for load balancing and high availability scenarios. Apache HTTP Server, Lighttpd, Varnish, and Squid do not provide the same level of specialized load balancing capabilities as HAProxy.

Q183: To enhance the reliability of data storage in their IT infrastructure, an organization is setting up a RAID configuration on a Linux server. They want to implement a configuration that provides both redundancy and improved read performance. Which RAID level should they choose?

A) RAID 0

B) RAID 1

C) RAID 5

D) RAID 6

E) RAID 10

F) RAID 50

Answer: E

Explanation: RAID 10, also known as RAID 1+0, is a configuration that combines the features of RAID 1 (mirroring) and RAID 0 (striping). It provides redundancy by mirroring data across pairs of disks, which ensures that if one disk fails, the data can still be accessed from its mirror. Additionally, it offers improved read performance by distributing the data across multiple disks, allowing simultaneous reads. This configuration is ideal for environments where both high availability and performance are critical. RAID 5 and RAID 6 offer redundancy with parity but do not match the performance of RAID 10 in terms of read speed. RAID 0 does not provide redundancy, while RAID 50 is more complex and typically used in larger-scale systems.

Q184: A financial services company is transitioning to a microservices architecture to improve the scalability and resilience of their applications. They have decided to deploy their services using containers managed by Kubernetes on Linux servers. Which component of Kubernetes is responsible for ensuring that the specified number of container replicas are running at any given time?
A) Kubelet

B) Etcd

C) Controller Manager

D) Scheduler

E) Kube-Proxy

F) API Server

Answer: C

Explanation: The Controller Manager in Kubernetes is responsible for ensuring that the desired state of the system matches the observed state. It includes the replication controller, which ensures that the specified number of replicas for a pod are running at any given time. If a pod fails or is removed, the Controller Manager will create a new pod to maintain the desired number of replicas. The Kubelet is responsible for managing containers on individual nodes, the Scheduler assigns pods to nodes, Etcd is the key-value store, Kube-Proxy manages network rules, and the API Server is the front end for the Kubernetes control plane.

Q185: True or False: In a Linux-based cloud environment, the implementation of Infrastructure as Code (IaC) ensures that any changes made to the infrastructure can be tracked, versioned, and rolled back if necessary.
A) True

B) False

Answer: A

Explanation: The statement is true. Infrastructure as Code (IaC) is a key practice in DevOps that enables the management and provisioning of infrastructure through code. This approach allows changes to be tracked and versioned using version control systems like Git, providing a clear history of who made changes and when. It also enables teams to roll back to previous versions of the infrastructure configuration in case of issues, ensuring consistency and reliability. By treating infrastructure as code, organizations can apply software development best practices to infrastructure management, including testing, continuous integration, and automated deployment, which significantly enhances the agility and stability of IT operations.

Q186: A mid-sized financial company uses a Linux-based server infrastructure to handle its customer transactions. The IT department has noticed sporadic issues with transaction processing, but these issues do not persist long enough for traditional monitoring to capture useful data. As the DevOps tools engineer, you are tasked with implementing a log management solution that can collect and analyze logs in near real-time from multiple servers to identify patterns that could be causing these transaction delays. Which tool would be most suitable for this task, considering ease of deployment, scalability, and real-time log processing capabilities?

A) Logstash

B) rsyslog

C) Splunk

D) Graylog

E) Fluentd

F) Syslog-ng

Answer: A

Explanation: Logstash is a powerful tool designed to collect, process, and forward log data in real-time. It is part of the Elastic Stack (ELK Stack), which is widely used for log management and analysis due to its scalability and ability to handle large volumes of data efficiently. Logstash can ingest data from multiple sources simultaneously, even in a distributed infrastructure like that of the financial company described. It offers a variety of plugins for input, filtering, and output, making it highly customizable to fit specific needs. Additionally, Logstash's integration with Elasticsearch and Kibana provides a complete solution for searching, analyzing, and visualizing log data, which is crucial for identifying and resolving transaction processing issues quickly.

Q187: When setting up a centralized logging server using Syslog-ng on a Linux server, which configuration file is primarily edited to define the sources, destinations, and log paths?

A) /etc/syslog-ng/syslog-ng.conf

B) /etc/rsyslog.conf

C) /etc/logrotate.conf

D) /var/log/syslog-ng.conf

E) /etc/syslog-ng.conf

F) /usr/local/etc/syslog-ng.conf

Answer: A

Explanation: The primary configuration file for Syslog-ng is typically located at /etc/syslog-ng/syslog-ng.conf. This file is where you define all the sources (where logs are coming from), destinations (where logs should be sent), and paths (the flow of logs from sources to destinations). Syslog-ng is a highly flexible logging daemon that can be configured to handle logs from various sources and forward them to different destinations, making it an ideal choice for centralized logging setups. It supports advanced log filtering, parsing, and classification, which are essential for managing and analyzing large volumes of log data effectively.

Q188: While configuring logrotate on a Linux system to manage log files, an administrator wants to ensure that rotated log files are compressed to save disk space. Which directive should be included in the logrotate configuration to achieve this?

A) compress

B) rotate

C) create

D) delaycompress

E) copytruncate

F) notifempty

Answer: A

Explanation: The 'compress' directive in the logrotate configuration file instructs logrotate to compress the rotated log files using gzip by default. This is a common practice to save disk space, especially when dealing with large log files. Logrotate is a powerful utility that automates the process of log file rotation, compression, and removal, which helps in managing disk space and ensuring that logs do not grow indefinitely. By using the 'compress' directive, administrators can ensure that older logs are stored in a more space-efficient manner without losing critical data.

Q189: In a distributed microservices environment, you need to aggregate logs from various Docker containers running on different hosts. This aggregated log data should then be forwarded to a centralized location for analysis. Which of the following tools is specifically designed to handle log data from containerized environments and can forward these logs to different destinations?

A) Prometheus

B) Grafana

C) Fluentd

D) Nagios

E) ELK Stack

F) Zabbix

Answer: C

Explanation: Fluentd is specifically designed to collect and forward log data from various sources, including containerized environments such as Docker. It is highly efficient in aggregating logs from multiple services and forwarding them to centralized locations like

Elasticsearch, Amazon S3, or other databases for analysis. Fluentd's lightweight architecture and the availability of a wide range of plugins make it suitable for handling logs in distributed microservices architectures. It can be easily integrated with Kubernetes and Docker, providing developers with a seamless experience in managing logs from containerized applications.

Q190: True or False: The Linux utility 'awk' can be used to filter and analyze log data based on specific patterns and fields within log entries.
A) True

B) False

Answer: A

Explanation: True. The 'awk' utility is a powerful text processing tool in Linux that is commonly used for pattern scanning and processing. It is particularly useful for analyzing log files as it allows users to specify patterns to search for within log entries and manipulate the data fields. 'awk' can be used to extract specific columns from log entries, perform calculations, and apply filters to display only the relevant information. This capability makes it an invaluable tool for system administrators and DevOps engineers who need to quickly analyze and extract insights from log data.

Q191: In a mid-sized company, the IT department is tasked with setting up a secure web server. The server will host sensitive client data, and it is crucial to protect this information from unauthorized access and data breaches. The team decides to implement a firewall and conduct regular vulnerability scans. As part of the security hardening process, they want to ensure that only essential services are running and that all unnecessary ports are closed. The company uses a Linux-based server, and you are asked to audit the current network configuration to identify potential security risks. Which tool or command would be most effective for listing all currently open ports and the services associated with them on a Linux system?

A) netstat -tuln

B) lsof -i

C) nmap localhost

D) ps aux

E) iptables -L

F) ss -s

Answer: A

Explanation: The command netstat -tuln is specifically designed to display all currently open ports and the services listening on those ports on a Linux system. This includes both TCP and UDP ports, which are denoted by the flags -t and -u, respectively. The -l flag ensures that only listening sockets are shown, and -n displays the numerical addresses instead of resolving hostnames, which speeds up the process and provides a clearer view of the ports in use. While lsof -i can also show open ports, it provides less focus on network configuration compared to netstat. The nmap localhost command is used for scanning ports from an external perspective, not listing them from a local standpoint. ps aux lists processes but doesn't focus on network ports. iptables -L shows firewall rules but doesn't directly list open ports. Finally, ss -s gives a summary of socket statistics and is not primarily used for listing currently open ports with associated services.

Q192: A company has recently experienced a breach where attackers gained access through an unpatched vulnerability in a widely-used software package. To prevent similar incidents, the IT team is implementing a policy to ensure all software is up-to-date with the latest security patches. Which Linux command can be used to list all upgradable packages on a system using the APT package manager?

A) apt-get update

B) apt-get upgrade

C) apt-get dist-upgrade

D) apt list --upgradable

E) dpkg --get-selections

F) apt-cache show

Answer: D

Explanation: The command apt list --upgradable is used to list all packages on a Debian-based system that have available updates. This command provides a concise and clear output of packages that can be upgraded, allowing the system administrator to decide which packages should be updated to maintain security. apt-get update is used to update the package lists from repositories, not to list upgradable packages. apt-get upgrade is used to perform the upgrade of packages but doesn't list them beforehand. apt-get dist-upgrade also performs upgrades but with more complex dependency handling. dpkg --get-selections lists all installed packages but not specifically upgradable ones. apt-cache show provides information about specific packages and isn't related to listing upgradable packages.

Q193: To enhance system security, a Linux server administrator is tasked with auditing user accounts to identify any potential security risks. This includes checking for accounts without passwords, those with empty passwords, and accounts that have not been accessed recently. Which command can be used to list all user accounts on a Linux system that have an empty password field in the /etc/shadow file?

A) grep '^[^:]:[!]' /etc/shadow

B) awk -F: '($2==""){print $1}' /etc/shadow

C) grep '^[^:]::' /etc/shadow

D) awk -F: '($2=="!!"){print $1}' /etc/shadow

E) cat /etc/passwd

F) getent passwd

Answer: C

Explanation: The grep '^[^:]::' /etc/shadow command is used to identify user accounts that have an empty password field in the /etc/shadow file. The /etc/shadow file contains encrypted passwords for user accounts, and an entry with two consecutive colons (::) indicates an empty password. This is a critical security risk as it allows unauthorized access without authentication. The other commands either check for different conditions or do not specifically target the empty password field scenario. awk -F: '($2==""){print $1}' /etc/shadow might seem correct but doesn't account for the specific syntax of /etc/shadow entries. grep '^[^:]:[!]' /etc/shadow checks for disabled accounts. awk -F: '($2=="!!"){print $1}' /etc/shadow looks for locked accounts. cat /etc/passwd displays user information but not password status. getent passwd retrieves entries from the passwd database but does not check passwords.

Q194: A system administrator wants to enforce the principle of least privilege on a Linux server by ensuring that users have access only to the commands and files necessary for their roles. To audit the current user permissions, which command can be used to list the access control lists (ACLs) set on a specific file or directory?

A) ls -l

B) getfacl

C) chmod

D) setfacl

E) chown

F) umask

Answer: B

Explanation: The getfacl command is used to retrieve the access control lists (ACLs) associated with a file or directory on a Linux system. ACLs provide a more fine-grained permission mechanism compared to the traditional owner/group/other model, enabling specific user access rights to be set on files and directories. This is crucial for auditing and enforcing least privilege by ensuring that only authorized users can access sensitive resources. The ls -l command displays basic permissions but does not show ACLs. chmod is used to change permissions, not to list them. setfacl is used to set or modify ACLs, while getfacl is used for listing them. chown changes file ownership, and umask sets default permission values for new files.

Q195: A Linux server administrator needs to verify that a set of security policies has been applied correctly to all servers in the infrastructure. This includes ensuring that remote root login is disabled to minimize potential security breaches. True or False: The configuration file /etc/ssh/sshdconfig should have the entry PermitRootLogin no to achieve this security policy.

A) True

B) False

Answer: A

Explanation: The PermitRootLogin no entry in the /etc/ssh/sshdconfig file is a configuration setting in OpenSSH server that explicitly disables remote root login over SSH. Disabling root login is an essential security measure to protect a server from unauthorized access and potential brute force attacks targeting the root user. By ensuring that root cannot log in directly, it forces users to authenticate with a less privileged account and then use sudo or similar mechanisms to execute administrative tasks. This configuration enhances security by adding another layer of protection and accountability, as all administrative actions can be traced back to individual user accounts. The sshdconfig file must be edited with root privileges, and changes require a restart of the SSH service to take effect.

Q196: A mid-sized e-commerce company is planning to migrate its application to a multi-machine setup to handle increased traffic and ensure high availability. The current setup consists of a single server hosting both the application and the database. The company wants to distribute the web application across multiple web servers and move the database to a dedicated server. Additionally, they plan to implement a load balancer to distribute incoming traffic evenly across the web servers. The IT team is tasked with configuring the network and ensuring seamless communication between the application and database servers. What is the most crucial step to ensure secure communication between all servers in this multi-machine architecture?

A) Implementing a VPN to secure the communication channels between the servers.

B) Configuring SSH keys for passwordless login between servers.

C) Using NFS to share the database files across the web servers.

D) Setting up a firewall to restrict traffic only between known servers.

E) Configuring a cron job to sync the server clocks periodically.

F) Installing fail2ban to protect against brute force attacks.

Answer: A

Explanation: Implementing a VPN (Virtual Private Network) is crucial in a multi-machine setup to ensure secure communication across the servers. A VPN encrypts the data transmitted over the network, protecting it from interception and eavesdropping. In a scenario where the application is distributed across multiple servers and a dedicated database server, ensuring secure data transmission is paramount to protect sensitive information, such as user credentials and transaction data. While other options like SSH keys and firewalls contribute to security, they do not provide the comprehensive encryption and protection of data in transit that a VPN offers. Additionally, setting up a VPN can simplify network management by creating a secure, single-point entry, especially when integrating with a load balancer. It's a fundamental step in securing multi-machine architectures.

Q197: When configuring a multi-machine environment, which tool is most appropriate for automating the deployment and configuration of multiple servers simultaneously?

A) rsync

B) cron

C) Ansible

D) top

E) grep

F) df

Answer: C

Explanation: Ansible is an open-source automation tool that is particularly suited for automating the deployment and configuration of servers in a multi-machine environment. It uses a simple, human-readable language (YAML) to describe the automation jobs, known as playbooks. Ansible is agentless, meaning it does not require any software to be installed on the target machines, making it easy to manage large-scale deployments. It also supports idempotency, ensuring that changes are applied consistently and repeatedly, which is crucial for maintaining system state across multiple servers. Other tools listed, such as rsync and cron, are not designed for comprehensive deployment automation across multiple machines.

Q198: A company is using a multi-machine setup for its application, with different components running on separate servers. The system administrator needs to ensure that the time is synchronized across all machines to avoid logging discrepancies and other time-sensitive issues. Which service should be configured to achieve this?
A) iptables

B) NTP

C) DHCP

D) FTP

E) LDAP

F) SMTP

Answer: B

Explanation: NTP (Network Time Protocol) is used to synchronize the clocks of computers over a network. In a multi-machine setup, having synchronized time across all servers is essential to maintain accurate logs, manage time-sensitive transactions, and ensure that cron jobs and other scheduled tasks execute at the correct times. Discrepancies in system time can lead to errors, inconsistencies, and security vulnerabilities. NTP is designed for precisely this purpose, providing a reliable method to keep system clocks in sync. Other services like FTP or SMTP serve entirely different purposes, such as file transfer and email delivery, respectively.

Q199: In a multi-machine architecture, an organization uses a centralized logging server to collect logs from various application servers. Which of the following is the most appropriate protocol to use for transmitting logs to the centralized server?

A) HTTP

B) FTP

C) SMTP

D) Syslog

E) NFS

F) HTTPS

Answer: D

Explanation: Syslog is a standardized protocol used to send log or event messages to a centralized server for storage. It is widely used in multi-machine setups to collect logs from various devices or applications in one place, facilitating easier monitoring, troubleshooting, and analysis. Syslog allows devices to send event messages to a logging server in a standardized format, which can be processed and reviewed by administrators. Other listed protocols, such as HTTP and FTP, are not designed for log transmission but serve different purposes like web communication and file transfer, respectively.

Q200: True or False: In a multi-machine setup, using shared storage solutions like NFS (Network File System) is the best approach to ensure database consistency across multiple application servers.

A) True

B) False

Answer: B

Explanation: Using NFS or similar shared storage solutions for database consistency across multiple application servers is generally not recommended. Databases require transactions and data integrity mechanisms that shared file systems like NFS do not natively provide. Instead, databases use synchronization protocols and clustering technologies to ensure consistency and integrity. Implementing a database cluster or using replication features are better approaches to maintaining consistency across application servers. Shared storage solutions are more suited for static file sharing rather than dynamic data with high concurrency and transactional needs.

Q201: A mid-sized financial services company is migrating its applications to a container-based infrastructure to improve scalability and deployment speed. The team is aware of the potential security threats associated with container images and wants to ensure that their images are secure before deployment. They have decided to implement a strategy to minimize these risks but are unsure about the best practices regarding user privileges within the containers. The team needs guidance on how to configure user privileges to enhance security.

A) Run all applications as the root user within the container to simplify management.

B) Use a non-root user within the container for running applications to limit access.

C) Disable user namespaces to prevent privilege escalation.

D) Set user namespace mapping to allow containers to run with root privileges on the host.

E) Utilize the same user ID (UID) across all containers for consistency.

F) Use capabilities to allow non-root users to perform privileged operations.

Answer: B

Explanation: Running applications as the root user within a container poses significant security risks because if an attacker gains access to the container, they can potentially control the host system. Using a non-root user is a fundamental security practice that limits the damage an attacker could do if they compromised the container. By defining and running processes as a non-root user, even if a container is exploited, the attacker's actions are restricted to the permissions of that non-root user. It is essential to configure the

Dockerfile to specify a USER directive that changes to a non-root user, thus providing an extra layer of security.

Q202: Which of the following is a security risk associated with using untrusted container images from public repositories?

A) Increased likelihood of image corruption during download.

B) Potential exposure to vulnerabilities or malicious code.

C) Reduced performance of the container due to image size.

D) Incompatibility issues with the host's kernel version.

E) Difficulty in managing networking configurations.

F) Challenges in maintaining consistent environment variables.

Answer: B

Explanation: Using untrusted container images from public repositories introduces the risk of incorporating vulnerabilities or malicious code into your environment. These images may contain outdated libraries, compromised packages, or backdoors that could lead to security breaches. It is vital to verify the source of container images, use trusted repositories, and regularly scan images for vulnerabilities using tools like Clair or Trivy. Organizations should also consider signing their images and employing image policies to ensure only verified and scanned images are deployed.

Q203: True or False: Enabling Linux kernel capabilities within a container can help enhance security by providing fine-grained access control to the processes running inside the container.

A) True

B) False

Answer: A

Explanation: Linux kernel capabilities allow for fine-grained access control by breaking down the privileges of the root user into distinct units, which can be independently enabled or disabled. This means specific capabilities can be granted to processes without giving full root access, thus limiting the potential attack surface. For instance, a process might be allowed to bind to network ports without being given full network administration privileges. This approach helps in adhering to the principle of least privilege, enhancing the security posture of containers.

Q204: A security audit of your containerized applications has highlighted the need to ensure that only authorized images are run in the production environment. What is the most effective measure to implement this requirement?

A) Regularly update the base images to the latest version.

B) Use image signing and verification to allow only signed images.

C) Set resource limits on containers to prevent overconsumption.

D) Enable SELinux in enforcing mode for all containers.

E) Apply security patches to the host operating system.

F) Utilize namespaces to isolate containers from each other.

Answer: B

Explanation: Image signing and verification is a critical security measure that ensures only authorized and trusted images are deployed in the production environment. By signing images, you can verify their integrity and authenticity, preventing the deployment of tampered or unauthorized images. Tools like Docker Content Trust (DCT) or Notary can be used to manage and verify image signatures. This practice is essential in maintaining a secure supply chain, ensuring that only images from trusted sources are used, which significantly reduces the risk of running compromised images in production.

Q205: When configuring a container runtime security policy, what is the primary benefit of using seccomp profiles?

A) They allow containers to communicate with each other more efficiently.

B) They provide a mechanism to restrict system calls available to the container.

C) They enhance the performance of the containerized application.

D) They simplify the process of container network configuration.

E) They ensure container logs are stored securely.

F) They enable more flexible container resource allocation.

Answer: B

Explanation: Seccomp (Secure Computing Mode) profiles are used to filter and restrict the system calls that a containerized application can make to the host kernel. By defining a whitelist of allowed system calls, seccomp profiles help limit the attack surface and effectively mitigate the risk of kernel exploits. This mechanism provides an additional layer of security by ensuring that even if a containerized application is compromised, its ability to interact with the host system is severely restricted. Implementing seccomp is part of a defense-in-depth strategy, crucial for maintaining a secure container environment.

Q206: A mid-sized tech company is migrating its applications from local servers to a cloud-based infrastructure. They are considering implementing a Continuous Integration/Continuous Deployment (CI/CD) pipeline to streamline their software development and deployment processes. The operations team needs to choose a suitable software component that can integrate with existing Linux systems and support automation of builds, testing, and deployment. Their main priorities are ease of integration with various source code repositories and container orchestration platforms like Kubernetes. Which tool should the operations team choose to best meet these requirements?

A) Jenkins

B) Ansible

C) Puppet

D) Chef

E) Nagios

F) ELK Stack

Answer: A

Explanation: Jenkins is a widely-used open-source automation server that supports building, deploying, and automating any project. It is known for its ease of integration with a variety of version control systems like Git, SVN, and Mercurial, as well as its strong plugin ecosystem that includes support for container orchestration platforms such as Kubernetes. Jenkins can automate tasks associated with building, testing, and deploying software, making it an ideal choice for setting up a CI/CD pipeline. While Ansible, Puppet, and Chef are powerful configuration management tools, they are not primarily designed for CI/CD. Nagios is a monitoring system, and the ELK Stack is used for logging and analytics.

Q207: Which of the following is a primary feature of Docker that facilitates software deployment in Linux environments?

A) Configuration Management

B) Containerization

C) Continuous Monitoring

D) Virtual Machines

E) Network Security

F) Load Balancing

Answer: B

Explanation: Docker is a platform that uses containerization to enable developers to package applications along with their dependencies into a single container. This approach ensures that the application can run consistently across different computing environments. Containerization is Docker's primary feature, allowing for rapid deployment and scaling of applications without the overhead of traditional virtual machines. Unlike virtual machines, containers share the same operating system kernel, making them more lightweight and efficient. Configuration management, continuous monitoring, network security, and load balancing are functionalities associated with different tools and are not the main focus of Docker.

Q208: A large e-commerce company uses various Linux-based servers to host their applications. The systems administrator is tasked with improving the observability of application performance and system health. After evaluating several options, they decide to implement a tool that offers real-time monitoring and alerting, integrates well with Linux, and provides a comprehensive dashboard for visualization. Which tool is the most appropriate choice for these requirements?

A) Prometheus

B) Ansible

C) Terraform

D) Grafana

E) Chef

F) Jenkins

Answer: A

Explanation: Prometheus is an open-source monitoring and alerting toolkit that is particularly well-suited for complex and dynamic environments like Linux-based server infrastructures. It provides powerful data model and query language (PromQL) for real-time monitoring and alerting, allowing users to create detailed dashboards and visualizations. Prometheus is designed for reliability and efficiency, allowing it to handle a large volume of metrics, making it an ideal choice for monitoring applications and system health. Grafana is often used alongside Prometheus for visualization, but it doesn't provide the same monitoring and alerting capabilities by itself. Ansible, Terraform, and Chef are primarily configuration management and orchestration tools, while Jenkins is used for CI/CD.

Q209: A Linux administrator needs to automate the deployment of applications across hundreds of servers. The chosen tool should have robust support for Linux systems, be capable of handling complex workflows, and integrate well with existing CI/CD pipelines. Which tool should they implement to accomplish these objectives?

A) Ansible

B) Kubernetes

C) ELK Stack

D) Terraform

E) Nagios

F) Grafana

Answer: A

Explanation: Ansible is a powerful automation tool that is particularly well-suited for deploying applications across multiple Linux servers. It uses a simple syntax written in YAML known as playbooks, which allows administrators to define configurations and orchestrate complex workflows. Ansible is agentless, meaning it only requires SSH access to the servers, making it easy to integrate into existing Linux-based infrastructures. It also integrates well with CI/CD pipelines to automate deployment processes. Kubernetes is more focused on container orchestration, Terraform is used for infrastructure as code, and Grafana and ELK Stack are used for visualization and logging, respectively. Nagios is primarily a monitoring tool.

Q210: True or False: The purpose of using a Linux package manager is to facilitate the installation, update, and removal of software packages on a Linux system.

A) True

B) False

Answer: A

Explanation: A Linux package manager is an essential tool for managing software on a Linux system. It automates the process of installing, updating, and removing software packages, ensuring that all dependencies are handled correctly. Package managers like APT (Advanced Package Tool) for Debian-based systems and YUM (Yellowdog Updater Modified) for Red Hat-based systems streamline software management tasks, reduce the risk of conflicts and errors, and provide users with access to a wide repository of software. This functionality is crucial for maintaining system stability and ensuring that software is kept up to date with the latest security patches and features.

Q211: Your company is migrating its microservices-based application to Kubernetes for better scalability and management. The application consists of multiple services that communicate with each other and rely on stable network identities. You need to ensure that these services can find each other using DNS and have stable endpoints despite potential changes in the number of pods or their IP addresses. Which Kubernetes feature should you primarily rely on to achieve this?

A) Persistent Volumes

B) ConfigMaps

C) Ingress Controllers

D) Services

E) Network Policies

F) StatefulSets

Answer: D

Explanation: In Kubernetes, a Service is an abstraction that defines a logical set of Pods and a policy by which to access them, typically through stable DNS names and IP addresses. When dealing with microservices that need reliable communication, Services provide a stable interface despite changes in the underlying pod IP addresses. This is crucial in dynamic environments where pods can be scaled up or down, and their IPs can change frequently. Services use labels to select the pods they route traffic to, ensuring that the correct pods can always be accessed with a consistent network endpoint, which aligns perfectly with the needs of microservice architectures.

Q212: In Kubernetes architecture, you need to define how containers are organized into pods, and how these pods are scheduled across nodes. Which component of the Kubernetes control plane is responsible for deciding on which node a pod should run?

A) kube-proxy

B) kubelet

C) etcd

D) kube-scheduler

E) controller-manager

F) kubectl

Answer: D

Explanation: The kube-scheduler is the component of the Kubernetes control plane responsible for assigning pods to nodes. It takes into account various factors like resource requirements, policy constraints, affinity, anti-affinity specifications, data locality, and more. The scheduler ensures that the workload is distributed evenly across nodes and that the pod placement respects any constraints defined in the pod specifications. It plays a critical role in optimizing resource utilization and maintaining the desired state of the cluster.

Q213: True/False: In Kubernetes, a ReplicaSet is primarily used to manage the deployment and scaling of stateful applications.

A) True

B) False

Answer: B

Explanation: A ReplicaSet is primarily used to maintain a stable set of replica Pods running at any given time for stateless applications. It ensures that a specified number of pod replicas are running at all times, and it handles scaling and self-healing by replacing failed pods. Stateful applications, on the other hand, require persistent storage and stable network identities, which are managed by a StatefulSet. StatefulSets offer additional guarantees about the ordering and uniqueness of pods, which are essential for stateful applications that maintain data or require consistent network identities.

Q214: A company is using Kubernetes to deploy applications and wants to segment network traffic between different namespaces for security reasons. Which Kubernetes feature would best help achieve this?

A) ServiceAccount

B) Network Policies

C) PodSecurityPolicy

D) Resource Quotas

E) Role-Based Access Control (RBAC)

F) ConfigMaps

Answer: B

Explanation: Network Policies in Kubernetes are used to control the traffic between pods and to or from the external world. They allow you to define rules for pod communication, providing a way to segment traffic for security purposes. By using Network Policies, you can specify which pods can communicate with each other and which can access external services. This is particularly useful for isolating traffic between different namespaces, ensuring that only authorized communication is allowed, thereby enhancing the security posture of the applications running in the cluster.

Q215: Imagine you are working for a financial services company that has strict compliance requirements. You need to ensure that all sensitive customer data is encrypted and only accessible to specific pods within a Kubernetes cluster. Which feature should you use to securely provide this sensitive data to the pods?

A) Secrets

B) Persistent Storage

C) ConfigMaps

D) DaemonSets

E) Deployments

F) Ingress

Answer: A

Explanation: In Kubernetes, Secrets are used to manage sensitive information like passwords, OAuth tokens, and SSH keys. Secrets provide a secure way to pass sensitive data to pods without embedding it directly in the container image or the pod specification. Kubernetes stores Secrets in etcd in an encoded format and provides mechanisms to restrict access to them. By using Secrets, you can ensure that sensitive customer data is accessible only to specific pods that have the necessary permissions, in compliance with strict security and compliance requirements. This helps in maintaining the confidentiality and integrity of sensitive information while adhering to best practices for data management in Kubernetes.

Q216: A company is deploying a microservices architecture using Docker Swarm mode to manage their containers. They want to ensure high availability and scalability across multiple data centers. The operations team must configure the network settings to allow inter-service communication securely and efficiently. Additionally, they need to ensure that the deployment can handle rolling updates without downtime. How should they configure the Docker Swarm cluster to meet these requirements?

A) Use the default bridge network and configure iptables manually for security.

B) Utilize an overlay network with encrypted traffic to connect services across nodes.

C) Deploy each service with a fixed number of replicas and update manually.

D) Configure the services to use host networking for better performance.

E) Use a single manager node for simplicity and faster updates.

F) Disable auto-lock feature for seamless node addition and removal.

Answer: B

Explanation: The best approach for this scenario is to utilize an overlay network with encrypted traffic. Overlay networks in Docker Swarm span across all nodes in the Swarm and enable services to communicate securely and efficiently, accommodating the inter-service communication requirement across multiple data centers. The encrypted traffic ensures that the data transmitted between services is secure. This network configuration also supports service discovery and load balancing, which are critical for high availability and scalability. By using Docker's built-in capabilities for rolling updates, the operations team can update services with zero downtime. The other options either compromise security or do not support dynamic scaling and seamless updates.

Q217: What command would you use to initialize a Docker Swarm on a new manager node?

A) docker swarm start

B) docker swarm init

C) docker swarm create

D) docker swarm setup

E) docker swarm new

F) docker swarm launch

Answer: B

Explanation: The command to initialize a Docker Swarm on a new manager node is docker swarm init. This command sets up the Docker host as a manager node, effectively creating a new Swarm cluster if one does not already exist. It configures the initial Swarm settings and generates a join token that can be used by worker nodes to join the Swarm. The other options do not represent valid Docker commands for initializing a Swarm.

Q218: True or False: In Docker Swarm mode, every node in the cluster must be a manager node to ensure fault tolerance.
A) True

B) False

Answer: B

Explanation: In Docker Swarm mode, not every node must be a manager to ensure fault tolerance. While manager nodes are responsible for maintaining the cluster state and orchestrating services, worker nodes handle the execution of tasks. For fault tolerance, it is essential to have an odd number of manager nodes (typically three or five) to maintain quorum, which allows the cluster to continue operating even if some manager nodes fail. Worker nodes do not participate in the consensus process and can be added as needed to scale out the workload.

Q219: You are tasked with setting up a Docker Swarm cluster that requires secure node communication and automatic failover. Which command would you run on a new node to join it as a manager node to an existing Swarm?

A) docker swarm join --as-manager

B) docker swarm join --manager

C) docker swarm join --role manager

D) docker swarm add --manager

E) docker swarm join --promote

F) docker swarm join --leader

Answer: B

Explanation: To join a new node as a manager to an existing Swarm, the correct command is docker swarm join --manager. This command adds the node to the Swarm with manager permissions, allowing it to participate in the management of the cluster. The join token for a manager must be used, which is different from the worker node token. This setup ensures secure communication among nodes and enables automatic failover capabilities as the manager nodes share the responsibility of maintaining the cluster state.

Q220: A tech startup is utilizing Docker Swarm to manage its containerized applications. They want to ensure that all service updates occur without service disruption. Which Docker Swarm feature should they leverage to achieve this goal?

A) Manual scaling

B) Rolling updates

C) Service restart

D) Paused deployment

E) Parallel updates

F) Container snapshot

Answer: B

Explanation: To ensure that service updates occur without service disruption, the startup should leverage Docker Swarm's rolling updates feature. Rolling updates allow services to be updated incrementally, replacing old tasks with new ones one at a time or in small batches. This process minimizes downtime and maintains service availability throughout the update process. Docker Swarm manages the load balancing and ensures that there are always enough running instances to handle incoming requests, making it ideal for maintaining uninterrupted service during updates.

Q221: A mid-sized company is transitioning its infrastructure monitoring to Prometheus. The team is concerned about managing the configuration of exporters across their heterogeneous environment consisting of various Linux distributions. They want to ensure that metrics are consistently collected without manual intervention whenever a new server is deployed. The team is considering using Prometheus' service discovery features to automate this process. Which of the following service discovery mechanisms would be most suitable for them to use, given their environment primarily uses static IPs and DNS records?

A) Consul

B) Kubernetes

C) DNS-based service discovery

D) Zookeeper

E) etcd

F) EC2 Service Discovery

Answer: C

Explanation: Prometheus offers various service discovery mechanisms to automate configuration management. In a setting where static IPs and DNS records are prevalent, DNS-based service discovery is highly suitable. This method leverages DNS SRV records to discover targets dynamically, which is ideal for environments where DNS is already integrated and used for service management. Unlike other methods such as Consul or Kubernetes, which require additional setup and are more suited for dynamic, containerized environments, DNS-based discovery is straightforward and leverages existing infrastructure, making it cost-effective and easy to implement. This method also minimizes manual configuration efforts, aligning with the team's goals of consistency and automation.

Q222: Select the most accurate statement about the Prometheus data model and its functionality.

A) Prometheus uses a hierarchical data model similar to Graphite.

B) Prometheus stores data as time series identified by metric name and set of key-value pairs.

C) Prometheus requires an external database for long-term storage.

D) All metric data in Prometheus must be pushed to it from applications.

E) Prometheus uses a NoSQL database to store its data.

F) Prometheus data model is based on relational database principles.

Answer: B

Explanation: Prometheus fundamentally stores data as time series, which are uniquely identified by a metric name and a set of key-value pairs, known as labels. This flexible data model allows for high dimensionality in metrics, providing powerful querying capabilities. Unlike Graphite's hierarchical model, Prometheus' label-based approach allows for more sophisticated aggregation and filtering. Prometheus is designed to be a standalone system and does not require external databases for its core functionality, although external storage solutions can be integrated for long-term data retention. Data is typically pulled from target systems, not pushed, which aligns with Prometheus' design principles of reliability and simplicity.

Q223: You are tasked with configuring Prometheus in a highly secure environment where network policies are very restrictive. The security team insists on minimizing open ports and requires all HTTP communications to be encrypted. Which configuration option best meets these requirements for securing Prometheus communications?

A) Use basic authentication for all Prometheus endpoints.

B) Employ a reverse proxy with SSL termination to handle HTTPS.

C) Configure Prometheus to use a non-standard port.

D) Enable IP whitelisting for access control to Prometheus.

E) Deploy Prometheus behind a VPN and only allow internal access.

F) Implement SSH tunneling for Prometheus communications.

Answer: B

Explanation: In secure environments, encrypting communications is crucial. Prometheus itself does not natively support HTTPS, requiring either a reverse proxy setup or external tools for encryption. Using a reverse proxy with SSL termination is a common and effective method to secure HTTP communications by offloading the TLS/SSL processing to the proxy server. This approach allows for HTTPS connections to the Prometheus endpoints without modifying Prometheus itself. While basic authentication and IP whitelisting can add layers of security, they do not encrypt the traffic. Deploying behind a VPN or using SSH tunneling can secure access but involves more complex setup and maintenance, making a reverse proxy with SSL termination the most straightforward and robust solution for HTTPS encryption.

Q224: Evaluate the following statement: "Prometheus uses a push-based model for collecting metrics from its targets, which makes it ideal for monitoring dynamic environments like cloud-native applications."

A) True

B) False

Answer: B

Explanation: This statement is false. Prometheus uses a pull-based model for collecting metrics, where it actively scrapes metrics from target endpoints at specified intervals. This design choice facilitates easy monitoring of ephemeral targets typical in dynamic, cloud-native environments, as Prometheus can automatically discover and scrape new instances through service discovery mechanisms. The pull-based model also ensures that Prometheus can handle the targets' availability, reducing the risk of overload on target systems. While push-based models are sometimes used with Prometheus through its Pushgateway, this is generally for short-lived jobs and not the primary mechanism for metric collection.

Q225: A retail company is using Prometheus to monitor their e-commerce platform. They have noticed an increase in the cardinality of their metrics due to the dynamic nature of their services, leading to performance issues. To mitigate this, they want to optimize their Prometheus setup. Which of the following is the best approach to reduce metric cardinality without losing critical monitoring data?

A) Increase the retention period of the Prometheus database.

B) Use recording rules to pre-aggregate high-cardinality metrics.

C) Deploy additional Prometheus instances to distribute the load.

D) Reduce the scrape interval to decrease data volume.

E) Use external storage solutions for high-cardinality metrics.

F) Disable label joins in PromQL queries.

Answer: B

Explanation: High cardinality in Prometheus can lead to increased memory and storage consumption, affecting performance. Recording rules are an effective strategy to manage this by pre-aggregating metrics with high cardinality. By aggregating metrics that are frequently queried, Prometheus can reduce the number of time series it needs to store and query, optimizing performance without sacrificing important monitoring data. This approach allows for the preservation of critical insights while ensuring that the system remains efficient. Increasing retention or deploying additional instances may alleviate some strain but do not address the fundamental issue of high cardinality. Reducing the scrape interval decreases data resolution, potentially losing important information, while external storage solutions are more suited for long-term retention rather than cardinality reduction. Disabling label joins does not impact cardinality directly and may limit query capabilities.

Q226: A mid-sized software company is implementing a Continuous Integration (CI) pipeline to automate the process of building, testing, and deploying their applications. Their current setup involves a Jenkins CI server running on a Linux machine, and they want to ensure that the source code repository is always synchronized with the latest code changes made by the developers. The company uses Git for version control and aims to trigger the CI pipeline automatically whenever new code is pushed to the main branch. Which Git feature can be used to achieve this automated triggering of the Jenkins pipeline? ###

A) Git Hooks

B) Git Submodules

C) Git Rebase

D) Git Bisect

E) Git Cherry-pick

F) Git Stash

Answer: A

Explanation: Git hooks are custom scripts that are triggered by certain events in the Git lifecycle, such as committing changes, merging branches, or pushing code. They are highly useful for automating tasks like deploying code or triggering CI pipelines. In this scenario, a post-receive hook on the Git server can be configured to send a web request to the Jenkins server whenever new code is pushed to the main branch. This web request can trigger a Jenkins job, effectively integrating Git with Jenkins for a seamless CI process. Git submodules, rebase, bisect, cherry-pick, and stash serve different purposes and are not suited for automating CI pipeline triggers.

Q227: In a typical Continuous Delivery (CD) pipeline, what is the primary purpose of the staging environment? ###

A) To replace the development environment for testing

B) To provide a backup for the production environment

C) To host the final version of the application for end-users

D) To replicate the production environment for final testing

E) To serve as a sandbox for developers to experiment

F) To act as a version control system for deployment scripts

Answer: D

Explanation: The staging environment is a critical component in a Continuous Delivery pipeline. Its primary purpose is to closely replicate the production environment to test the application in conditions that mimic the live environment as closely as possible. This helps identify potential issues that might arise in production, allowing developers and testers to ensure the application is ready for deployment. Unlike development or sandbox environments, the staging environment is not meant for experimentation or development; it is a final checkpoint to validate application stability and performance before moving to production.

Q228: A development team is incorporating a Continuous Integration (CI) system that frequently executes automated tests on a Linux-based infrastructure. They notice that test execution is significantly slowing down due to the high number of test cases. What Linux-based solution could be implemented to improve the test execution time without reducing the number of tests? ###

A) Use 'nice' command to prioritize test processes

B) Implement test parallelization using GNU Parallel

C) Schedule tests during low-traffic hours using 'at'

D) Utilize swap space to handle test data overflow

E) Use tmux to manage multiple test sessions

F) Install more RAM to increase system capacity

Answer: B

Explanation: GNU Parallel is a shell tool for executing jobs in parallel using one or more computers. In the context of a Continuous Integration system, it can significantly reduce test execution time by running multiple test cases concurrently rather than sequentially. By utilizing GNU Parallel, the development team can efficiently distribute the workload across available CPU cores, achieving better performance and faster feedback from their CI system. The 'nice' command adjusts the scheduling priority of processes but does not inherently improve execution time. Scheduling tests during low-traffic hours, using swap space, tmux, or adding RAM may help but are not as directly effective as parallelizing the workload.

Q229: True/False: In a Continuous Integration (CI) process, the primary goal is to ensure that every code change automatically triggers a build and test cycle, providing immediate feedback to developers. ###

A) True

B) False

Answer: A

Explanation: The essence of Continuous Integration is to automate the process of building and testing code changes as soon as they are integrated into the main codebase. This immediate feedback loop is crucial for detecting errors early in the development cycle, thus reducing the time and effort required to fix issues. CI tools are configured to monitor the version control system for code changes and to automatically execute build scripts and test suites, ensuring that any new errors or issues are quickly identified and communicated to the developers. This practice helps maintain code quality and minimizes integration problems.

Q230: A company is using a Continuous Delivery (CD) pipeline to manage the deployment of their web application hosted on a Linux server. They want to ensure zero downtime during deployments. Which deployment strategy is most appropriate for achieving this goal?

A) Blue-Green Deployment

B) Rolling Deployment

C) Canary Deployment

D) Recreate Deployment

E) Shadow Deployment

F) Big Bang Deployment

Answer: A

Explanation: Blue-green deployment is a strategy designed to ensure zero downtime during application deployment. It involves maintaining two identical environments: blue and green. At any given time, one environment (e.g., blue) is live and serving all production traffic, while the other (e.g., green) is idle. During deployment, the new version of the application is deployed to the idle environment. Once testing and validation are complete, traffic is switched to the new environment, making it live. This approach eliminates downtime and allows for quick rollback if needed. Rolling, canary, recreate, shadow, and big bang deployments have their advantages but do not inherently guarantee zero downtime.

Q231: In a mid-sized company, the DevOps team is tasked with automating the deployment of a web application across multiple environments, including development, testing, and production. They decide to use Puppet for configuration management. One of the team members suggests organizing the configuration code using manifests and classes to ensure consistency and reusability. The web application requires a specific version of Apache, certain firewall rules, and a custom configuration file for the virtual host. How should the team structure their Puppet code to achieve this?

A) Create a single manifest file with all configurations.

B) Use a class for Apache installation, another class for firewall rules, and a third class for the virtual host configuration.

C) Write separate manifest files for each environment.

D) Use a module to encapsulate all configurations but avoid using classes.

E) Define resource types for Apache, firewall, and virtual host in one class.

F) Use templates for each component and include them in a single manifest file.

Answer: B

Explanation: In Puppet, using classes is a best practice for organizing configuration code. By creating a separate class for each distinct aspect of the configuration (Apache installation, firewall rules, and virtual host configuration), the team can ensure modularity and reusability. This approach allows for clear separation of concerns and makes it easier to manage dependencies and updates. Each class can be applied to nodes as needed, promoting consistency across environments. Manifests are used to declare resources, but classes provide a higher level of abstraction and organization within modules, which are collections of manifests and data. This structure aligns with Puppet's design philosophy and facilitates scalable and maintainable infrastructure management.

Q232: A DevOps engineer is using Chef to manage a fleet of servers. The company has a policy that any configuration changes should be tested in a staging environment before being applied to production. Which Chef component should the engineer use to group recipes and apply them conditionally based on the environment?

A) Environments

B) Roles

C) Data Bags

D) Resources

E) Attributes

F) Templates

Answer: A

Explanation: Chef Environments are used to define different settings and attributes depending on the environment, such as staging, production, or development. By using environments, a DevOps engineer can apply specific configurations to nodes based on their environment. This allows for testing changes in a staging environment before promoting them to production. Environments can be used to override attributes and control version constraints for cookbooks, ensuring that only tested and approved configurations are applied in production. Roles and data bags are also Chef components but serve different purposes: roles are used to define server roles and data bags store global data. Resources, attributes, and templates are used within recipes but do not provide environment-specific control.

Q233: Choose the correct statement regarding the use of cookbooks in Chef.

A) Cookbooks can only contain recipes.

B) Cookbooks cannot include templates.

C) Cookbooks allow for versioning, which is essential for maintaining different states of infrastructure.

D) Cookbooks are limited to defining node attributes.

E) Cookbooks are exclusively used for testing configurations.

F) Cookbooks cannot be shared between teams.

Answer: C

Explanation: Cookbooks in Chef are the fundamental units of configuration and policy distribution. They can contain recipes, templates, files, attributes, libraries, and more. One of the key features of cookbooks is versioning, which is crucial for managing changes and ensuring stability across different environments. By versioning cookbooks, teams can maintain different states of their infrastructure, test changes safely, and roll back if necessary. This capability is essential for continuous integration and deployment practices in a DevOps environment. Cookbooks can be shared and reused across teams and projects, promoting collaboration and consistency.

Q234: In the context of Puppet, identify the true statement.
A) Classes in Puppet can only be defined within modules.

B) Manifests in Puppet are exclusively used for defining node-specific configurations.

C) Recipes are a central concept in Puppet for organizing code.

D) Cookbooks are used in Puppet for managing configurations.

E) Puppet supports conditional logic in manifests through the use of templates.

F) Manifests are the basic building blocks of Puppet configurations.

Answer: F

Explanation: In Puppet, manifests are files that contain Puppet code and are the basic building blocks for configurations. They are written in the Puppet language and define the desired state of the system by declaring resources, classes, and variables. Manifests can be applied directly to nodes or included within modules. Classes can be defined within manifests or modules, not exclusively in modules, and are used to group related configurations. Puppet does not have a concept of recipes or cookbooks; these terms are specific to Chef. Puppet supports conditional logic through its language features, not templates, which are used for dynamic file content generation.

Q235: True or False: In Chef, a recipe is a collection of resources that describes a particular configuration or policy.

A) True

B) False

Answer: A

Explanation: In Chef, a recipe is indeed a collection of resources that describes a specific configuration or policy for a system. Recipes are written in Ruby and are used to define the steps necessary to bring a system to a desired state. They include resource declarations that specify actions to be taken, such as installing packages, creating files, or starting services. Recipes can be included in cookbooks and can call other recipes, allowing for modular and reusable configuration management. This makes them a fundamental component in Chef's infrastructure automation framework.

Q236: In a rapidly growing tech company, the microservices architecture has been adopted to allow for better scalability and management of services. The company has several microservices running in a containerized environment using Docker on multiple Linux servers. The DevOps team is tasked with implementing a service discovery mechanism to allow these microservices to dynamically find and communicate with each other without hardcoding IP addresses. The team decides to use Consul for service discovery, and they need to configure it on the Linux servers. What command should the team use to start the Consul agent in client mode on each service node?

A) consul agent -server -node=<nodename> -bind=<nodeip> -data-dir=/var/consul

B) consul agent -node=<nodename> -bind=<nodeip> -data-dir=/var/consul

C) consul agent -client -node=<nodename> -bind=<nodeip> -data-dir=/var/consul

D) consul agent -dev -node=<nodename> -bind=<nodeip> -data-dir=/var/consul

E) consul agent -config-dir=/etc/consul.d -node=<nodename> -bind=<nodeip>

F) consul agent -join=<serverip> -node=<nodename> -bind=<nodeip> -data-dir=/var/consul

Answer: C

Explanation: In a service discovery setup with Consul, it's essential to differentiate between the server and client roles of the Consul agents. The server nodes maintain the state of the cluster, while client nodes are primarily responsible for forwarding queries to the server nodes. When starting a Consul agent in client mode, the -client flag specifies that the agent should run as a client. The -node flag assigns a unique identifier to the node, and the -bind flag sets the IP address that the agent will advertise to other nodes. The -data-dir flag specifies where Consul will store its data. Using these flags correctly ensures that the Consul agents can communicate effectively, allowing services to discover each other dynamically without hardcoded IP addresses.

Q237: Which of the following tools is primarily used for service discovery and configuration management in a Linux-based containerized environment?
A) Prometheus

B) ELK Stack

C) Docker Swarm

D) Consul

E) Grafana

F) Jenkins

Answer: D

Explanation: Consul is a tool specifically designed for service discovery and configuration management. It provides several key features such as service registration, health checking, and a distributed key-value store. These features make it particularly well-suited for dynamic environments like containerized applications where services need to discover each other at runtime. Prometheus and Grafana are more focused on monitoring and visualization, while Docker Swarm is primarily a container orchestration tool. The ELK Stack is used for logging, and Jenkins is a CI/CD tool, all of which serve different purposes than service discovery.

Q238: In a typical Linux-based Kubernetes setup, which component is responsible for providing service discovery within the cluster?
A) etcd

B) kube-proxy

C) kube-apiserver

D) CoreDNS

E) kubelet

F) Helm

Answer: D

Explanation: CoreDNS is the component responsible for service discovery within a Kubernetes cluster. It acts as the DNS server that Kubernetes uses to resolve service names to IP addresses. CoreDNS integrates with Kubernetes to provide DNS-based service discovery by serving DNS records based on the service and pod configurations. While etcd is used as a backing store for all cluster data, including service discovery data, it is not directly responsible for resolving service names. kube-proxy, kube-apiserver, and kubelet have other roles related to network routing, API management, and node management, respectively. Helm is a package manager for Kubernetes applications and does not handle service discovery.

Q239: True or False: In a Linux environment, service discovery can only be achieved by using dedicated tools like Consul or etcd.
A) True

B) False

Answer: B

Explanation: Service discovery in a Linux environment can be implemented using various methods and is not limited to dedicated tools like Consul or etcd. While these tools provide robust solutions for dynamic service discovery, other methods such as using DNS for static service registration, leveraging service meshes like Istio, or even using environment variables and configuration files can also achieve service discovery. Each method has its use cases, advantages, and limitations, and the choice depends on the specific requirements of the environment and the architecture of the application.

Q240: In a Docker-based microservices architecture running on Linux, a team decides to use environment variables for service discovery. Which of the following is a potential downside of this approach?
A) Increased security

B) Lack of scalability

C) Simplified configuration management

D) Easier debugging processes

E) Automatic service registration

F) Reduced network overhead

Answer: B

Explanation: Using environment variables for service discovery in a Docker-based microservices architecture can lead to scalability issues. This approach typically requires services to have predefined knowledge of each other's addresses or endpoints, which can become cumbersome as the number of services increases. It does not support dynamic changes easily if services are added, removed, or scaled up and down, as the environment variables would need to be updated accordingly. This lack of scalability can become a significant operational overhead compared to dynamic service discovery solutions like Consul or Kubernetes, which automatically handle service registration and discovery without requiring manual updates to environment variables.

Q241: In a mid-sized tech company, the development team has recently adopted agile methodologies to enhance software delivery. The team uses continuous integration and continuous deployment (CI/CD) pipelines to automate the deployment process. They are currently facing issues with the speed of deployment, as the integration tests take too long to execute. The team lead suggests using a Linux-based solution to parallelize these tests to improve deployment speed. Which Linux feature or tool is most appropriate for this task?

A) cron jobs

B) xargs

C) tmux

D) GNU Parallel

E) systemd

F) rsync

Answer: D

Explanation: In an agile environment, especially when using CI/CD pipelines, it is crucial to optimize the speed and efficiency of processes like integration tests. GNU Parallel is a tool that allows you to run shell jobs in parallel, which is particularly useful in testing scenarios where multiple test scripts can be executed concurrently. By parallelizing test execution, GNU Parallel can significantly reduce the overall time required for testing, which is a common bottleneck in deployment processes. Unlike cron jobs, which are used for scheduling, or rsync, which is for file synchronization, GNU Parallel directly addresses the need to run multiple processes simultaneously, providing an efficient solution for the team's problem.

Q242: When implementing agile methodologies in software development, which of the following Linux commands is most suitable for monitoring real-time logs to quickly identify issues during a deployment process?
A) tail

B) grep

C) awk

D) sed

E) find

F) cat

Answer: A

Explanation: In an agile development environment, rapid feedback is essential. The tail command, especially with the -f option (tail -f), is ideal for monitoring real-time logs. This command allows developers and engineers to view new entries in a log file as they are appended, which is crucial during deployment to quickly identify and address any issues. While grep, awk, and sed are powerful for processing text, they do not inherently provide real-time log monitoring. Similarly, find and cat are used for locating files and displaying file contents, respectively, without real-time capabilities.

Q243: In the context of agile software development, the principle of 'fail fast' is often emphasized to ensure rapid iterations and improvements. Which Linux command can be used to simulate a network failure during testing to validate the application's resilience?
A) iptables

B) ifconfig

C) netstat

D) route

E) ping

F) traceroute

Answer: A

Explanation: The 'fail fast' principle in agile software development encourages testing applications under various failure scenarios to ensure robustness and prompt recovery. The iptables command is a Linux utility that allows the configuration of the network packet filtering rules. By setting specific rules, you can simulate network failures or block certain types of traffic to test how an application behaves under such conditions. This is an essential part of stress testing and helps in identifying potential points of failure. Unlike ifconfig, netstat, route, ping, and traceroute, iptables directly manipulates packet filtering and can effectively simulate network disruptions.

Q244: True/False: Agile software development inherently requires the use of Linux-based systems for effective implementation.
A) True

B) False

Answer: B

Explanation: Agile software development is a methodology focused on iterative development, collaboration, and adaptability, and it is not inherently tied to any specific operating system, including Linux. While Linux offers many tools and environments that can facilitate agile practices, such as automation scripts, CI/CD pipelines, and open-source software, agile methodologies can be implemented on various platforms, including Windows and macOS. The choice of operating system depends on the specific needs and context of the development team, rather than a requirement of the agile framework itself.

Q245: A DevOps engineer is tasked with setting up a development environment that supports agile practices, including frequent builds and automated testing. The team uses Git for version control and Jenkins for CI/CD. Which Linux command best supports their need for managing project dependencies efficiently in this scenario?

A) make

B) gcc

C) cmake

D) apt-get

E) chmod

F) tar

Answer: D

Explanation: Managing project dependencies efficiently is crucial in an agile environment, where frequent builds and automated testing are common. The apt-get command is a powerful package management utility in Debian-based Linux distributions. It is used to install, update, and remove packages, ensuring that all necessary dependencies for a project are met. This is particularly important when setting up development environments or deploying applications, as it automates the management of required software libraries and tools. While make, gcc, and cmake are essential for building and compiling applications, they do not manage dependencies. chmod alters file permissions, and tar is used for archiving, neither of which directly address dependency management.

Q246: Your company, TechInnovate, is transitioning to a DevOps model to improve the collaboration between the development and operations teams. You have been tasked with setting up a continuous integration/continuous deployment (CI/CD) pipeline using Jenkins and Docker. The developers need to ensure that their applications are compatible across different environments by using containerization. One of the requirements is that each build process must include unit testing and code quality checks. Once the code passes these checks, the application should be automatically deployed to a staging server for further testing. Which of the following steps would best fit into the CI/CD pipeline to achieve this goal?

A) Set up a Jenkins job that only compiles the code and then deploys it directly to the production server.

B) Create a Jenkins job that runs unit tests and code quality checks before packaging the application into a Docker image.

C) Use Jenkins to manually trigger the build process and deploy it after approval from the operations team.

D) Configure Jenkins to build the application, but perform unit testing manually by developers.

E) Utilize Jenkins to deploy directly to the production server without any testing to speed up the deployment process.

F) Implement a separate Jenkins job for each stage: building, testing, and deployment, but skip unit tests to save time.

Answer: B

Explanation: In a DevOps environment, automation of the build, test, and deployment processes is crucial to ensure speed and reliability. Option B describes a process where a Jenkins job is set up to perform unit testing and code quality checks before packaging the application into a Docker image. This ensures that only code that passes predefined quality metrics is deployed, reducing the likelihood of introducing bugs into the staging or production environments. Containerization with Docker ensures that the application runs consistently across different environments. By automating these processes, TechInnovate can achieve the desired improvements in collaboration and integration between development and operations teams.

Q247: Which of the following statements correctly describes a fundamental principle of DevOps?

A) DevOps mandates that only the operations team is responsible for security.

B) DevOps encourages continuous collaboration between development and operations teams.

C) In DevOps, testing is performed only after all development work is completed.

D) DevOps limits the use of automation to the deployment phase.

E) DevOps focuses exclusively on increasing the speed of software deployments.

F) DevOps requires the use of a specific set of tools and technologies.

Answer: B

Explanation: A key principle of DevOps is the continuous collaboration and integration between development and operations teams. This collaborative approach aims to break down silos that traditionally exist between these teams, allowing for more effective communication, faster problem resolution, and more efficient workflows. By fostering a culture of shared responsibility, DevOps helps ensure that both development and operations are aligned towards common goals such as quality, performance, and user satisfaction. Unlike traditional methodologies, DevOps emphasizes ongoing interaction, feedback, and iteration throughout the software development lifecycle.

Q248: True or False: In a DevOps environment, infrastructure as code (IaC) allows teams to manage and provision computing infrastructure through machine-readable definition files, rather than physical hardware configuration or interactive configuration tools.

A) True

B) False

Answer: A

Explanation: The principle of Infrastructure as Code (IaC) is a cornerstone of DevOps practices. IaC enables teams to define and manage their infrastructure using code, which can be versioned and treated just like application software. This approach allows for repeatability, scalability, and reliability, as infrastructure can be provisioned and configured in a consistent manner across different environments. IaC facilitates automation and reduces the likelihood of human error associated with manual setup and configuration. By treating infrastructure as code, DevOps teams can apply software development practices such as version control, testing, and continuous integration to their infrastructure management processes.

Q249: In a DevOps setup, you are asked to automate the deployment of applications using Ansible. Which of the following Ansible features can help you ensure that the deployment process is idempotent, meaning that running it multiple times won't have unintended side effects?

A) Ansible Vault

B) Ansible Playbooks

C) Ansible Galaxy

D) Ansible Tower

E) Ansible Roles

F) Ansible Modules

Answer: F

Explanation: Ansible Modules are designed to be idempotent, which means they can be run multiple times without changing the result beyond the initial application. This property is crucial in a DevOps environment where automation scripts might be executed multiple times in different environments or due to retriggered deployments. Modules handle the logic for checking the current state of the system and making changes only when necessary, thus preventing unintended alterations or duplications. This feature of Ansible Modules ensures that your deployments are reliable and consistent, a critical aspect of DevOps practices.

Q250: You are part of a team working on a large-scale project that requires frequent deployments. The team has decided to adopt a DevOps approach to improve efficiency. One of the challenges is ensuring that every team member can replicate the production environment on their local machines for development and testing purposes. What strategy would best address this challenge?

A) Use different configuration files for each environment and manually edit them.

B) Implement virtual machines for each developer to mimic the production environment.

C) Encourage developers to manually configure their environments to match production.

D) Develop and distribute a set of scripts to automate the environment setup process.

E) Leverage containerization to create consistent development environments across all machines.

F) Set up a centralized server where developers can test their code directly in the production environment.

Answer: E

Explanation: Leveraging containerization is the most effective strategy for creating consistent development environments across all machines. Tools like Docker allow developers to encapsulate application dependencies and configurations within containers, ensuring that the same environment is reproduced on any system that runs the container. This eliminates discrepancies between development, testing, and production environments, a common source of bugs and deployment issues. Containerization also simplifies sharing and versioning of environments, enhancing team collaboration and efficiency, which are core objectives of a DevOps approach.

Q251: A rapidly growing e-commerce company is experiencing frequent downtime, which is affecting their revenue. They have decided to implement Service-Level Objectives (SLOs) and Service-Level Agreements (SLAs) to improve their service reliability and customer satisfaction. The team needs to define clear SLOs for their web server uptime and response time. The web server runs on Linux, and you have been tasked with monitoring these metrics using command-line tools. Which Linux command is most appropriate for continuously monitoring the uptime and response times of the web server to ensure it meets its SLOs?   ---

A) uptime

B) top

C) curl

D) ping

E) netstat

F) vmstat

Answer: C

Explanation: When you need to monitor the uptime and response times of a web server, curl is the most appropriate tool. curl can be used to send requests to the web server and measure the time taken to receive a response. This allows you to track the response time, a critical component of your SLOs. The -w option in curl can be used to format the output to display the time metrics, such as timeconnect and timetotal, which help in monitoring the server's responsiveness. Other options like uptime provide system uptime and load averages but do not offer insights on web server response times. ping checks network connectivity and latency but not the web server's specific response time to HTTP requests. Therefore, curl is suitable for ensuring the server meets its SLOs for uptime and response times.

Q252: In the context of defining SLAs for a cloud-based application hosted on Linux servers, which element is critical to include to ensure that the SLA is comprehensive and enforceable?   ---

A) A list of all installed software packages

B) Detailed server hardware specifications

C) A clear definition of service availability metrics

D) A log of all user login attempts

E) The server's geographical location

F) A schedule for server maintenance

Answer: C

Explanation: A comprehensive and enforceable SLA must include a clear definition of service availability metrics. These metrics define the expected performance and reliability standards that the service provider must meet. Service availability metrics typically include uptime percentages, response time commitments, and definitions of downtime. These metrics form the basis for measuring whether the service provider is fulfilling the contractual obligations agreed upon with the client. Other elements, such as server specifications or maintenance schedules, may support the SLA but do not directly define the service level commitments.

Q253: True or False: SLAs and SLOs are interchangeable terms in the context of service management.   ---

A) True

B) False

Answer: B

Explanation: The statement is false. SLAs (Service-Level Agreements) and SLOs (Service-Level Objectives) are related but distinct concepts in service management. An SLA is a formal agreement between a service provider and a customer that outlines the expected level of service, including metrics such as uptime, performance, and response times. It often includes penalties or compensations if the service levels are not met. On the other hand, an SLO is a specific, measurable objective that is part of the SLA. It defines the target level of service performance (e.g., 99.9% uptime) but does not include the legal and financial terms that an SLA does. Therefore, while SLOs are components of SLAs, they are not interchangeable.

Q254: You are tasked with setting up a monitoring system on a Linux server to ensure that the organization meets its SLA for application performance. Which of the following tools can be used to measure and report on system and application performance metrics regularly?   ---
A) awk

B) grep

C) sar

D) sed

E) diff

F) hexdump

Answer: C

Explanation: sar (System Activity Reporter) is a powerful tool for measuring and reporting on system and application performance metrics on Linux. It can collect data on CPU usage, memory usage, I/O activities, network load, and other system activities over time. This makes it an ideal tool for monitoring whether the system is meeting the performance metrics defined in an SLA. The data collected by sar can be used to generate reports and alerts, helping administrators to ensure that the application performance aligns with the SLA requirements. Other tools like awk, grep, and sed are used for text processing and do not provide system monitoring capabilities.

Q255: A global enterprise has multiple data centers and needs to establish SLAs for different geographic regions, each with varying network performance characteristics. As a DevOps engineer, you must ensure that the SLAs for these regions are realistic and achievable. Which factor is most crucial to consider when setting the SLAs for each region?

A) The cultural preferences of the region

B) The number of servers in each data center

C) The average network latency and bandwidth

D) The software development lifecycle processes

E) The types of applications hosted in the region

F) The time zone differences

Answer: C

Explanation: When establishing SLAs for different geographic regions, the average network latency and bandwidth are critical factors to consider. These network performance characteristics directly impact the ability to deliver services at the agreed-upon levels. Different regions may have varying levels of network infrastructure quality, which affects latency and bandwidth. Understanding these differences allows for setting realistic and achievable SLAs that account for the inherent network limitations of each region. While other factors like the number of servers or applications hosted may influence operations, they do not directly impact the SLA's core metrics related to network performance.

Q256: An organization is migrating its infrastructure to the cloud and needs to automate the initialization of its virtual machines across different cloud environments. They have chosen cloud-init for this purpose. The DevOps team is tasked with creating a configuration that allows the installation of a web server, setting up a specific user with SSH access, and ensuring that the VM's hostname is set correctly according to a predefined naming convention. Part of the team is unsure how to correctly structure the cloud-init configuration file to meet these requirements. Which part of the cloud-init configuration file handles the installation of packages like a web server?   ---

A) runcmd

B) bootcmd

C) packages

D) writefiles

E) sshimportid

F) user-data

Answer: C

Explanation: Cloud-init is a framework that allows for the initialization of cloud instances as they are launched. The 'packages' directive in a cloud-init configuration file specifies packages that should be installed using the package manager of the distribution. This is particularly useful for ensuring that necessary software, such as a web server, is installed immediately upon VM initialization. The 'packages' section is straightforward, allowing for a list of packages to be defined that the system package manager will then install. This approach is both efficient and ensures consistent environments across multiple VMs.

Q257: In the cloud-init configuration context, which directive is responsible for executing commands after all other cloud-init stages have been completed, ensuring that the system is fully up and running?   ---
A) runcmd

B) bootcmd

C) finalmessage

D) writefiles

E) ds-identify

F) cloud-config

Answer: A

Explanation: In cloud-init, the 'runcmd' directive is specifically designed to execute commands at the very end of the cloud-init process. This ensures that the system is fully initialized and all other configurations have been applied before these commands are run. It is typically used for tasks that require the system to be in a fully operational state, such as starting services or running scripts that depend on other configurations. This stage is crucial in scenarios where the order of operations impacts the system's functionality or when certain services need to be restarted or modified after initial setup.

Q258: True/False: Cloud-init can be used to set the hostname of a virtual machine during its initialization process. ---
A) True

B) False

Answer: A

Explanation: Cloud-init has the capability to set the hostname of a virtual machine during its initialization process. This is achieved through the 'hostname' directive within the cloud-init configuration file. By specifying the desired hostname, cloud-init configures the system's hostname as part of its early stages of initialization. This feature is particularly important for maintaining consistent naming conventions across cloud environments, essential for network management and identification purposes. It ensures that each instance is uniquely identifiable in the network right from its creation.

Q259: A company is deploying a new cloud-based service and needs to ensure that specific configurations are applied to every instance at boot. This includes adding a new SSH key for a user, installing specific applications, and modifying configuration files. Given the need for these tasks to be automated upon instance startup, which cloud-init configuration module is responsible for updating SSH keys?   ---

A) sshauthorizedkeys

B) sshimportid

C) runcmd

D) bootcmd

E) users

F) writefiles

Answer: B

Explanation: The 'sshimportid' directive in cloud-init is used to import SSH keys for users on the system. This directive is particularly useful in cloud environments where instances need to be accessed securely via SSH. By specifying a service like Launchpad or GitHub, or by directly providing a URL to a key, cloud-init can automatically fetch and install public SSH keys for specified users. This feature ensures secure access to the instance without manual intervention, an essential aspect of deploying services in a cloud environment where security and automation are pivotal.

Q260: You are working for a tech company that provides infrastructure as a service (IaaS). Your team is tasked with ensuring that every virtual machine instance launched with your service has a specific file, /etc/company.conf, with predefined content. The file must be written at the boot time of each new instance. Which cloud-init module should you use to achieve this?

A) runcmd

B) writefiles

C) bootcmd

D) cloud-config

E) sethostname

F) packages

Answer: B

Explanation: The 'writefiles' module in cloud-init is used to create or overwrite files on the filesystem as part of the initialization process. This module allows for specifying the path, content, permissions, and ownership of the file. In this scenario, using 'writefiles' ensures that /etc/company.conf is created with the predefined content every time a new virtual machine instance is launched. This approach is essential for maintaining consistency across instances, especially in environments where configuration files are critical for application performance or security. It provides a reliable method to enforce configuration settings across a distributed infrastructure.

Q261: A financial services company is deploying a new application in a cloud environment that relies on several virtual machines (VMs) for different services such as databases, application servers, and web servers. The application is expected to experience variable loads throughout the day, and the company wants to ensure efficient use of resources while maintaining high availability. The cloud provider offers snapshotting, pausing, cloning, and resource limit configuration features for VMs. Considering the need for backup and rapid scaling, which feature should the company prioritize to ensure quick recovery from VM failures without significant downtime?

A) Snapshotting

B) Pausing

C) Cloning

D) Resource limits

E) Load balancing

F) Automated scaling

Answer: A

Explanation: Snapshotting is a critical feature in cloud environments, especially for applications requiring high availability and rapid recovery options. By taking snapshots of VMs, the company can ensure that a complete state of the VM, including the operating system, applications, and data at a specific point in time, is captured. This allows for quick restoration in case of a failure, minimizing downtime. While cloning can be useful for creating new instances, it is snapshotting that provides the recovery point for existing instances. Pausing is irrelevant for failure recovery, resource limits manage resource usage but not recovery, load balancing manages traffic but not VM state, and automated scaling adjusts resources but doesn't restore VM states.

Q262: Pausing a virtual machine in a cloud environment releases all allocated resources, which can be reallocated to other instances, thereby saving costs.
A) True

B) False

Answer: B

Explanation: Pausing a virtual machine does not release all allocated resources. When you pause a VM, the CPU is halted, and the state of the VM is saved in RAM, meaning that RAM is not freed up. Consequently, while some CPU resources might be freed, memory resources remain allocated, and thus, pausing does not fully release resources for reallocation to other instances. This action is often used for scenarios where temporary suspension is needed without shutting down the VM, but it does not translate to cost savings as compared to stopping or hibernating the VM, where resources are fully released.

Q263: Which command would you use to create a snapshot of a KVM-based virtual machine while it is running, ensuring data consistency?

A) virsh pause

B) virsh snapshot-create-as

C) virsh save

D) virsh clone

E) virsh undefine

F) virsh destroy

Answer: B

Explanation: The virsh snapshot-create-as command is used to create a snapshot of a KVM-based virtual machine. It ensures that the snapshot is consistent by capturing the VM's state at the moment the snapshot is taken. This is crucial for live systems where downtime is not an option. The command supports creating consistent snapshots even while the VM is running by using internal or external snapshots depending on the storage configuration. Other commands do not provide snapshot functionality: virsh pause suspends the VM, virsh save saves the VM state to a file, virsh clone creates a copy of the VM, virsh undefine removes VM definition, and virsh destroy stops the VM immediately.

Q264: A company is evaluating the use of resource limits on their virtual machines to prevent any single instance from consuming excessive resources and impacting other instances. What Linux feature is typically used to enforce resource limits on VMs managed by a hypervisor like KVM?

A) cpuset

B) cgroups

C) ulimit

D) nice

E) ionice

F) setrlimit

Answer: B

Explanation: cgroups (control groups) is a Linux kernel feature that limits, accounts for, and isolates the resource usage (CPU, memory, disk I/O, etc.) of a collection of processes. In the context of virtual machines managed by hypervisors like KVM, cgroups are commonly used to enforce resource limits. This ensures that no single VM can monopolize system resources, protecting the performance of other VMs on the same host. While cpuset is a part of cgroups for CPU isolation, it is not the comprehensive mechanism for resource limits. ulimit and setrlimit are more relevant for individual processes rather than VMs. nice and ionice adjust the priority of processes but do not enforce hard resource limits.

Q265: A retail company uses virtualization to run multiple instances of their online store application. They need to rapidly replicate their application servers to handle seasonal traffic spikes. Which virtualization feature best supports this requirement by allowing the creation of new instances based on an existing one?

A) Snapshotting

B) Pausing

C) Cloning

D) Resource limits

E) Live migration

F) Network bridging

Answer: C

Explanation: Cloning is the virtualization feature that is best suited for rapidly replicating application servers. By cloning an existing VM, the company can quickly create new instances with the same configurations, software, and data, making it ideal for handling traffic spikes. This process is faster than setting up a new VM from scratch and ensures consistency across instances. Snapshotting is more about capturing the state of a VM for backup purposes, while pausing, resource limits, live migration, and network bridging do not directly address the need for rapid replication of VMs. Cloning provides a practical solution for scaling applications in response to increased demand.

Q266: A medium-sized e-commerce company is using Jenkins to automate its CI/CD pipeline. The development team has requested that build artifacts from the successful runs of a job be reused in another job to improve efficiency. They also need to ensure that the artifacts have unique identifiers for traceability and auditing. The company plans to use Jenkins plugins to achieve this. Given these requirements, which Jenkins plugin combination should the company use to meet both needs?

A) Pipeline Plugin and Docker Pipeline Plugin

B) Fingerprint Plugin and Job DSL Plugin

C) Copy Artifact Plugin and Fingerprint Plugin

D) Docker Pipeline Plugin and Artifact Deployer Plugin

E) Build Pipeline Plugin and Job Import Plugin

F) Copy Artifact Plugin and Artifact Deployer Plugin

Answer: C

Explanation: The company's requirements involve reusing build artifacts in another job while ensuring that the artifacts have unique identifiers. The Copy Artifact Plugin is specifically designed to allow Jenkins jobs to copy artifacts from another job, which addresses the need to reuse build artifacts. The Fingerprint Plugin is used to track artifacts across jobs by assigning unique identifiers, thereby meeting the traceability and auditing requirements. This combination of plugins efficiently handles both reuse and traceability of build artifacts in Jenkins.

Q267: The Copy Artifact Plugin in Jenkins is primarily used to:

A) Create a backup of Jenkins configuration files.

B) Copy artifacts from one build to another.

C) Integrate Jenkins with Docker.

D) Generate build reports.

E) Deploy artifacts to a remote server.

F) Monitor Jenkins system health.

Answer: B

Explanation: The Copy Artifact Plugin is a Jenkins plugin that allows developers to copy artifacts from one Jenkins job/build to another. This functionality is essential in scenarios where different stages of a pipeline need to share or reuse outputs from previous stages. It streamlines the process of artifact management within Jenkins, making it easier to maintain and automate complex build pipelines. This plugin does not perform tasks such as backup creation, Docker integration, or system health monitoring, which are outside its scope.

Q268: When implementing Docker in a Jenkins pipeline using the Docker Pipeline Plugin, which of the following best describes a key feature of this integration?

A) Automatically deploys Docker containers to a Kubernetes cluster.

B) Allows Jenkins to build and run Docker images as part of a Jenkins job.

C) Monitors Docker container logs in real-time within Jenkins.

D) Provides Jenkins with a GUI for managing Docker services.

E) Encrypts Docker images during the build process.

F) Synchronizes Jenkins jobs with Docker Hub repositories.

Answer: B

Explanation: The Docker Pipeline Plugin allows Jenkins to interact with Docker containers during the execution of a pipeline. It provides Jenkins with the ability to build, run, and manage Docker images as part of a Jenkins job. This integration is crucial for building containerized applications and allows for consistent, portable environments across different stages of the CI/CD pipeline. The plugin does not inherently provide GUI management or real-time log monitoring features, nor does it handle encryption or synchronization with Docker Hub by itself.

Q269: An organization is using Jenkins to manage its CI/CD workflow and has implemented the Fingerprint Plugin. They want to ensure that their artifacts are tracked for audit purposes. Which of the following statements about the Fingerprint Plugin is correct?

A) It creates a backup of the Jenkins job configuration.

B) It automatically deletes unused artifacts after a build.

C) It assigns a unique identifier to artifacts for tracking purposes.

D) It integrates Jenkins with cloud storage solutions.

E) It enhances Jenkins' security by encrypting artifacts.

F) It provides role-based access controls for Jenkins projects.

Answer: C

Explanation: The Fingerprint Plugin in Jenkins is designed to assign unique identifiers to build artifacts. This feature is critical for tracking artifacts across different jobs and builds, ensuring that the artifacts can be audited and traced back to their source. The plugin helps maintain a record of which artifacts were produced by which builds, facilitating better management and traceability within the CI/CD pipeline. It does not handle backup creation, automatic deletion, cloud integration, encryption, or access control, which are tasks outside its intended purpose.

Q270: True/False: The Docker Pipeline Plugin in Jenkins allows for the direct integration and management of Docker containers within Jenkins jobs without the need for additional scripting or configuration.

A) True

B) False

Answer: B

Explanation: While the Docker Pipeline Plugin provides powerful capabilities for integrating Docker within Jenkins jobs, it does not completely eliminate the need for additional scripting or configuration. Users must define how Docker containers are built, run, and managed within their Jenkins pipelines using the appropriate DSL syntax. The plugin provides the necessary functions and methods to facilitate these operations but requires users to script the specific steps required for their workflow. Therefore, while it significantly simplifies the process, some level of scripting and configuration is still necessary.

Q271: A tech company is migrating its infrastructure to the cloud and plans to use Packer to automate the creation of machine images for both development and production environments. The team needs to ensure that images are consistent across environments and easily maintainable. They also want to integrate the process with their existing CI/CD pipeline which includes Jenkins for automated builds. Which feature of Packer should be leveraged to meet these requirements and why?   ---

A) Use of Packer's Post-Processor feature to automatically upload images to multiple cloud providers.

B) Implementation of Packer's Variable Interpolation to manage different environment configurations.

C) Integration of Packer with the Ansible provisioner to ensure configuration management.

D) Utilization of Packer's Build Artifacts feature to store intermediate build files.

E) Application of Packer's Template Validation to ensure template accuracy before builds.

F) Usage of Packer's HCL2 (HashiCorp Configuration Language) for defining reusable modules.

Answer: B

Explanation: Packer's Variable Interpolation feature is crucial in managing different environment configurations while maintaining consistency across images. By defining variables in the template, the same Packer configuration can be used for both development and production environments, with specific values being injected at build time. This approach not only ensures consistency but also simplifies maintenance by reducing duplication in configuration files. Integrating this with Jenkins in a CI/CD pipeline allows for seamless automation of image builds, making the entire process efficient and reliable.

Q272: In Packer, which component is responsible for defining the specific cloud provider or platform where the machine image will be created?   ---
A) Builder

B) Provisioner

C) Post-Processor

D) Artifact

E) Template

F) Variable

Answer: A

Explanation: The Builder component in Packer is responsible for defining the specific cloud provider or platform where a machine image will be created. Each builder has its own set of configuration options and is platform-specific. For instance, there are builders for AWS, Google Cloud, Azure, and more. The builder is a crucial part of the Packer template as it dictates how and where the image is built, ensuring that the resulting image is compatible with the target environment.

Q273: A development team wants to ensure that Packer templates are syntactically correct before initiating a build process within their continuous integration workflow. Which Packer command should they incorporate into their CI/CD pipeline to achieve this?   ---

A) packer inspect

B) packer validate

C) packer build

D) packer fmt

E) packer init

F) packer test

Answer: B

Explanation: The packer validate command is used to check the syntax and basic structure of a Packer template before initiating the build process. This command ensures that the template is correctly formatted and that all required fields are present. By incorporating packer validate into a CI/CD pipeline, the development team can automatically verify the correctness of their templates as part of their build process, preventing build failures due to template errors.

Q274: In a Packer configuration, true or false: The provisioner section is responsible for defining how the virtual machine should be destroyed after the build process completes.   ---

A) True

B) False

Answer: B

Explanation: False. The provisioner section in a Packer configuration is responsible for defining how software and configurations are installed on the machine during the build process. It is used to prepare the machine by installing necessary software, services, and configurations. The destruction or cleanup of the virtual machine after the build is typically handled by the platform's native features or by a post-processor if additional actions are required. The provisioner does not manage the destruction of the machine.

Q275: A company has a requirement to build custom machine images for different application versions and store them securely. They want to ensure that the images are not publicly accessible and are version-controlled. Which Packer feature will best address this need?

A) Use of the file provisioner to upload versioned application files.

B) Implementation of a post-processor to upload images to a private repository.

C) Utilization of Packer's logging feature to track image versions.

D) Adoption of Packer's built-in security features to protect image data.

E) Application of environment variables to control image access permissions.

F) Configuration of Packer's artifact storage to manage image versions.

Answer: B

Explanation: Implementing a post-processor to upload images to a private repository is the best approach to ensure that images are securely stored and version-controlled. Packer's post-processors can be configured to upload the finalized image to a private repository, such as a private Docker registry or cloud-specific storage, where access permissions can be tightly controlled. This ensures that images are not publicly accessible and can be versioned according to the company's requirements. The use of a private repository also allows for robust version management and access control, meeting the security and operational needs of the company.

Q276: A medium-sized e-commerce company uses a microservices architecture deployed on a Kubernetes cluster to manage its online transactions and inventory systems. The DevOps team is planning to upgrade the Kubernetes version in the production environment to leverage new features and security improvements. Before proceeding, they need to ensure the upgrade does not disrupt existing services or degrade performance. The team identifies that the current kube-proxy configuration might be a key factor influencing network performance during the upgrade. Which of the following actions should the team take to assess and mitigate the impact of the Kubernetes upgrade on service operations?   ---

A) Evaluate the impact of the upgrade using a canary deployment strategy.

B) Directly upgrade the production cluster to minimize downtime.

C) Increase the number of nodes in the cluster to handle potential failures.

D) Set up a parallel testing environment and conduct a full stress test.

E) Review and optimize kube-proxy configuration before the upgrade.

F) Roll back the upgrade immediately if any issue arises post-upgrade.

Answer: D

Explanation: Before upgrading a Kubernetes cluster, it is crucial to understand the potential impact on service operations. Conducting a full stress test in a parallel testing environment allows the team to simulate the production environment without affecting live services. This approach helps in identifying potential points of failure and performance bottlenecks that might occur due to the upgrade. A canary deployment, while useful for gradual rollouts, might not expose all issues. Direct upgrades can pose risks of service downtime, and increasing nodes might not address the root causes of any performance degradation. Reviewing kube-proxy configuration is beneficial but should be done as part of a comprehensive testing strategy. Immediate rollback is a reactive measure and should not be the first step in risk mitigation.

Q277: During a routine update of a load balancer configuration in a Linux environment, a system administrator needs to apply changes without causing any interruption to the active connections. Which command is most appropriate for gracefully reloading the configuration?   ---

A) kill -9 <processid>

B) systemctl restart <servicename>

C) systemctl reload <servicename>

D) kill -HUP <processid>

E) systemctl status <servicename>

F) reboot

Answer: C

Explanation: The systemctl reload <servicename> command is specifically designed to reload the configuration of a service without interrupting active connections, which is essential in maintaining service availability during configuration changes. Unlike systemctl restart, which would stop and then start the service (disrupting active connections), reload attempts to apply the new configuration gracefully. The kill -HUP command can also be used to signal processes to reload their configuration, but systemctl provides a more consistent and service-aware approach. The other options either forcefully terminate the process or do not apply configuration changes.

Q278: A DevOps engineer is tasked with reducing the downtime of a critical web application during a planned database server upgrade. The application and database server run on separate Linux hosts. To ensure minimal downtime, the engineer decides to implement a high-availability database solution. Which of the following strategies is most suitable for maintaining service operations during the upgrade?   ---

A) Implementing a load balancer in front of the database server.

B) Setting up a master-slave replication with automatic failover.

C) Scheduling the upgrade during off-peak hours.

D) Utilizing a single-node database backup and restore process.

E) Switching to a NoSQL database for faster performance.

F) Enabling database caching to reduce load during upgrades.

Answer: B

Explanation: Implementing a master-slave replication setup with automatic failover is a robust strategy for maintaining database availability during upgrades. This setup ensures that if the master database server goes down, a slave can automatically take over, minimizing downtime and maintaining service operations. Load balancers typically distribute traffic and do not directly handle database failover scenarios. Scheduling upgrades during off-peak hours reduces user impact but does not address downtime directly. A single-node backup and restore process would result in downtime during restoration. Switching to a NoSQL database is a complex change that is not specifically aimed at reducing downtime during upgrades. Database caching can improve query performance but does not inherently ensure high availability during server upgrades.

Q279: True/False: To ensure that a service configuration change on a Linux server does not impact operational service availability, it is essential to restart the service after applying the changes.   ---

A) True

B) False

Answer: B

Explanation: In many cases, it is not necessary to restart a service to apply configuration changes. Instead, reloading the service configuration allows the changes to take effect without interrupting the service. The ability to reload rather than restart is a critical feature for maintaining service availability, as it avoids downtime associated with stopping and starting the service. This capability is particularly important in environments where high availability is required and service interruptions must be minimized.

Q280: A financial services firm uses a Linux-based system to handle transaction processing. The IT department is considering implementing a configuration management tool to streamline the deployment of software updates and configuration changes across its servers. In selecting a tool, which of the following features is most critical for minimizing the impact of changes on service operations?

A) Multi-cloud support

B) Declarative configuration model

C) Integration with CI/CD pipelines

D) Support for containers and microservices

E) High-level scripting capabilities

F) Advanced monitoring and alerting features

Answer: B

Explanation: A declarative configuration model is crucial for minimizing the impact of changes on service operations. This model allows administrators to define the desired state of the system, and the configuration management tool ensures that the system conforms to this state. This approach reduces the risk of configuration drift and errors, as changes are managed in a consistent and predictable manner. While multi-cloud support, CI/CD integration, and container support are valuable, they do not directly address maintaining service stability and consistency. High-level scripting and monitoring are useful for automation and visibility but are not as pivotal as the declarative model in minimizing operational impact.

Q281: Understanding the role of documentation in change management is critical for maintaining service reliability. A mid-sized company is using a combination of custom scripts and third-party tools to manage its cloud infrastructure. Recently, they experienced several service outages due to undocumented changes in their deployment scripts. Management has decided to implement a structured change management process. Which of the following documentation practices will most effectively help in mitigating such issues? -
--

A) Maintain a detailed changelog for each script and tool used, including the purpose, author, and date of each change.

B) Keep all documentation in a private repository accessible only to the development team to ensure security.

C) Document only the major changes in a centralized wiki to reduce the documentation workload.

D) Use a version control system without additional documentation, as commit messages suffice for tracking changes.

E) Implement a strict approval process that requires management sign-off for all changes without additional documentation.

F) Create a checklist for developers to follow, ensuring that all changes are verbally communicated in team meetings.

Answer: A

Explanation: Maintaining a detailed changelog for each script and tool is an effective documentation practice. It ensures that all changes, including minor ones, are recorded with relevant information such as purpose, author, and date. This helps in tracking changes and understanding the impact, which is crucial for troubleshooting and preventing outages. A private repository limits accessibility and can hinder collaboration, while a centralized wiki with only major changes may omit important details. Relying solely on commit messages or verbal communication can lead to incomplete records. An approval process without documentation fails to provide the necessary context for changes.

Q282: In the context of continuous integration/continuous deployment (CI/CD), documentation plays a pivotal role. Which practice should be adopted to ensure that the CI/CD pipeline is well-documented and easily maintainable? --

A) Document only the CI/CD configuration files and omit any associated scripts to reduce complexity.

B) Use inline comments within the pipeline scripts and configuration files to describe each step and its purpose.

C) Keep a separate document detailing the pipeline setup and its dependencies, stored in a different repository.

D) Rely on the CI/CD tool's default documentation for pipeline setup, without additional customization.

E) Create a video tutorial explaining the pipeline setup, replacing written documentation.

F) Document the pipeline setup only when onboarding new team members to save time.

Answer: B

Explanation: Inline comments within pipeline scripts and configuration files are a practical documentation practice. They provide immediate context and understanding of each step's purpose and functionality, which is critical for quick reference and maintenance. While detailed separate documents are useful, they can become outdated if not regularly updated. Relying solely on default documentation or video tutorials can be insufficient for specific customizations. Documentation should be a continuous process, not just reserved for onboarding.

Q283: A company is implementing Infrastructure as Code (IaC) using tools like Terraform and Ansible to automate their deployments. They have noticed that their teams struggle with understanding the infrastructure setup and dependencies. To improve this, the company decides to enhance their documentation practices. Which approach is best suited to address this issue?

A) Maintain a high-level architecture diagram without detailed documentation to simplify the overview.

B) Document each resource's configuration in the IaC scripts, including its purpose and dependencies.

C) Rely on comments in the code to provide necessary documentation, avoiding separate documents.

D) Use a third-party tool to auto-generate documentation from the IaC scripts without manual input.

E) Create a centralized document listing all resources but without any detailed descriptions.

F) Focus on training sessions rather than documentation to improve understanding of the infrastructure.

Answer: B

Explanation: Documenting each resource's configuration directly within the IaC scripts is an effective approach to enhance understanding. This practice ensures that each resource's purpose and dependencies are clear to anyone reading the scripts, facilitating easier maintenance and collaboration. A high-level architecture diagram is useful but lacks detail. Auto-generated documentation may miss context, while centralized documents without details or relying solely on training sessions may not provide comprehensive coverage.

Q284: True/False - Comprehensive documentation is unnecessary for well-known Linux commands as their usage is commonly understood.   ---
A) True

B) False

Answer: B

Explanation: Comprehensive documentation is essential even for well-known Linux commands. While basic usage might be commonly known, advanced options, specific configurations, and context-specific usage often require detailed documentation. This ensures that all team members, regardless of experience level, can effectively and consistently use these commands within specific environments or scripts. Additionally, documentation aids in training, troubleshooting, and knowledge transfer, contributing to more reliable and efficient operations.

Q285: A financial services company is required to comply with strict regulatory standards, necessitating thorough documentation of all IT operations. The company plans to automate its compliance reporting. Which documentation approach will best support this automation effort?

A) Keep manual logs and update them periodically for compliance audits.

B) Use a centralized logging system that automatically documents all changes and operations.

C) Document compliance-related operations in a shared spreadsheet for easy access.

D) Implement a policy where all compliance documentation is handled by a dedicated team manually.

E) Use a third-party compliance tool without integrating it into existing documentation practices.

F) Restrict compliance documentation to high-level summaries to meet minimum requirements.

Answer: B

Explanation: A centralized logging system that automatically documents all changes and operations is the most effective approach for supporting automated compliance reporting. This system ensures that all relevant data is captured in real-time, reducing the risk of human error and ensuring completeness. Manual logs and shared spreadsheets are prone to oversight and may not be timely. Relying solely on a dedicated team or third-party tool without integration can lead to gaps in documentation. High-level summaries do not provide the detail necessary for thorough compliance reporting.

Q286: A mid-sized software company specializing in e-commerce platforms is preparing to deploy a critical update to its payment processing system. The company has a robust Continuous Integration/Continuous Deployment (CI/CD) pipeline, which includes automated testing and deployment processes. However, they have experienced issues in the past with failed deployments affecting their production environment. The company's DevOps team decides to implement a rollback strategy to mitigate potential risks associated with the new deployment. They need a strategy that allows them to quickly revert to a stable state if the deployment encounters issues, minimizing downtime and preserving customer satisfaction. Which of the following strategies would best achieve this goal?

A) Implement a blue-green deployment strategy to switch back to the previous version.

B) Use a rolling deployment strategy without any rollback mechanism.

C) Perform a canary deployment with manual rollback plans.

D) Rely solely on virtual machine snapshots for rollback.

E) Use a feature flag system to toggle the new features on or off.

F) Manually back up the database before deployment and restore it if issues occur.

Answer: A

Explanation: Blue-green deployment is a technique that involves maintaining two separate environments: one that is live (blue) and one that is idle (green). During deployment, the new version is deployed to the idle environment. Once testing and validation confirm the new version is stable, traffic is switched from the live environment to the idle one, making it live. If any issues arise, traffic can be switched back to the original environment, facilitating a quick rollback to the previous stable state. This strategy minimizes downtime and allows for thorough testing before fully committing to the new version. Other options, like rolling deployments or canary deployments without automated rollbacks, do not provide the same level of assurance for rapid recovery. Virtual machine snapshots and database backups, while useful, generally do not provide the same speed and flexibility as a blue-green deployment strategy.

Q287: A DevOps engineer is tasked with setting up a rollback mechanism for a critical application running on a Kubernetes cluster. Which tool or approach would be most appropriate to achieve automated rollbacks of failed deployments in this environment?

A) Use Kubernetes' kubectl rollout undo command.

B) Implement Jenkins pipelines with manual rollback steps.

C) Use systemd service rollback features.

D) Implement a script to redeploy old container images manually.

E) Configure an Ansible playbook for rollback automation.

F) Use Git hooks to reverse code changes.

Answer: A

Explanation: Kubernetes provides built-in support for managing deployments and their rollouts. The kubectl rollout undo command is specifically designed to revert a deployment to a previous state. This command leverages Kubernetes' deployment history, allowing for a straightforward and efficient rollback process. This built-in functionality is particularly advantageous because it integrates seamlessly into the Kubernetes ecosystem, providing a robust and automated solution for managing deployment states. Other options, such as using Jenkins or Ansible, require additional setup and do not integrate as natively with Kubernetes' capabilities. Systemd and Git hooks are not applicable in a Kubernetes context for managing application rollbacks.

Q288: An organization is evaluating rollback strategies to incorporate into their existing deployment process. They need a strategy that ensures minimal data loss and quick recovery times. Which rollback strategy should they choose?
A) Versioned backups with periodic snapshots.

B) Hot standby database with automatic failover.

C) Immutable infrastructure deployments.

D) Docker image version control.

E) Automated database schema migrations.

F) Feature toggles with gradual rollout.

Answer: B

Explanation: A hot standby database with automatic failover is a highly effective rollback strategy for organizations that prioritize minimal data loss and quick recovery times. This approach involves maintaining a secondary database that is continuously updated with the primary database's changes. In the event of a failure, the system can automatically switch to the standby database, ensuring continuity and minimizing downtime. This strategy is particularly beneficial for systems with stringent uptime and data integrity requirements. Versioned backups and snapshots, while helpful, do not offer the same immediacy in failover scenarios. Immutable infrastructure and Docker image version control focus more on the application layer rather than data continuity. Feature toggles, while useful for toggling features on and off, do not inherently provide data recovery capabilities.

Q289: Consider the following statement: "A rollback strategy is crucial in continuous deployment to ensure that any deployment that introduces critical issues can be swiftly reversed to maintain system stability and availability." Is this statement true or false?
A) True

B) False

Answer: A

Explanation: The statement is true. In the context of continuous deployment, where changes are frequently and automatically deployed to production environments, the risk of introducing issues increases. A rollback strategy is essential to manage this risk effectively. It allows teams to revert to a previous stable state quickly if a deployment causes problems, thereby maintaining system stability and availability. Rollback strategies can include various methods, such as blue-green deployments, canary deployments, or using tools like Kubernetes' rollback features. By having a well-defined rollback plan, organizations can ensure that they can quickly respond to deployment failures, minimizing downtime and preserving the user experience.

Q290: A company is concerned about the potential impact of failed deployments on their customer-facing services. They are considering implementing a rollback strategy that involves using feature flags to manage the introduction of new features. What is an important consideration when using feature flags for rollbacks?

A) Ensure the feature flags are hardcoded into the application.

B) Use a centralized feature flag management system.

C) Deploy feature flags after the main deployment.

D) Rely on feature flags to manage database schema changes.

E) Use feature flags only for backend services.

F) Manually update feature flags in the source code repository.

Answer: B

Explanation: When using feature flags as part of a rollback strategy, it is crucial to have a centralized feature flag management system. This system allows for real-time control over which features are active or inactive without the need to redeploy the application. Centralized management provides flexibility and rapid response capabilities, enabling teams to toggle features on and off across various environments efficiently. This approach is particularly beneficial for managing the user experience during deployments and rollbacks. Hardcoding feature flags or relying solely on them for managing database schema changes can lead to complications and reduced flexibility. Similarly, deploying feature flags after the main deployment or updating them manually in the source code repository would negate their primary advantage of agility and speed in managing feature rollouts and rollbacks.

Q291: A mid-sized e-commerce company is experiencing issues with their application performance during peak shopping times. They have a distributed architecture with multiple microservices running on Kubernetes. Logs are generated by various applications and stored in a centralized logging system using Elasticsearch. The team wants to integrate these logs with their monitoring system, Prometheus, to create alerts based on specific log patterns and metrics. Which method would best facilitate this integration to allow for efficient alerting and monitoring of log data?

A) Use Promtail to push logs from Elasticsearch to a Prometheus instance.

B) Configure Elasticsearch to send logs directly to Prometheus using a webhook.

C) Set up a Logstash pipeline to send logs to Prometheus through a custom exporter.

D) Use Grafana Loki alongside Prometheus for log aggregation and querying.

E) Install a Prometheus agent in the Kubernetes cluster to scrape logs from Elasticsearch.

F) Implement a custom script to parse logs from Elasticsearch and push metrics to Prometheus.

Answer: D

Explanation: The integration of logging with monitoring systems is crucial for maintaining application performance and reliability, especially in a distributed architecture like Kubernetes. Grafana Loki is a log aggregation system that is designed to work seamlessly with Prometheus. Loki does not index the contents of the logs but instead indexes the labels, which makes it cost-effective and efficient. By using Loki, logs can be aggregated and queried alongside metrics in Grafana, allowing for seamless alerting and monitoring. This integration provides a unified view of logs and metrics, facilitating troubleshooting and performance analysis without the need for complex pipelines or custom scripts. Promtail, a client for Loki, can be used to collect logs and push them to Loki, but it is not directly compatible with Elasticsearch. Therefore, using Grafana Loki alongside Prometheus is the most efficient and effective method for integrating logs with the monitoring system in this scenario.

Q292: What is the primary purpose of using the fluentd logging tool in a Linux-based environment?

A) To monitor the CPU and memory usage of applications.

B) To collect and centralize logs from various sources.

C) To provide real-time alerts based on system metrics.

D) To automate the deployment of applications.

E) To manage network configurations and bandwidth.

F) To execute scheduled tasks and cron jobs.

Answer: B

Explanation: Fluentd is an open-source data collector designed to simplify and unify log data collection, processing, and aggregation across various sources in a Linux-based environment. Its primary purpose is to collect logs from disparate sources, unify them, and then send them to a centralized storage location or logging system. Fluentd supports a wide range of input and output plugins, making it highly versatile and adaptable for different logging needs. Unlike monitoring tools that focus on metrics like CPU and memory usage, Fluentd handles log data, providing a flexible solution for log management, which is essential for troubleshooting, auditing, and compliance in complex IT environments.

Q293: In a Linux environment, which command would you use to forward system logs to a remote syslog server for integration with a centralized monitoring system?

A) journalctl --forward

B) logger --remote

C) syslogd -R

D) rsyslogd -c

E) systemctl forward-logs

F) rsyslogd -r

Answer: C

Explanation: To forward system logs to a remote syslog server, the syslogd -R command is commonly used in Linux environments. This command configures the syslog daemon to send logs to a specified remote server. The -R option specifically allows the syslog daemon to forward logs to another host, which can then be integrated into a centralized monitoring system. This approach is widely used for centralizing log management, enabling administrators to monitor and analyze logs from multiple systems in one place. The rsyslog, an enhanced version of syslog, also supports remote logging, but the syslogd -R method is a traditional and straightforward approach for this purpose.

Q294: A Linux-based organization is using a combination of Prometheus and Grafana for monitoring their infrastructure. They want to create alerts based on specific patterns found in the logs generated by their applications. Which tool or method should they use to extract these log patterns and transform them into metrics that can be consumed by Prometheus?

A) Use the metricbeat tool to collect logs and convert them into metrics.

B) Implement Fluentd with a custom plugin to transform logs into Prometheus metrics.

C) Deploy a Prometheus exporter to directly parse log files.

D) Utilize Logstash with a Prometheus output plugin.

E) Integrate Filebeat with a Prometheus module.

F) Use a Kibana dashboard to visualize log patterns and export them to Prometheus.

Answer: B

Explanation: To extract log patterns and transform them into metrics for Prometheus, using Fluentd with a custom plugin is an effective solution. Fluentd is a versatile data collector that can parse log data and transform it into various formats, including metrics that Prometheus can consume. By implementing a custom plugin, Fluentd can be configured to identify specific log patterns and convert them into meaningful metrics. This approach allows for the seamless integration of logs and metrics, enabling the organization to create alerts based on log data. While Logstash and Metricbeat are also capable of processing logs, Fluentd's flexibility and extensibility make it particularly suitable for this task in a Linux environment.

Q295: True or False: The integration of logging and monitoring systems is primarily used to reduce the volume of logs stored in a system.
A) True

B) False

Answer: B

Explanation: The integration of logging and monitoring systems is not primarily aimed at reducing the volume of logs stored in a system. Instead, it is designed to enhance the visibility and manageability of system operations by correlating log data with performance metrics. This integration allows for more effective troubleshooting, proactive alerting, and comprehensive analysis of system behavior. By combining logs and metrics, organizations can gain deeper insights into the health and performance of their systems, leading to improved reliability and faster incident resolution. While managing log volume may be a consideration, it is not the primary goal of integrating logging with monitoring systems.

Q296: In a mid-sized company that recently transitioned to a DevOps culture, the IT operations team is tasked with enhancing system reliability and performance. They need to establish a monitoring solution that not only identifies issues in real-time but also integrates seamlessly with their current Linux-based infrastructure. The team is considering various tools that offer comprehensive insights into system health, resource usage, and potential bottlenecks. The solution should support automation and alerting to ensure quick responses to incidents. Which tool should the IT operations team implement to achieve these goals?   ---

A) Zabbix

B) Wireshark

C) Jenkins

D) Puppet

E) Docker

F) Git

Answer: A

Explanation: Zabbix is a robust monitoring tool specifically designed for real-time monitoring of servers, networks, and applications. It is well-suited for Linux environments and provides comprehensive data collection, visualization, and alerting capabilities. Zabbix's strengths lie in its ability to track performance metrics such as CPU, memory, disk space, and network utilization, which are crucial for maintaining system reliability and performance. Its seamless integration with Linux systems allows for efficient automation of monitoring tasks and immediate alerting in case of anomalies, making it ideal for a company adopting a DevOps approach.

Q297: The IT operations team is considering implementing Infrastructure as Code (IaC) to enhance their automation capabilities. They are evaluating different tools and approaches to manage their Linux infrastructure. Which of the following tools is primarily used for IaC in a Linux environment? ---

A) Ansible

B) Nagios

C) Grafana

D) Splunk

E) Snort

F) Kibana

Answer: A

Explanation: Ansible is a powerful tool primarily used for Infrastructure as Code (IaC) in Linux and other environments. It allows IT operations teams to automate the provisioning, configuration, and management of infrastructure using simple, human-readable YAML files. Ansible's agentless architecture and ease of use make it an ideal choice for implementing IaC, enabling teams to automate repetitive tasks, enforce consistency, and reduce the potential for human error. It integrates well with other DevOps tools and can manage a wide range of resources, ensuring efficient and reliable infrastructure management.

Q298: Consider a Linux-based IT infrastructure where the primary goal is to ensure maximum uptime and performance for critical applications. The IT operations team is evaluating solutions for automating system updates and patches to minimize downtime. Which of the following strategies should be prioritized to achieve this goal? ---

A) Implementing a rolling update strategy

B) Scheduling updates during peak hours

C) Disabling automatic updates entirely

D) Using a single server for all applications

E) Manually applying updates without automation

F) Ignoring update notifications

Answer: A

Explanation: Implementing a rolling update strategy is a powerful approach to ensure maximum uptime and performance for critical applications in a Linux-based IT infrastructure. This strategy involves updating systems incrementally, one at a time, or in small groups, to minimize the impact on overall system availability. By doing so, IT operations can ensure that at least some instances of the application are always available, even during updates. This approach reduces downtime, allows for testing of updates on a smaller scale before full deployment, and helps in quickly identifying and rolling back problematic updates.

Q299: True/False: In the context of IT operations, achieving high availability is primarily focused on minimizing the Mean Time to Repair (MTTR) rather than maximizing the Mean Time Between Failures (MTBF).   ---
A) True

B) False

Answer: B

Explanation: Achieving high availability in IT operations is primarily focused on maximizing the Mean Time Between Failures (MTBF) rather than minimizing the Mean Time to Repair (MTTR). While both MTBF and MTTR are important metrics, high availability strategies prioritize extending the time between failures to ensure continuous service delivery. This involves implementing redundancy, failover solutions, and proactive monitoring to prevent failures from occurring in the first place. On the other hand, MTTR focuses on reducing the time it takes to recover from a failure, which is also important but secondary to preventing the failures themselves.

Q300: An organization with a diverse set of Linux servers is looking to implement a centralized logging solution to improve their IT operations' efficiency in diagnosing issues across their infrastructure. They want a tool that can aggregate logs from various sources, provide search and analytics capabilities, and support alerting based on specific log patterns. Which of the following tools best meets these requirements?

A) Logstash

B) Wireshark

C) Chef

D) Kubernetes

E) Vagrant

F) Terraform

Answer: A

Explanation: Logstash is a key component of the ELK stack (Elasticsearch, Logstash, Kibana) and is specifically designed for log aggregation and processing. It can collect logs from various sources across a Linux-based infrastructure, parse and enrich them, and then store them in a centralized repository such as Elasticsearch. With Logstash, IT operations can set up complex queries and analytics to diagnose issues efficiently and configure alerts based on specific log patterns to proactively address potential problems. Its ability to integrate with various data sources and provide real-time insights makes it an ideal choice for centralized logging solutions in diverse environments.

Q301: Identify the tool that is a lightweight, agentless automation tool that relies on SSH to manage and configure systems, often used for automated system configuration and software installation.   ---
A) Puppet

B) Chef

C) Terraform

D) Ansible

E) SaltStack

F) Jenkins

Answer: D

Explanation: Ansible is an open-source automation tool that is known for its simplicity and ease of use, especially in environments where agentless configuration management is preferred. It uses SSH for communication with nodes, making it lightweight and easy to deploy since it doesn't require any agent software to be installed on the client machines. Ansible is widely used for tasks such as automated system configuration, software installation, and orchestration. It uses YAML-based playbooks that define the desired state of systems, which are then executed over SSH, ensuring that actions are idempotent. The other options listed either rely on agents, focus on different aspects of DevOps, or are used for purposes other than configuration management, such as continuous integration.

Q302: On a Linux system, you need to ensure that a script is executed automatically after any package installation or removal operation using the apt package manager. Which configuration file should be modified to achieve this?

A) /etc/apt/apt.conf

B) /etc/apt/apt.conf.d/local

C) /etc/apt/apt.conf.d/99custom

D) /etc/apt/apt-post-install.sh

E) /etc/apt/apt.conf.d/50unattended-upgrades

F) /etc/apt/apt.conf.d/01autoremove

Answer: C

Explanation: The apt package manager on Debian-based systems, such as Ubuntu, allows for custom scripts to be executed through configuration files. To ensure a script is executed after every package operation, one can create or modify a file in the /etc/apt/apt.conf.d/ directory. The file 99custom can be used to define hooks or scripts that should run after package operations. By placing a script in this file, one can utilize the DPkg::Post-Invoke or DPkg::Post-Invoke-Success options to specify a command that will be executed after package installations or removals. This approach allows for additional custom operations to be seamlessly integrated into the package management process. The other listed files and directories are either not relevant to this configuration or are used for different purposes.

Q303: True or False: In the context of automated system configuration, ensuring idempotency means that applying the same operation multiple times will yield the same result without causing unintended changes.
A) True

B) False

Answer: A

Explanation: Idempotency is a crucial concept in automated system configuration and management. It refers to the property of operations that can be applied multiple times without changing the result beyond the initial application. In other words, an idempotent operation ensures that running a configuration script or tool repeatedly will not produce any additional changes after the first execution, assuming the system is already in the desired state. This is essential for predictable and consistent configuration management, as it prevents unintended side effects or states when operations are re-applied. Tools like Ansible, Puppet, and Chef are designed to be idempotent, allowing configurations to be safely re-applied and maintained over time.

Q304: Your organization is preparing to deploy a major update to its web application, which is hosted on a cluster of Linux servers. The DevOps team has decided to implement a change management process to ensure a smooth transition. As part of the process, you need to make certain that changes to the configuration files on the servers are tracked and can be rolled back if necessary. Given the need for version control and rollback capabilities, which tool or method would be most appropriate to manage this requirement?

A) Use a simple backup script to copy configuration files to a separate directory before making changes.

B) Implement a Git repository to track changes to configuration files.

C) Use the rsync command to synchronize configuration files to a remote server.

D) Utilize a spreadsheet to manually document changes to configuration files.

E) Configure a cron job to archive configuration files daily.

F) Employ system snapshots to capture the entire server state before changes.

Answer: B

Explanation: Implementing a Git repository is the most suitable method for tracking changes to configuration files. Git provides version control, allowing you to see the history of changes, who made them, and why. This ability to track changes and roll back to previous versions is crucial in a change management process, especially when dealing with configuration files on Linux servers. While backups, synchronization, manual documentation, and snapshots have their uses, they don't offer the fine-grained control, collaboration, and rollback capabilities of a version control system like Git.

Q305: The IT department of a financial services company needs to implement a change management process for its Linux-based transaction processing system. The system is critical and must remain highly available. Changes must be documented, tested, and approved before deployment. Which of the following steps is NOT typically part of a formal change management process?
A) Documenting the change request and its purpose.

B) Testing the change in a production environment immediately.

C) Reviewing the change by an authorized change advisory board.

D) Scheduling the change implementation during a planned maintenance window.

E) Recording the change in a centralized change management system.

F) Implementing a rollback plan in case the change fails.

Answer: B

Explanation: Testing a change in a production environment immediately is not a typical part of a formal change management process. Changes should be tested in a development or staging environment first to identify any potential issues without impacting the live system. Only after successful testing and approval should the change be deployed to production. Other steps like documentation, review, scheduling, and rollback planning are standard components of a structured change management process to ensure changes are made safely and efficiently.

Q306: True or False: In a change management process, it is considered best practice to deploy changes directly to the production environment to minimize downtime.
A) True

B) False

Answer: B

Explanation: Deploying changes directly to the production environment is not considered best practice due to the risks involved. Such an approach can lead to unexpected downtime and disruptions if issues arise. Best practices involve deploying changes to a staging or testing environment first, allowing for thorough testing and validation before moving to production. This process helps ensure that any potential issues are identified and resolved without impacting the users or the stability of the production environment.

Q307: An e-commerce company is experiencing frequent issues with unapproved changes to its Linux server configurations, causing downtime. To address this, the company decides to implement a strict change management policy. Which principle should be prioritized to ensure both control over changes and operational efficiency?

A) Allow only senior administrators to make changes without documentation.

B) Require changes to be documented, reviewed, and approved before implementation.

C) Implement a no-changes policy during business hours to avoid disruptions.

D) Allow developers to make immediate changes when issues arise without approvals.

E) Schedule all changes during off-peak hours without prior testing.

F) Permit all changes to be made directly in the production environment for speed.

Answer: B

Explanation: Requiring changes to be documented, reviewed, and approved before implementation is the principle that strikes a balance between control and operational efficiency. This approach ensures that all changes are necessary, well-planned, and vetted by knowledgeable stakeholders, reducing the risk of errors and downtime. While other options might offer speed or convenience, they compromise the integrity and stability of the system by bypassing important checks and balances that are essential in a robust change management process.

Q308: A software development company is transitioning to a DevOps model and needs to establish a change management process for its Linux-based environments. The company wants to automate as much of the process as possible to reduce manual effort and errors. Which tool would best support the automation of change management tasks, such as tracking changes and enforcing approval workflows?

A) Ansible

B) Jenkins

C) Puppet

D) Redmine

E) Subversion

F) Nagios

Answer: D

Explanation: Redmine is a project management tool that can be used to automate change management tasks, such as tracking changes and enforcing approval workflows. It provides features like issue tracking, project wikis, and customizable workflows, making it well-suited for managing change requests and approvals. While Ansible, Jenkins, and Puppet are powerful tools for automation and configuration management, they are not specifically designed for managing the process and documentation aspects of change management. Subversion is a version control system, and Nagios is a monitoring tool, neither of which directly address the automation of change management processes.

Q309: A mid-sized software development company is in the process of implementing a continuous deployment pipeline for their microservices architecture. The company uses a mix of different technologies, including Docker containers, Jenkins for CI/CD, and Ansible for configuration management. The Operations team is tasked with ensuring that any service updates are automatically deployed to production with minimal downtime. The team needs to set up a process that will allow new Docker images to be pulled and run seamlessly on their production servers. Which of the following commands should the team include in their deployment script to ensure that the new Docker container runs using the latest image version while gracefully stopping the old container?

A) docker run -d --name myapp myapp:latest

B) docker stop myapp && docker rm myapp && docker run -d --name myapp myapp:latest

C) docker pull myapp:latest && docker run -d --name myapp --rm myapp:latest

D) docker stop myapp && docker pull myapp:latest && docker run -d --name myapp myapp:latest

E) docker pull myapp:latest && docker stop myapp && docker run -d --name myapp myapp:latest

F) docker run --restart always -d --name myapp myapp:latest

Answer: D

Explanation: In a continuous deployment scenario where Docker containers are used, it is crucial to ensure that the latest image is pulled and the existing container is stopped properly before starting a new one with the updated image. The command sequence includes stopping the existing container, pulling the latest image, and then running a new container with the updated image. This ensures no downtime as the old container is stopped gracefully before the new one starts. Option D correctly orders these operations to prevent potential conflicts or downtime.

Q310: In the context of continuous deployment, which of the following statements is true regarding the use of feature toggles in service operations?

A) Feature toggles help in reducing the risk by allowing features to be tested in production without affecting users.

B) Feature toggles are primarily used to improve application security by disabling unused features.

C) Implementing feature toggles increases the deployment time due to added complexity.

D) Feature toggles are used to permanently remove features from an application.

E) Feature toggles require a complete re-architecture of the deployment pipeline.

F) Feature toggles can only be implemented in monolithic applications.

Answer: A

Explanation: Feature toggles, also known as feature flags, are a powerful tool in continuous deployment. They allow new features to be deployed to production and tested in real-world conditions without exposing them to all users. This reduces risk by providing a way to test features in production environments and roll them back if issues arise, without requiring a new deployment. They do not inherently increase deployment time or complexity if implemented correctly and can be used in both monolithic and microservices architectures.

Q311: Determine whether the following statement is true or false: "In a continuous deployment pipeline, rollback strategies are unnecessary because all deployments are automatically successful."

A) True

B) False

Answer: B

Explanation: Continuous deployment pipelines aim to automate the deployment process but do not guarantee that every deployment will be successful. Rollback strategies are essential to manage and mitigate risks associated with failed deployments. They ensure that systems can quickly revert to a stable state in case a deployment introduces critical issues. Effective rollback mechanisms, such as maintaining previous versions of a service or using blue-green deployments, are critical aspects of a robust continuous deployment strategy.

Q312: A retail company uses Jenkins for their continuous deployment pipeline and needs to implement an approval step before deploying to production. This step should ensure that a manager reviews and approves the deployment. Which Jenkins feature or plugin should be used to implement this functionality?

A) Jenkins Blue Ocean

B) Jenkins Pipeline

C) Jenkins Multibranch Pipeline

D) Jenkins Build Pipeline Plugin

E) Jenkins Promoted Builds Plugin

F) Jenkins Role Strategy Plugin

Answer: E

Explanation: The Jenkins Promoted Builds Plugin is designed to add manual approval steps to a Jenkins job. It allows defining conditions under which a build is promoted to the next stage, such as a deployment to production. This feature is particularly useful in continuous deployment pipelines where a human approval step is necessary to ensure that changes meet certain criteria or policies before being deployed to production environments. The plugin integrates seamlessly with Jenkins pipelines to enable this functionality.

Q313: In a continuous deployment setup using Kubernetes to manage deployments of containerized applications, which of the following commands will correctly update a Kubernetes deployment to use a new image version, ensuring zero downtime?

A) kubectl apply -f deployment.yaml

B) kubectl set image deployment/myapp myapp=myapp:v2

C) kubectl update deployment myapp --image=myapp:v2

D) kubectl replace -f deployment.yaml

E) kubectl patch deployment myapp --patch '{"spec": {"template": {"spec": {"containers": [{"name": "myapp", "image": "myapp:v2"}]}}}}'

F) kubectl rollout restart deployment myapp --image=myapp:v2

Answer: B

Explanation: The kubectl set image command is used to update the image of a container in a Kubernetes deployment. By specifying the new image version, Kubernetes will handle the rolling update process, which ensures zero downtime by gradually replacing old pods with new ones. This built-in feature of Kubernetes helps maintain service availability and reliability during updates, crucial aspects of continuous deployment practices.

Q314: A manufacturing company relies on a complex system of interconnected services running on Linux servers to control its production line. Recently, they experienced a major incident where a critical service became unresponsive, leading to a halt in production. As a DevOps Tools Engineer, you are tasked with implementing an incident response plan to prevent such occurrences in the future. Which initial step should you prioritize in developing an effective incident response plan?

A) Set up automated scripts to restart services when they go down

B) Conduct a root cause analysis for every incident

C) Establish clear communication channels and protocols

D) Implement a version control system for all configurations

E) Train all team members on incident management tools

F) Develop a detailed inventory of all production systems

Answer: C

Explanation: An effective incident response plan begins with establishing clear communication channels and protocols. This step ensures that when an incident occurs, there is a predefined method for communicating the incident's details, which helps in coordinating the response efforts. It is crucial that all team members know whom to contact and how information will be disseminated during an incident. While root cause analysis, inventory management, and training are essential components of incident management, they are subsequent steps. Automated scripts and version control are more about incident prevention and post-incident learning. Clear communication forms the backbone of incident response, enabling quick mobilization and efficient problem resolution.

Q315: In the context of incident response and management on Linux systems, which command is most suitable for monitoring real-time system performance to quickly identify a sudden spike in resource usage?
A) df -h

B) netstat -tuln

C) top

D) ps aux

E) du -sh

F) crontab -l

Answer: C

Explanation: The top command is specifically designed for real-time monitoring of system performance on Linux systems. It provides a dynamic view of the system's processes, displaying information such as CPU usage, memory usage, and process identifiers. This makes it an ideal tool for identifying sudden spikes in resource usage, which can be indicative of an incident. Other commands like df -h, netstat -tuln, and ps aux provide useful system information but do not offer the real-time dynamic monitoring capabilities necessary for incident response. du -sh and crontab -l serve different purposes related to disk usage and scheduled tasks, respectively.

Q316: A company uses a centralized logging system to manage logs from various Linux servers. They face challenges in correlating logs across different services during an incident. What is the best practice for ensuring logs from different services can be effectively correlated?

A) Implement log rotation to manage log file sizes

B) Use a consistent timestamp format across all logs

C) Store logs in a distributed database for redundancy

D) Enable verbose logging for detailed information

E) Set up a separate logging server for each service

F) Use log compression to save storage space

Answer: B

Explanation: Using a consistent timestamp format across all logs is crucial for effective log correlation, especially during incident response. This practice allows logs from different services and systems to be easily compared and analyzed in chronological order. When incidents occur, being able to correlate logs accurately is essential for understanding the sequence of events and pinpointing the root cause. While log rotation, storage, verbosity, and compression are important for log management, they do not facilitate the correlation of logs. A consistent timestamp ensures that logs from different sources can be aligned and understood in context.

Q317: True or False: Regular drills and simulations of incident response scenarios are unnecessary for teams that have detailed documentation and automated monitoring in place.

A) True

B) False

Answer: B

Explanation: Regular drills and simulations are crucial even for teams with detailed documentation and automated monitoring. These exercises help ensure that all team members understand their roles during an incident and can effectively execute the response plan. Simulations provide a controlled environment to practice and refine incident response strategies, which can reveal potential gaps or weaknesses in the documentation or automation. Moreover, they build confidence and improve communication among team members. Documentation and monitoring are valuable resources, but hands-on practice is key to ensuring a team is prepared to respond efficiently to real incidents.

Q318: In the event of a security incident where unauthorized access to a Linux server is detected, which immediate action should be taken to prevent further unauthorized activity?

A) Power off the server immediately to prevent data loss

B) Notify all users and require password changes

C) Isolate the server from the network

D) Update all system packages to the latest version

E) Perform a full system backup

F) Install a new firewall rule to block all incoming traffic

Answer: C

Explanation: When unauthorized access is detected, the immediate priority is to prevent further unauthorized activity, which is best achieved by isolating the server from the network. This action stops the attacker from continuing their activities and potentially spreading to other systems. While notifying users and updating packages are important steps, they are not immediate actions. Powering off the server can result in data loss and hinder forensic analysis. A full system backup and new firewall rules are preventive or post-incident measures rather than immediate responses. Isolating the server minimizes risk and allows for a thorough investigation to determine the breach's scope and impact.

Q319: In a rapidly growing tech startup, the DevOps team is implementing an alerting system to enhance the reliability and responsiveness of their services. The team has set up a system using Prometheus and Alertmanager to monitor critical application metrics. Recently, they noticed an increase in the latency of alerts, which has led to delayed responses to incidents. Upon investigation, they found that most alerts are not reaching the on-call engineers in a timely manner due to configuration issues. The team wants to ensure that alerts are prioritized and delivered promptly to the right people. Which configuration change should they consider to reduce alert latency and ensure proper notification delivery?

A) Increase the scrape interval of Prometheus to collect data more frequently.

B) Use a different alerting tool instead of Alertmanager.

C) Configure Alertmanager to use a high-availability setup.

D) Increase the notification timeout in Alertmanager.

E) Disable grouping in Alertmanager to send alerts immediately.

F) Reduce the retention time of metrics in Prometheus.

Answer: E

Explanation: Alertmanager's primary role is to manage alerts sent by client applications such as Prometheus, including deduplication, grouping, and routing them to the correct receiver integrations such as email, PagerDuty, or Slack. In this scenario, the delay in alerts reaching the on-call engineers can be attributed to the grouping mechanism in

Alertmanager. By default, Alertmanager groups similar alerts to reduce noise, but this can introduce latency. Disabling or properly configuring alert grouping can help in sending alerts immediately as they occur, thus reducing latency. This approach ensures that critical alerts are delivered promptly without being held up by the grouping process.

Q320: In the context of alerting systems, what is the primary purpose of using a "dead man's switch"?

A) To automate the escalation process when alerts are not acknowledged.

B) To verify that the alerting system itself is functioning correctly.

C) To automatically restart services that have failed.

D) To ensure high availability of services.

E) To prioritize critical alerts over informational ones.

F) To reduce the number of false positive alerts.

Answer: B

Explanation: A "dead man's switch" is a mechanism used in alerting systems to ensure that the alerting infrastructure itself is operational. It typically involves sending regular alerts or heartbeats that are expected to be received by an alerting system. If the alerting system does not receive these heartbeats, it assumes that there is a problem with the alerting infrastructure, prompting an investigation. This is crucial for maintaining the reliability of the alerting system, as it helps identify issues in the alert delivery process itself, ensuring that alerts about actual incidents will be delivered correctly.

Q321: True or False: In Linux-based alerting systems, configuring alerts to trigger on the absolute value of metrics is generally more effective than triggering on changes or anomalies in the metric values.
A) True

B) False

Answer: B

Explanation: In alerting systems, triggering alerts based on changes or anomalies in metric values is often more effective than on absolute values. This approach, known as anomaly detection, helps in identifying unusual behavior that could indicate a problem, even if the absolute metric values are within expected ranges. Anomalies can highlight performance degradation or other issues before they reach critical levels. Monitoring for changes rather than static thresholds can lead to more meaningful alerts, reducing the number of false positives and enhancing the relevance of alerts to the on-call engineers.

Q322: Which Linux command is commonly used to test the configuration of an alerting rule in a Prometheus setup before deploying it in a production environment?

A) curl

B) promtool

C) netstat

D) dig

E) ping

F) systemctl

Answer: B

Explanation: Prometheus provides a command-line tool called promtool that is used to validate configurations, including those for alerting rules. This tool helps ensure that the syntax and structure of the configuration files are correct before they are deployed in a production environment. Using promtool to test alerting rules can prevent misconfigurations that might lead to missed alerts or incorrect alert behavior. This is an essential step in the configuration process, especially in a production environment where the reliability of the alerting system is crucial.

Q323: In an environment using Nagios for alerting, an engineer needs to ensure that alerts are sent only when a service is down for more than 5 minutes. Which configuration option should be modified to achieve this?

A) maxcheckattempts

B) notificationinterval

C) retryinterval

D) servicenotificationperiod

E) checkfreshness

F) checkinterval

Answer: A

Explanation: In Nagios, the maxcheckattempts directive is used to specify the number of times a service check must fail before an alert is generated. By adjusting this value in conjunction with the checkinterval, which determines how often the checks are performed, an engineer can configure Nagios to only send alerts if a service remains down for a specified period, such as 5 minutes. For instance, if the checkinterval is set to 1 minute and maxcheckattempts is set to 6, an alert will only be sent if the service check fails 6 times consecutively, effectively implementing a 5-minute threshold for alerting. This configuration helps to reduce the number of false positives due to transient issues.

Q324: In a mid-sized technology company, the DevOps team is tasked with improving the efficiency of their infrastructure management operations. They decide to implement automation to streamline the deployment and configuration of their Linux-based servers. The goal is to reduce manual intervention, minimize downtime, and ensure consistency across different environments. The team evaluates several automation tools and needs to decide on one that is most compatible with their current tech stack, which includes Ansible, Jenkins, and Docker. Which tool should the team choose to seamlessly integrate with their existing tools and enhance automation across their infrastructure?

A) Puppet

B) Chef

C) SaltStack

D) Terraform

E) Kubernetes

F) Nagios

Answer: D

Explanation: Terraform is an open-source infrastructure as code software tool that provides a consistent CLI workflow to manage hundreds of cloud services. It allows users to define both cloud and on-prem resources in human-readable configuration files that can be versioned, reused, and shared. With its ability to integrate seamlessly with Ansible, Jenkins, and Docker, Terraform is an excellent choice for a team looking to enhance automation across their infrastructure. It provides more infrastructure provisioning capabilities compared to configuration management tools like Ansible and Chef, and is more focused on the infrastructure layer than Kubernetes, which is more container orchestration-focused. Nagios is mainly used for monitoring, thus not aligning with the primary goal of infrastructure automation.

Q325: Which of the following benefits is NOT commonly associated with implementing automation in service operations on Linux-based systems?

A) Enhanced security through reduced human error

B) Improved system reliability and uptime

C) Greater flexibility in manual configuration adjustments

D) Consistency in system configuration across multiple environments

E) Faster deployment times

F) Reduction in operational costs

Answer: C

Explanation: nan

Q326: True or False: Implementing automation in service operations can lead to a decrease in team collaboration and communication, as tasks are handled by automated processes rather than individuals.

A) True

B) False

Answer: B

Explanation: While it may seem that automating tasks could reduce the need for communication, the opposite is often true. Automation requires effective collaboration and communication during the design and implementation phases to ensure that automated processes are aligned with business goals and technical requirements. Furthermore, regular updates and maintenance of automated systems necessitate ongoing communication among team members. Automation often shifts the focus of team interactions from routine task execution to more strategic discussions, enhancing collaboration and planning.

Q327: A DevOps engineer is tasked with setting up a continuous integration and deployment pipeline for a new microservices application on a Linux server. The engineer needs to ensure that the infrastructure setup is idempotent and can be easily rolled back in case of failures. Which of the following tools is best suited for achieving these requirements?

A) Jenkins

B) Ansible

C) Docker Compose

D) Git

E) Kubernetes

F) Systemd

Answer: B

Explanation: Ansible is a tool that excels in configuration management and infrastructure automation due to its declarative nature and idempotency. Idempotency ensures that applying the same configuration multiple times results in the same state, which is crucial for reliable infrastructure setup. Ansible's playbooks allow for easy rollback of configurations, making it a strong candidate for setting up continuous integration and deployment pipelines where consistency and rollback capabilities are essential. While Jenkins is great for CI/CD, it is not inherently designed for idempotent infrastructure configuration. Docker Compose and Kubernetes are more suited for managing application containers rather than infrastructure as a whole.

Q328: You are a systems administrator responsible for managing a fleet of Linux servers in a large organization. Your team is considering implementing a configuration management tool to automate server provisioning and configuration. The tool must support agentless operation, have a simple learning curve, and integrate well with existing shell scripts. Which tool best meets these requirements?

A) Chef

B) Puppet

C) Ansible

D) SaltStack

E) Terraform

F) CFEngine

Answer: C

Explanation: Ansible is known for its simplicity, agentless architecture, and ease of integration with existing shell scripts. It uses SSH for communication, eliminating the need for a dedicated agent on each managed node, which simplifies deployment and maintenance. Ansible's YAML-based playbooks are easy to understand and write, making it an accessible choice for teams new to configuration management. Chef and Puppet require agents on nodes and have steeper learning curves due to their domain-specific languages. SaltStack and CFEngine also use agents, and while Terraform is excellent for provisioning, it is not a configuration management tool.

Q329: A financial services company has recently transitioned to a DevOps model to improve its software development and delivery processes. As part of this transition, they have implemented CI/CD pipelines using Jenkins and Docker. The operations team has noticed that the feedback loop between the development and operations teams is not as effective as intended, resulting in delayed deployments and increased error rates. The company is also using Prometheus for monitoring and Grafana for visualizations. Which action should the DevOps team prioritize to enhance the feedback loops and service improvement?

A) Increase the frequency of team meetings to discuss deployment issues.

B) Implement automated alerts from Prometheus to notify teams of anomalies.

C) Use Docker Swarm to manage their containerized applications.

D) Migrate monitoring to a cloud-based solution for better scalability.

E) Integrate Jenkins with Slack to provide real-time build notifications.

F) Schedule regular training sessions on new DevOps tools for the team.

Answer: B

Explanation: To enhance the feedback loops, the DevOps team should focus on providing real-time, actionable insights to both development and operations teams. By implementing automated alerts from Prometheus, teams can be promptly notified of performance anomalies or failures, allowing them to act quickly and address issues before they impact users. Automated alerts help reduce the time between detection and resolution, thereby improving the overall service quality. Other options, such as increasing meeting frequency or migrating monitoring solutions, do not directly address the immediacy and efficiency of feedback that is essential in a DevOps environment.

Q330: In the context of service improvement, a feedback loop is an essential component in DevOps practices. True or False: Feedback loops in DevOps are only concerned with gathering metrics for software development teams and do not involve operations.
A) True

B) False

Answer: B

Explanation: Feedback loops in DevOps are a critical component that involves both development and operations teams. They are designed to provide continuous, actionable insights that help in refining processes, improving code quality, and enhancing system performance. Operations teams use feedback loops to monitor infrastructure, detect anomalies, and optimize deployments. The integration of feedback from both development and operations ensures that teams can collaborate effectively to improve service delivery and reliability.

Q331: Which Linux command can be used to create a text file containing system logs, which are then analyzed to provide feedback for service improvement?
A) cat /var/log/syslog > analysis.txt

B) tail -f /var/log/syslog > analysis.txt

C) cp /var/log/syslog analysis.txt

D) touch /var/log/syslog > analysis.txt

E) grep "error" /var/log/syslog > analysis.txt

F) echo /var/log/syslog > analysis.txt

Answer: E

Explanation: The grep command is used to search for specific patterns in files, such as error messages in system logs, which are critical for analyzing and understanding system behavior. By redirecting the output of grep to a text file, teams can create a focused dataset containing only relevant information for further analysis. This data can be used to generate insights and feedback on system performance, helping to identify issues and drive service improvements. Other commands like cat or cp would copy the entire log file without filtering for specific content.

Q332: A manufacturing company is using a DevOps approach to ensure the reliability of their IoT devices. They have set up a feedback loop system with Nagios for monitoring and Logstash for log management. After a recent update, they noticed an increase in downtime. As a DevOps engineer, what would be the most effective first step in utilizing the feedback loop to address this issue?
A) Adjust the thresholds for Nagios alerts to reduce false positives.

B) Conduct a full system rollback to the previous stable version.

C) Analyze logs using Logstash to identify patterns associated with downtime.

D) Increase the frequency of Nagios checks to detect issues faster.

E) Update all IoT devices to the latest firmware version.

F) Schedule a maintenance window to manually inspect the IoT devices.

Answer: C

Explanation: Analyzing logs using Logstash is a crucial first step in understanding the root cause of the increased downtime. Logstash can aggregate and parse logs from various sources, allowing the team to identify patterns and correlations related to the downtime. By pinpointing specific errors or anomalies, the team can develop a targeted response to address the issue. Adjusting alert thresholds or increasing check frequency could be supplementary actions but should be informed by insights gained from log analysis.

Q333: Which command would you use to continuously monitor a log file for changes, providing real-time feedback for immediate action in a Linux environment?

A) head /var/log/syslog

B) watch /var/log/syslog

C) less /var/log/syslog

D) tail -f /var/log/syslog

E) open /var/log/syslog

F) read /var/log/syslog

Answer: D

Explanation: The tail -f command is used to monitor changes to a file in real-time, making it an invaluable tool for observing live logs on a Linux system. This command outputs the latest lines of a file and continuously updates the display as new entries are added. It is particularly useful for monitoring log files during active troubleshooting or when immediate feedback is needed for ongoing processes. Other commands like head or less are used for static viewing and do not provide real-time updates.

Q334: In a mid-sized company, the DevOps team is responsible for ensuring that the continuous integration/continuous deployment (CI/CD) pipeline functions smoothly. Recently, they encountered an issue where new deployments led to increased error rates in production, causing significant downtime. The team decided to incorporate more rigorous testing into their CI/CD pipeline to catch issues early. They are considering various testing strategies to implement. Which type of testing should be prioritized in the pipeline to ensure that new code changes do not break existing functionality?

A) Unit Testing

B) Integration Testing

C) Smoke Testing

D) Load Testing

E) Security Testing

F) User Acceptance Testing

Answer: B

Explanation: Integration testing is crucial in a CI/CD pipeline as it focuses on verifying the interactions between different modules or components of a system. While unit tests are essential for validating individual pieces of code, integration tests ensure that these pieces work together as expected. In a complex system, changes in one module can inadvertently affect others, leading to issues like the increased error rates mentioned. By prioritizing integration testing, the team can catch these interaction-related bugs before they reach production, thus minimizing downtime and maintaining system reliability. This approach aligns well with the goals of a DevOps team to promote consistency, reliability, and efficiency in software delivery.

Q335: A DevOps engineer is tasked with implementing automated testing in a legacy application that has been running in production for several years. The application lacks comprehensive documentation, and the engineer is unsure about the dependencies between its components. What is the best initial step in the testing process to gain an understanding of the application's behavior?

A) Implement end-to-end testing to simulate user journeys.

B) Conduct exploratory testing to identify undocumented features.

C) Perform static code analysis to evaluate code quality.

D) Develop unit tests for individual functions.

E) Set up a sandbox environment for testing.

F) Initiate a code review with the original developers.

Answer: C

Explanation: Static code analysis is an effective starting point for understanding a legacy application's behavior, especially when documentation is lacking. This method involves examining the source code without executing it, allowing the engineer to identify potential issues, such as code smells, complexity, and dependencies between components. Static analysis tools can provide insights into the structure and quality of the code, helping the engineer to prioritize areas requiring further exploration and testing. This foundational understanding is crucial before diving into dynamic testing methods like unit or end-to-end testing, ensuring that subsequent efforts are well-informed and targeted.

Q336: An e-commerce company has recently transitioned its infrastructure to a cloud-based environment. As part of this transition, the DevOps team is tasked with ensuring that the new system can handle peak loads during sales events. Which type of testing should be emphasized to confirm the system's ability to maintain performance under high traffic conditions?
A) Unit Testing

B) Integration Testing

C) Load Testing

D) Smoke Testing

E) Functional Testing

F) Regression Testing

Answer: C

Explanation: Load testing is essential for assessing how a system performs under expected peak load conditions. For an e-commerce platform, ensuring that the system can handle high traffic volumes during sales events is critical to maintaining a positive user experience and maximizing sales. Load testing involves simulating a high number of concurrent users and transactions to identify performance bottlenecks and ensure that the system's scalability meets business demands. By focusing on load testing, the DevOps team can proactively address potential issues related to server capacity, response times, and stability, thereby ensuring a robust infrastructure capable of supporting peak loads.

Q337: A newly hired DevOps engineer is reviewing the existing service operation practices at their company. They notice that the team currently uses manual testing for all their updates, leading to delays and human error. The engineer proposes a shift to automated testing. What is a key advantage of automated testing in service operations?

A) Eliminates the need for any human oversight.

B) Guarantees zero defects in production.

C) Provides faster feedback on code changes.

D) Reduces the initial investment in testing.

E) Ensures compliance with all industry standards.

F) Simplifies the code review process.

Answer: C

Explanation: Automated testing provides faster feedback on code changes, a significant advantage over manual testing. In service operations, rapid feedback is crucial as it allows for quick identification and resolution of issues before they impact production. Automated tests can be integrated into the CI/CD pipeline, enabling continuous validation of the code with every commit. This efficiency reduces the time between code development and deployment, enhances team productivity, and minimizes the risk of human error. While automated testing does not guarantee zero defects or eliminate the need for human oversight, it significantly improves the speed and reliability of the testing process, which is vital for maintaining service quality.

Q338: In the context of service operations testing, it's essential to verify that the system's functionalities meet the specified requirements. This verification process can be classified into two broad categories: verification and validation. Verification ensures the product is built correctly, while validation ensures the right product is built. True or False: Validation testing is primarily concerned with the internal workings of the system, such as code and algorithm correctness.

A) True

B) False

Answer: B

Explanation: Validation testing is concerned with ensuring that the system meets the business and user requirements, focusing on the external behavior of the system rather than its internal workings. It involves checking whether the right product is being built according to the user's needs and expectations. This contrasts with verification, which focuses on the internal aspects like code correctness, algorithms, and system architecture to ensure the product is built correctly. Therefore, validation testing includes activities like user acceptance testing and functional testing, which are more aligned with user satisfaction and requirement fulfillment.

Q339: A software development company is preparing to release a new version of their web application. To minimize risk, they want to implement a deployment strategy that allows them to test the new version in a production environment with a small subset of users before rolling it out to everyone. They have heard about canary deployments and blue-green deployments but are unsure which approach to take. The team needs a strategy that allows for quick rollback if issues are detected and involves minimal downtime. They use a Linux-based infrastructure with Docker containers to manage their application deployments. Which deployment strategy should they choose to best meet their needs?

A) Canary deployment using Docker Swarm

B) Blue-green deployment using Kubernetes

C) Rolling update deployment using Ansible

D) Canary deployment with feature flags

E) Blue-green deployment with Jenkins

F) In-place upgrade with Docker Compose

Answer: A

Explanation: A canary deployment involves releasing the new version of an application to a small subset of users before making it available to everyone. This approach allows the team to monitor the new version's performance and quickly rollback if any issues are detected. Using Docker Swarm for a canary deployment is suitable in this situation as Docker provides built-in support for managing containerized applications, easily allowing the team to direct a portion of traffic to the new version. This strategy minimizes downtime because the old version remains active while the new version is rolled out gradually. Blue-green deployments are also viable but might involve more downtime as they require switching between environments. Rolling updates and in-place upgrades are less flexible in rollback situations. Feature flags could be part of the strategy, but alone do not provide the infrastructure-level deployment capabilities needed here.

Q340: A DevOps engineer is tasked with implementing a blue-green deployment strategy for a high-availability web service running on a Linux server. Which of the following tools or techniques is least likely to be directly involved in managing the DNS switch between blue and green environments?
A) HAProxy

B) iptables

C) Route 53

D) Ansible Playbooks

E) Consul

F) Nginx

Answer: D

Explanation: In a blue-green deployment, the DNS switch between the blue and green environments is crucial for directing traffic to the correct version of the application. Tools like HAProxy, Route 53, Consul, and Nginx are commonly used to manage traffic and DNS configurations. HAProxy and Nginx can act as load balancers, Route 53 is AWS's DNS service, and Consul can be used for service discovery and health checks. These tools are directly involved in managing DNS or traffic routing. iptables, although primarily a firewall tool, can also be used to redirect traffic. Ansible Playbooks, however, are primarily used for configuration management and automation rather than direct DNS management, making them the least likely to be involved directly in the DNS switch.

Q341: A company utilizes a canary deployment strategy for their applications and has configured their Linux servers to support this approach. They have observed that the network traffic distribution does not reflect the anticipated gradual increase to the canary release. What could be a possible cause of this issue in a Linux-based environment?

A) Misconfigured load balancer

B) Incorrect DNS settings

C) Insufficient server resources

D) Outdated SSL/TLS certificates

E) Network latency issues

F) Lack of application logging

Answer: A

Explanation: A canary deployment strategy relies heavily on correctly configured network components to gradually route traffic to the new version of the application. A misconfigured load balancer could result in improper distribution of traffic, leading to either too much or too little being routed to the canary release. This would prevent the team from observing the canary release's performance under expected conditions. DNS settings typically resolve domain names and are less involved in traffic distribution. While server resources, SSL/TLS certificates, and network latency can affect application performance, they are unlikely to be the root cause of traffic distribution issues. Lack of logging would affect monitoring and debugging but not the traffic flow itself.

Q342: In a blue-green deployment strategy, the "blue" environment is currently live serving production traffic. The "green" environment has been updated with the latest release and is ready to go live. Which of the following actions should be performed next to ensure a smooth transition with minimal downtime?

A) Update the load balancer to point to the green environment

B) Deploy the code to the blue environment

C) Increase the server resources for the green environment

D) Conduct a full backup of the blue environment

E) Scale down the blue environment

F) Run integration tests on the green environment

Answer: A

Explanation: In a blue-green deployment, the transition from the current production environment (blue) to the new environment (green) involves updating the load balancer to direct traffic to the green environment. This action ensures that users are seamlessly transitioned to the updated application with minimal downtime. Deploying code to the blue environment or increasing resources are not necessary steps in the context of the transition. Conducting a backup or scaling down are precautionary and post-transition actions, while running tests on the green environment should have been completed before the transition to ensure readiness for production traffic.

Q343: True/False: In a canary deployment, the term "canary" refers to deploying a new software version to a small subset of users to monitor its performance and detect any issues before a full rollout.
A) True

B) False

Answer: A

Explanation: The term "canary" in canary deployment is derived from the historical use of canaries in coal mines to detect toxic gases. In software deployment, this concept is applied by releasing a new version of an application to a small group of users initially. This allows for monitoring the new version's behavior and performance in a real-world environment while minimizing risk. If any issues arise, the deployment can be quickly rolled back, or adjustments can be made before the software is released to the entire user base. This method provides a safeguard against widespread issues by addressing them at a smaller scale first.

Q344: A multinational corporation is using a configuration management tool to maintain consistency across its servers in different regions. The company stores its configuration management data within a centralized version control system. During an audit, it was found that some services were experiencing downtime due to configuration drifts. As a DevOps Tools Engineer, you are tasked with ensuring that configuration drifts are minimized and that all services are consistently using the most updated configuration data. What is the best practice to achieve this?
A) Implement scheduled cron jobs to manually update server configurations weekly.

B) Use a continuous integration/continuous deployment (CI/CD) pipeline to automatically apply configuration changes.

C) Rely solely on manual inspections and audits to detect configuration drifts.

D) Configure servers to pull configuration updates from the version control system at startup only.

E) Use a configuration management tool to automatically enforce the desired state of servers continuously.

F) Perform quarterly configuration reviews and make manual adjustments as necessary.

Answer: E

Explanation: The best practice for minimizing configuration drifts and ensuring consistency is to use a configuration management tool that automatically enforces the desired state of servers continuously. This approach eliminates the need for manual updates and reviews, which are prone to human error and can lead to configuration drifts. By automatically applying configuration changes, you ensure that all servers are consistently using the most updated configuration data. This method also integrates well with DevOps practices, promoting automation and efficiency in managing configurations across different environments.

Q345: In the context of Linux-based configuration management, which of the following tools is specifically designed to track changes and manage versions of configuration files?

A) Ansible

B) Chef

C) Puppet

D) Git

E) Docker

F) Kubernetes

Answer: D

Explanation: Git is a version control system specifically designed to track changes and manage versions of files, including configuration files. While Ansible, Chef, and Puppet are configuration management tools that help automate and enforce configurations, they do not inherently track versions of files. Docker and Kubernetes are containerization and orchestration tools, respectively, and do not serve the primary purpose of version control. Using Git to manage configuration files ensures that changes are tracked, versioned, and can be reverted if necessary, which is crucial for maintaining consistency and accountability in configurations.

Q346: True or False: Using configuration management data to automate server setup can significantly reduce the time to deploy new services.

A) True

B) False

Answer: A

Explanation: Automating server setup using configuration management data can significantly reduce the time required to deploy new services. By defining configurations as code, configuration management tools can automatically provision and configure servers with minimal manual intervention. This automation ensures that servers are set up quickly and consistently according to predefined specifications, reducing the risk of errors and speeding up the deployment process. This approach aligns with DevOps principles of automation and continuous delivery, enabling faster and more reliable service deployments.

Q347: Which of the following is a common practice when using configuration management tools to enhance security for Linux servers?

A) Allowing unrestricted root access for all users to facilitate quick changes.

B) Storing configuration files in plain text on the server for easy editing.

C) Using environment-specific encrypted data bags to manage sensitive information like passwords.

D) Disabling all logging to prevent sensitive information from being recorded.

E) Implementing a single configuration for all environments to reduce complexity.

F) Manually applying security patches to each server.

Answer: C

Explanation: Using environment-specific encrypted data bags to manage sensitive information like passwords is a common practice to enhance security when using configuration management tools. This approach ensures that sensitive data is encrypted and protected, reducing the risk of unauthorized access. Configuration files containing sensitive information should never be stored in plain text, and unrestricted root access poses significant security risks. Logging is crucial for auditing and should not be disabled. Applying security patches and updates should be automated rather than manual to ensure all servers are consistently secured.

Q348: You are tasked with designing a configuration management strategy for a new project that will be deployed across multiple environments (development, testing, production). The project requires different configurations for each environment, and these configurations must be maintained in a secure and efficient manner. Which approach should you take to manage these environment-specific configurations?

A) Hard-code the configurations directly into the application code.

B) Use separate configuration files for each environment with manual synchronization.

C) Store all configurations in a single file and use conditional statements to apply them.

D) Utilize environment-specific configuration files managed through a version control system.

E) Apply configurations manually to each environment to ensure precision.

F) Use a cloud-based storage solution to manage all configurations externally.

Answer: D

Explanation: Utilizing environment-specific configuration files managed through a version control system is the most efficient and secure approach for managing configurations across multiple environments. This method allows for the separation of configurations for different environments, ensuring that changes in one environment do not unintentionally affect others. By using a version control system, you can track changes, manage versions, and ensure that configurations are applied consistently and securely. Hard-coding configurations or using manual methods increases the risk of errors and reduces flexibility, while a single configuration file with conditionals can become complex and error-prone.

Q349: Your company, TechSolutions Inc., is transitioning to a DevOps model and is keen on using dashboards for real-time monitoring of their service metrics. As a DevOps engineer, you are tasked with setting up a dashboard that integrates with multiple Linux servers to visualize CPU usage, memory consumption, and network activity in a unified view. The dashboard must be capable of alerting the operations team when CPU usage exceeds 85% for more than 5 minutes. Which tool would you choose to create this dashboard efficiently, considering ease of integration with Linux and availability of alerting features?

A) Grafana

B) Kibana

C) Nagios

D) Tableau

E) Prometheus

F) Cacti

Answer: A

Explanation: Grafana is widely used for creating interactive and dynamic dashboards. It seamlessly integrates with data sources like Prometheus, which can scrape metrics from Linux servers. Grafana excels in visualizing metrics such as CPU usage, memory, and network activity. It has robust alerting capabilities that enable notifications based on predefined thresholds, such as CPU usage exceeding 85% for a specific duration. This makes it an ideal choice for TechSolutions Inc. to monitor and alert on critical service metrics within a DevOps context.

Q350: You are configuring a dashboard to visualize service metrics collected from a set of Linux servers. To ensure the dashboard provides meaningful insights, which of the following steps should you prioritize when setting up the data source for your dashboard?

A) Configure data retention policies to ensure historical data is available

B) Set up authentication to secure access to the dashboard

C) Establish a connection to a time-series database storing the metrics

D) Customize the color scheme to match the company brand

E) Enable logging for all dashboard interactions

F) Schedule regular backups of dashboard configurations

Answer: C

Explanation: Establishing a connection to a time-series database is crucial for the dashboard to access real-time and historical service metrics. Time-series databases are optimized for storing and querying time-stamped data, making them ideal for tracking system performance over time. This connection ensures that the dashboard can pull the necessary data to visualize CPU, memory, and network usage, providing insights into system behavior and trends essential for proactive management.

Q351: When setting up a visualization dashboard for Linux server metrics, it is important to ensure that the dashboard reflects real-time data accurately. Which Linux command can be used to verify the network activity metrics being collected by the dashboard?

A) top

B) df

C) netstat

D) ifconfig

E) iostat

F) vmstat

Answer: C

Explanation: The netstat command is used to display network connections, routing tables, and interface statistics. It provides a comprehensive view of the network activity on a Linux server, which is essential for verifying the accuracy of network-related metrics displayed on the dashboard. By using netstat, you can cross-reference the collected network metrics with live system data to ensure that the dashboard is displaying real-time and accurate information.

Q352: True/False: When using Grafana to visualize metrics from Linux systems, it is possible to set alerts that can trigger notifications based on specific conditions of the metric data.
A) True

B) False

Answer: A

Explanation: Grafana supports alerting functionality, allowing users to set up alerts based on specific conditions related to the metric data it visualizes. This feature is highly beneficial for monitoring systems, as it enables proactive notifications when certain thresholds are met, such as high CPU usage or memory consumption. Alerts can be configured to send notifications through various channels like email, Slack, or other integrated services, thus ensuring the operations team is promptly informed of potential issues.

Q353: A large enterprise has deployed a Grafana dashboard for visualizing service metrics from its Linux servers. They notice that the dashboard performance is sluggish and suspect the issue lies with the underlying data source configuration. Which action is most likely to improve the performance of their Grafana dashboard?

A) Increase the polling frequency of the data source

B) Aggregate data points to reduce the volume of data

C) Add more panels to the dashboard

D) Use a higher resolution for the visualizations

E) Enable debug mode in Grafana

F) Increase the number of data sources

Answer: B

Explanation: Aggregating data points can significantly improve the performance of a Grafana dashboard. By reducing the volume of data that needs to be processed and visualized, the dashboard becomes more responsive. This is achieved by summarizing data over greater intervals or using pre-aggregated metrics, which reduces the load on both the data source and the Grafana server. This approach is particularly useful in large enterprises where high-frequency data collection can lead to performance bottlenecks.

Q354: A development team at a mid-sized e-commerce company is tasked with deploying a new feature that allows users to save items for later purchase. The feature is not fully tested and the team wants to roll it out incrementally to gather user feedback and ensure system stability. They decide to use feature flags to manage this deployment. What is the most effective way to implement feature flags for this scenario in a Linux environment?

A) Use a simple configuration file in the application directory to toggle the feature on and off.

B) Implement a database-driven feature flag system to allow real-time updates without redeploying the application.

C) Hardcode the feature flags into the application binary for increased security.

D) Use environment variables to control the feature flags, ensuring changes can be made without code modifications.

E) Deploy the feature to a separate server and route traffic selectively to that server.

F) Use a cloud provider's proprietary feature flagging service to manage the feature rollout.

Answer: B

Explanation: Implementing a database-driven feature flag system is the most effective approach in this scenario. By using a database, the team can update feature flags in real-time without needing to redeploy the application, providing them with the flexibility to enable or disable features quickly based on user feedback or system performance. This method also allows for more granular control, such as enabling the feature for a specific percentage of users or for specific user segments. While environment variables offer some flexibility, they require application restarts to take effect and lack the granularity offered by a database-driven approach. Hardcoding feature flags into the binary or using configuration files require redeployment and are not as dynamic. Routing traffic to a separate server complicates the architecture and may lead to inconsistency in user experience.

Q355: True or False: Feature flags can only be used for enabling or disabling features in a Linux environment.
A) True

B) False

Answer: B

Explanation: Feature flags are versatile tools that can be used for more than just enabling or disabling features. In a Linux environment, they can be employed to perform various functions such as facilitating A/B testing, enabling canary releases, and managing configuration changes without redeploying code. Feature flags can also assist in rolling back features quickly if issues arise, without affecting the rest of the system. They provide a mechanism for dynamic and granular control over the application behavior, making them a crucial part of modern DevOps practices.

Q356: In a microservices architecture deployed on Linux servers, a company wants to use feature flags to manage service dependencies. What is the best practice to ensure feature flags do not become a single point of failure?

A) Store feature flags in a centralized configuration management tool with high availability.

B) Use a distributed file system to store feature flags across all nodes.

C) Include feature flag configurations within each microservice's Docker container.

D) Cache feature flag values in memory to reduce dependency on external systems.

E) Use a separate microservice solely for managing feature flags.

F) Implement circuit breaker patterns within the application code.

Answer: A

Explanation: Storing feature flags in a centralized configuration management tool with high availability is the best practice to ensure they do not become a single point of failure. This approach provides resilience and redundancy, minimizing the risk of downtime if a single instance fails. High availability ensures that the feature flag management system can withstand failures and continue to operate, thus maintaining the stability and reliability of the service deployments. Distributed file systems and caching in memory may offer some benefits, but they do not provide the same level of robustness and may lead to inconsistency or stale data if not carefully managed.

Q357: During a complex deployment process on a Linux server, how can feature flags be used to mitigate risk and ensure a smooth release?

A) By using them to manage server resource allocation dynamically based on feature usage.

B) By deploying all new features at once and using feature flags to disable them if issues arise.

C) By controlling the rollout of new features to a small subset of users before a full release.

D) By using feature flags to test performance under peak load conditions.

E) By implementing them to switch between different database configurations seamlessly.

F) By leveraging them to automate the rollback process if the deployment fails.

Answer: C

Explanation: Using feature flags to control the rollout of new features to a small subset of users before a full release is an effective way to mitigate risk and ensure a smooth deployment. This strategy, often referred to as a canary release, allows the team to gather early feedback, monitor system performance, and identify potential issues in a controlled environment. If any problems are detected, the feature can be quickly disabled or adjusted before a wider audience is affected. This approach reduces the impact of potential failures and increases the likelihood of a successful deployment. Deploying all features at once increases risk, while dynamically managing resources or testing load conditions are indirect benefits rather than primary mitigation strategies.

Q358: When implementing feature flags in a Linux-based continuous integration/continuous deployment (CI/CD) pipeline, what is a critical factor to consider to ensure seamless integration and operation?

A) Ensuring feature flags are embedded directly within the source code repository.

B) Integrating feature flag checks within automated test scripts to validate feature behavior.

C) Using a third-party API to fetch feature flag states during deployment.

D) Maintaining a version-controlled feature flag configuration file.

E) Allowing each team member to modify feature flags as needed.

F) Storing feature flags in system environment variables for easy access.

Answer: B

Explanation: Integrating feature flag checks within automated test scripts is critical to validate feature behavior during the CI/CD process. This ensures that any changes in feature flags do not introduce unexpected behavior or regressions in the application. Automated tests can verify that features behave as expected when enabled or disabled, providing an additional layer of assurance before the deployment reaches production. While version-controlling feature flag configurations and using APIs can facilitate management, they do not directly address the need for validating application behavior. Allowing unrestricted modifications or embedding flags in the source code can lead to inconsistencies and potential deployment issues.

Q359: Your company has recently deployed a new web application that generates a large volume of logs daily. The logs are stored in multiple formats across different servers running Linux. The development team requires a centralized log management solution that allows them to easily search, filter, and analyze logs in real-time. Additionally, they need to be able to set alerts for specific log events. Which tool would best meet these requirements?

A) Logrotate

B) ELK Stack (Elasticsearch, Logstash, Kibana)

C) Syslog-ng

D) Rsyslog

E) Fluentd

F) Splunk

Answer: B

Explanation: The ELK Stack, consisting of Elasticsearch, Logstash, and Kibana, is a powerful suite of tools designed for log management. Elasticsearch is a search and analytics engine that can handle large volumes of data, Logstash is used for data processing and can collect logs from various sources, and Kibana provides a user-friendly interface for visualizing and analyzing logs. This stack is ideal for real-time log analysis, searching, and filtering, and it supports alerting through integration with tools like ElastAlert. In contrast, tools like Logrotate focus on log rotation for disk space management, and Syslog-ng and Rsyslog primarily handle log forwarding and collection without the advanced search and visualization capabilities of the ELK Stack.

Q360: A DevOps engineer wants to ensure that logs from a Linux server are forwarded to a central log management server. The server should use the default syslog protocol, and the configuration should be consistent with traditional syslog facilities. Which configuration file should the engineer modify to achieve this?

A) /etc/logrotate.conf

B) /etc/rsyslog.conf

C) /etc/syslog-ng/syslog-ng.conf

D) /etc/sysconfig/syslog

E) /etc/journal/journald.conf

F) /etc/elasticsearch/elasticsearch.yml

Answer: B

Explanation: The rsyslog service is a modern replacement for the traditional syslog service, providing advanced log processing capabilities while maintaining compatibility with traditional syslog protocols and facilities. The configuration file for rsyslog is typically located at /etc/rsyslog.conf. This file allows users to define rules for log forwarding, filtering, and processing. By modifying /etc/rsyslog.conf, a DevOps engineer can configure a Linux server to forward logs to a central log management server using the syslog protocol. Other options, such as /etc/logrotate.conf and /etc/journal/journald.conf, are related to log rotation and journal management, respectively, and do not pertain to syslog forwarding.

Q361: True/False: Fluentd is primarily designed for handling structured data, and it natively supports data collection from various sources, including databases, application logs, and system metrics.
A) True

B) False

Answer: A

Explanation: Fluentd is an open-source data collector designed for flexible and high-performance log and data processing. It is particularly well-suited for handling structured data and can collect logs from a wide range of sources, including application logs, databases, and system metrics. Fluentd uses a plugin architecture that supports over 500 plugins, enabling it to adapt to various data collection needs. Its ability to unify data collection and consumption allows for efficient log management and analysis, making it a popular choice for DevOps environments where integrated data processing is crucial.

Q362: A systems administrator needs to ensure that log files on a Linux server do not consume excessive disk space. The administrator decides to implement log rotation to automatically archive and compress logs. Which tool is best suited for this task, and how should it be configured for daily rotation?
A) Use the 'logrotate' tool with a 'daily' parameter in the configuration file.

B) Configure 'rsyslog' to limit log file sizes and rotate logs daily.

C) Use 'journalctl' with a size limit and daily rotation settings.

D) Set up 'syslog-ng' with daily rotation policies.

E) Implement 'fluentd' with file size and rotation plugins.

F) Use 'Logwatch' to manage log size and rotation.

Answer: A

Explanation: Logrotate is a widely-used utility on Linux systems for managing the automatic rotation and compression of log files. It is specifically designed to ease the administration of systems that generate large numbers of log files. By configuring logrotate with the 'daily' parameter in its configuration file, a systems administrator can set up daily rotation of log files. This helps in managing disk space effectively by archiving and, optionally, compressing old log files. While tools like rsyslog and syslog-ng can forward logs, they do not provide built-in log rotation and compression capabilities like logrotate does. Journalctl is used for viewing logs managed by systemd's journal, and fluentd focuses on log collection and processing, not rotation.

Q363: A technology startup wants to implement a scalable and distributed log management solution that can filter and process logs in real-time before sending them to a centralized log storage. They also want the solution to be highly extensible with plugins. Which tool should they choose?

A) Graylog

B) Logstash

C) Logrotate

D) Rsyslog

E) Kibana

F) Journalctl

Answer: B

Explanation: Logstash is part of the ELK Stack and is designed for real-time log collection, filtering, and processing. It is highly extensible and supports a wide range of plugins, making it ideal for a scalable and distributed log management solution. Logstash can collect logs from various sources, process them with its powerful filtering capabilities, and then forward them to a centralized storage, such as Elasticsearch, for indexing and analysis. Unlike Logrotate, which focuses on log rotation, or Kibana, which is used for visualization, Logstash provides the necessary functionality for real-time log processing and extensibility through plugins. Graylog is also a log management tool but is less suited for real-time processing compared to Logstash.

Q364: A software company is developing a new web application that will be deployed across multiple environments: development, testing, staging, and production. The staging environment is used to perform final testing before moving to production. It is crucial that the staging environment mirrors production as closely as possible to ensure any issues are identified and resolved prior to deployment. The company is using Docker containers to manage their applications. However, they notice that some configurations differ between staging and production, leading to unexpected behavior during deployment. What is the best practice to ensure that the staging environment accurately replicates the production environment using Docker?

A) Use separate Dockerfiles for staging and production with different configurations.

B) Create environment-specific scripts to modify container configurations post-deployment.

C) Utilize Docker Compose with environment variables to manage different settings for staging and production.

D) Manually adjust Docker container settings in the staging environment to match production.

E) Use a configuration management tool like Ansible to deploy containers with consistent configurations across environments.

F) Set up a cron job to periodically synchronize configuration files between staging and production.

Answer: C

Explanation: To ensure that the staging environment closely mirrors the production environment, it is essential to maintain consistency in configurations across both environments. Utilizing Docker Compose with environment variables is an effective approach to achieve this. By defining environment variables in a .env file or using Docker Compose's built-in support for environment-specific configurations, you can manage different settings for each environment without modifying the Dockerfiles. This method allows for easy swapping of configurations based on the environment, ensuring that staging accurately replicates production. Additionally, this approach minimizes manual intervention and reduces the risk of human error, providing a more streamlined and automated process for deploying consistent configurations across environments.

Q365: In a Linux-based application deployment pipeline, a staging environment is designed to test new updates before they are moved to production. Which practice can help ensure that the state of the application in staging is as close to production as possible?

A) Regularly snapshot the production database and restore it to the staging environment.

B) Update the staging environment only when there are major changes to the application.

C) Use a different operating system in staging to test compatibility across platforms.

D) Deploy to the staging environment after every commit to the version control system.

E) Only deploy security patches to the staging environment to avoid unnecessary changes.

F) Disable logging in the staging environment to improve performance.

Answer: A

Explanation: To ensure that the staging environment is as close to production as possible, regularly snapshotting the production database and restoring it to the staging environment is a critical practice. This approach helps maintain data consistency and ensures that any issues related to data handling, schema changes, or data integrity can be identified and addressed in staging before reaching production. It allows testers to work with real-world data scenarios, making the testing process more realistic and relevant. While frequent deployment to staging (e.g., after every commit) is beneficial for testing code changes, data consistency is best achieved through regular database synchronization between production and staging.

Q366: A team of DevOps engineers is responsible for managing a complex microservices architecture, hosted on a Linux-based cloud platform. They have implemented a staging environment to test microservices interactions before any production deployment. The team wants to ensure that their staging environment can also simulate traffic patterns similar to production. Which tool or method would be most appropriate for achieving this goal?

A) Use a HTTP load testing tool like Apache JMeter to simulate traffic in staging.

B) Implement a cron job that randomly triggers service endpoints in staging.

C) Utilize a network monitoring tool to observe traffic in production and manually replicate it in staging.

D) Employ a simple curl script to generate requests to staging endpoints periodically.

E) Set up a separate load balancer specifically for the staging environment.

F) Use a packet analyzer like Wireshark to clone production traffic into staging.

Answer: A

Explanation: Using a HTTP load testing tool like Apache JMeter is the most appropriate method for simulating traffic patterns in a staging environment. JMeter allows the team to create realistic load scenarios that mimic production traffic, including concurrent users, request rates, and complex workflows. By designing test plans that replicate production traffic patterns, the team can evaluate the performance and interactions of microservices under load, identify bottlenecks, and ensure the reliability of the application before deploying to production. Other methods, such as using curl scripts or cron jobs, do not provide the same level of control and sophistication in simulating realistic traffic patterns.

Q367: A DevOps engineer is tasked with setting up a new staging environment for a web application that uses multiple services and databases. The engineer decides to use a configuration management tool to automate the setup process, ensuring consistency and repeatability. Which of the following tools is NOT typically used for configuration management in this context?   Question 5 (True/False): In a Linux-based deployment pipeline, using a staging environment is essential for ensuring that any changes made in production will not cause unexpected issues or downtime.

A) Ansible

B) Puppet

C) Chef

D) Terraform

E) SaltStack

F) Git

Answer: A

Explanation: The use of a staging environment is a critical component in a Linux-based deployment pipeline, especially for complex applications. By having a staging environment that closely mirrors production, organizations can test new features, updates, and configurations in a controlled setting before deploying them to production. This practice helps identify and resolve potential issues that could lead to downtime or unexpected behavior in production. It acts as a safety net, allowing teams to validate changes and ensure that they meet quality standards without impacting end-users. Staging environments help mitigate risks associated with deployment, ultimately contributing to the stability and reliability of the production environment.

Q368: Your company is adopting a microservices architecture to enhance its e-commerce platform. Each service is managed by a dedicated team, and each team is responsible for the deployment and maintenance of its own service. The company has decided to use Git as the version control system for managing service configurations. Considering the need for collaboration, traceability, and rollback capabilities, what is the best practice for organizing the Git repositories to manage these configurations effectively?

A) Use a single repository for all services and configurations.

B) Use one repository per service, including both code and configurations.

C) Use a monorepo with submodules for each service configuration.

D) Use a separate repository for all configurations, distinct from code repositories.

E) Use feature branches within a single repository for each service.

F) Use a single repository with a distinct branch for each service.

Answer: B

Explanation: Using one repository per service, including both code and configurations, allows for modularity and independence in the management and deployment of each microservice. This structure supports the microservices architecture by enabling each team to work autonomously on their respective services. It enhances traceability, as each service's history is isolated to its repository, and facilitates rollback if needed. Having both code and configurations in the same repository simplifies version control and deployment processes, ensuring that the correct version of the configuration is always used with the code. This approach also aligns well with CI/CD practices, allowing each team to manage their deployment pipelines independently without affecting other services.

Q369: In a DevOps environment, which command would you use to clone a remote Git repository that contains service configurations onto your local machine?

A) git init

B) git commit

C) git clone

D) git pull

E) git fetch

F) git config

Answer: C

Explanation: The 'git clone' command is used to create a copy of an existing Git repository from a remote server onto a local machine. This is the first step in working with a repository, as it downloads all the files, branches, and commits from the remote repository. The 'git clone' command is essential for setting up a local development environment where you can make changes to service configurations, test them locally, and eventually push changes back to the remote repository. This process is central to managing configurations in a version-controlled manner, allowing for collaborative development and precise configuration management.

Q370: True or False: In a configuration management process using Git, it is best practice to commit large binary files directly into the repository to ensure all necessary assets are versioned.
A) True

B) False

Answer: B

Explanation: It is not advisable to commit large binary files directly into a Git repository because Git is optimized for tracking text changes rather than binary changes. Large binary files can significantly increase the repository size, slow down operations, and reduce performance. Instead, it is better to use Git LFS (Large File Storage) or store large assets in an external storage system designed for handling binaries, and then link them to the repository. This practice maintains the efficiency of Git operations and ensures that the repository remains manageable and performant for all users involved in the configuration management process.

Q371: While managing service configurations, you need to ensure that sensitive information such as API keys and passwords are not exposed in the Git repository. Which method is the most secure approach to prevent this from happening?

A) Include sensitive information in the .gitignore file.

B) Use Git hooks to remove sensitive information before committing.

C) Encrypt sensitive files before adding them to the repository.

D) Store sensitive information in environment variables, not in the repository.

E) Use a separate branch for sensitive information.

F) Use Git's built-in encryption feature for sensitive files.

Answer: D

Explanation: The most secure approach to prevent exposing sensitive information like API keys and passwords in a Git repository is to store such data in environment variables, rather than in the repository itself. This method keeps sensitive data out of the version control system entirely, minimizing the risk of accidental exposure. Environment variables can be managed securely in deployment tools or platforms, ensuring that the correct values are injected into applications at runtime. This method also aligns with best practices for configuration management, where configuration values are separated from the codebase to maintain security and flexibility across different environments.

Q372: A company is using Git to manage multiple configuration files for its Linux-based web services. To streamline the deployment process, they decide to implement Infrastructure as Code (IaC) practices. Which Git feature would be most beneficial in tracking changes to the infrastructure configurations over time and ensuring consistent deployment across environments?

A) Git branches

B) Git tags

C) Git submodules

D) Git merge

E) Git stash

F) Git rebase

Answer: B

Explanation: Git tags are particularly beneficial for tracking changes to infrastructure configurations over time and ensuring consistent deployment across environments. Tags in Git are used to mark specific points in the repository's history as important, which is often done to indicate a release or a stable version of the configuration. By tagging a commit that represents a stable and tested configuration, teams can easily reference and deploy consistent versions across different environments. This practice is an essential part of implementing Infrastructure as Code, as it ensures that deployments are reproducible and that any changes to infrastructure can be traced and audited over time. Tags provide a clear history of releases and are integral to maintaining a reliable deployment pipeline in a DevOps environment.

Q373: A company is using Vagrant to manage virtualized environments for its development team. The team has been tasked with setting up a new Vagrant environment that will automatically configure network settings to provide an IP address accessible from the host machine. This IP should be consistent regardless of where the Vagrant file is executed, and should allow SSH access from the host. The development environment must be isolated, with no direct access to the external internet for security reasons. Which Vagrant networking feature should the team use to meet these requirements?
A) Public network

B) Private network

C) Bridged network

D) Forwarded port

E) Host-only network

F) NAT network

Answer: B

Explanation: To meet the requirement of a consistent and accessible IP address from the host machine, the Vagrant private network option is the most suitable. A private network provides a stable IP address that is only accessible from the host machine, making it ideal for environments that need to be isolated from the external internet for security reasons. Unlike public or bridged networks, which connect to external networks, a private network ensures that the virtual machine is only accessible to the host, fulfilling the security constraint. Forwarded ports and NAT networks do not provide a consistent IP address and are more suited for different use cases, such as accessing specific services or enabling general internet access from the guest, respectively.

Q374: When using Vagrant to manage virtual machines, which command would you use to store the current state and configuration of a virtual machine so that it can be easily restored later?

A) vagrant save

B) vagrant backup

C) vagrant snapshot save

D) vagrant archive

E) vagrant export

F) vagrant pause

Answer: C

Explanation: The vagrant snapshot save command is used to capture the current state of a virtual machine managed by Vagrant. This snapshot can later be restored, allowing users to revert the virtual machine to the exact state it was in when the snapshot was taken. This is particularly useful for testing and development environments where consistent states need to be maintained or reverted to after changes. Other options like vagrant save or vagrant backup are not valid Vagrant commands, and vagrant export is used for packaging the environment into a reusable box, not for state management.

Q375: True or False: The Vagrantfile is a Ruby-based DSL (Domain Specific Language) file that allows users to configure and control all aspects of Vagrant environments, including storage, networking, and provisioning.
A) True

B) False

Answer: A

Explanation: The Vagrantfile is indeed a Ruby-based Domain Specific Language file that allows users to control various aspects of their Vagrant environments. This includes setting up virtual machine configurations such as CPU, memory, and storage, as well as configuring networking options like private and public networks. Additionally, the Vagrantfile is used to define provisioning scripts or tools, such as shell scripts or configuration management tools like Ansible or Puppet, to automate the setup of the environment. The flexibility and power of the Vagrantfile come from its basis in Ruby, which allows for complex logic and customization.

Q376: A development team is using Vagrant to create virtual environments for testing. They need to configure a shared folder between the host and guest machine that automatically updates on both ends when changes occur. Which Vagrant feature should the team use to achieve this functionality?
A) NFS synced folder

B) RSync synced folder

C) SMB synced folder

D) VirtualBox shared folder

E) GuestAdditions shared folder

F) FUSE mount

Answer: A

Explanation: The NFS (Network File System) synced folder feature in Vagrant allows for high-performance file sharing between the host and guest machines. It ensures that changes made in the shared folder on one side are automatically reflected on the other side. While RSync is another option, it is not suitable for real-time synchronization, as it requires manual or timed syncing. SMB and VirtualBox shared folders can also be used, but NFS is typically preferred for its performance and reliability, especially in Unix-based systems where NFS is native.

Q377: A company has several developers working on different operating systems, including Linux, Windows, and macOS. They need to ensure that all developers can access a shared Vagrant environment with consistent networking settings. Which Vagrant networking feature should be configured to ensure this level of cross-platform compatibility and access?
A) Public network with DHCP

B) Private network with static IP

C) Host-only network

D) Bridged network

E) NAT network with port forwarding

F) Internal network

Answer: E

Explanation: To ensure cross-platform compatibility and consistent access across different operating systems, a NAT network with port forwarding is the best option. This setup allows developers to access the Vagrant environment using a common port on their host machines, regardless of the underlying operating system. NAT provides an easy way to map host ports to guest ports, ensuring that services running inside the Vagrant environment are reachable from the host. This method is preferred over private or host-only networks, which might not offer the same level of flexibility and ease of configuration across different platforms.

Q378: You are a DevOps engineer at a large e-commerce company responsible for managing the infrastructure used by the development teams. The company uses Vagrant for creating and configuring lightweight, reproducible, and portable development environments. Recently, there has been a requirement to provision a virtual machine with a specific file structure and some configuration files necessary for the application to run. These files need to be copied from the host machine to the guest machine upon provisioning. You also need to ensure that this setup is automated and easily repeatable by different team members on their local machines. Which Vagrant provisioner would be the most appropriate to achieve this requirement?   ---
A) Shell

B) File

C) Ansible

D) Docker

E) Puppet

F) Chef

Answer: B

Explanation: The File provisioner in Vagrant is designed specifically to copy files and directories from the host machine to the guest machine. This makes it ideal for transferring configuration files, scripts, or any other necessary files that need to be present on the guest machine for the application to function correctly. The File provisioner ensures that the files are copied over at the time of provisioning, making the setup automated and consistent across different environments. Although other provisioners like Shell or Ansible can also accomplish file transfers, they are not as straightforward or efficient for simple file copying tasks as the File provisioner.

Q379: In a Vagrant-based environment, you need to ensure that upon provisioning, a set of initialization scripts is executed on the guest machine to install necessary software packages and perform system configurations. These scripts should be run with elevated privileges to ensure they can modify system settings and install software as required. Which Vagrant provisioner is best suited for executing these initialization scripts?   ---

A) File

B) Shell

C) Ansible

D) Docker

E) Puppet

F) Nginx

Answer: B

Explanation: The Shell provisioner in Vagrant allows you to run shell scripts on the guest machine, which is perfect for executing initialization scripts that install software packages and perform system configurations. The Shell provisioner can be configured to run scripts as a specific user, including with elevated privileges (e.g., using sudo), which is essential for tasks that require administrative access. While other provisioners like Ansible or Puppet can also manage system configurations, the Shell provisioner is the simplest and most direct method for running custom scripts during the provisioning process.

Q380: A company is transitioning to a microservices architecture and has decided to use Vagrant for local development environments. Developers need to test their microservices locally within Docker containers, and the development environment must be provisioned using a tool that supports Docker. Which Vagrant provisioner should be used to manage these Docker containers within the Vagrant environment?   ---

A) Shell

B) File

C) Ansible

D) Docker

E) Puppet

F) Kubernetes

Answer: D

Explanation: The Docker provisioner in Vagrant allows you to manage Docker containers directly within the Vagrant environment. This provisioner is specifically designed for interacting with Docker, enabling you to build, run, and manage containers as part of the Vagrant provisioning process. This integration is particularly useful in a microservices architecture where services are containerized, as it allows developers to replicate production-like environments on their local machines. The Docker provisioner simplifies the process of configuring and running Docker containers, making it the ideal choice for this scenario.

Q381: An organization is using Vagrant to manage virtual machine environments for development and testing. They have a requirement to use Ansible for configuration management and application deployment directly within the Vagrant provisioning process. This setup should not require Ansible to be pre-installed on the host machine. Is it possible to use the Ansible Local provisioner in this scenario?   ---

A) True

B) False

Answer: A

Explanation: The Ansible Local provisioner in Vagrant is designed to work within the guest machine, which means that Ansible does not need to be installed on the host machine. Instead, Ansible is installed and executed on the guest machine during the provisioning process. This is particularly useful in environments where installing Ansible on the host is not feasible or desirable. By using the Ansible Local provisioner, the configuration management and application deployment can be handled entirely within the Vagrant-managed virtual machine, ensuring consistency and reducing dependencies on the host environment.

Q382: You are tasked with setting up a development environment using Vagrant where different team members need to provision their environments using the same configuration management tool. The environment should be able to handle complex orchestration tasks and integrate well with various cloud providers. Which Vagrant provisioner would be best suited for this requirement to manage complex deployments and cloud integrations?

A) Shell

B) File

C) Ansible

D) Docker

E) Puppet

F) Terraform

Answer: C

Explanation: Ansible is a powerful configuration management tool that excels in handling complex orchestration tasks and integrates well with various cloud providers and services.

When used as a Vagrant provisioner, Ansible can manage not only the local development environment but also more complex infrastructure setups, including those involving cloud resources. Ansible's agentless architecture and extensive module library make it a versatile choice for managing a wide range of tasks and environments. While Terraform is also capable of managing infrastructure, it is not a Vagrant provisioner like Ansible, which integrates directly into the Vagrant workflow for provisioning and managing development environments.

Q383: A mid-sized e-commerce company is experiencing fluctuations in its web application performance, impacting customer experience. The DevOps team has decided to implement Prometheus to monitor application metrics and ensure real-time visibility into system health. They plan to use nodeexporter to collect hardware and OS metrics and push them to Prometheus. However, the team is unsure about how to configure Prometheus to scrape these metrics efficiently. As an experienced DevOps engineer, you are tasked with setting up the Prometheus configuration file. Which parameter in Prometheus's configuration file allows you to define the frequency at which Prometheus scrapes metrics from nodeexporter?

A) scrapeinterval

B) scrapetimeout

C) targetduration

D) jobname

E) staticconfigs

F) relabelconfigs

Answer: A

Explanation: Prometheus's configuration file, typically named prometheus.yml, includes a section where you define the scrape configuration for each job. The scrapeinterval parameter specifies how often Prometheus should scrape metrics from the target endpoints, such as nodeexporter. By default, this is set to 15 seconds but can be adjusted to meet the performance and monitoring needs of your application. This parameter is crucial for setting the right balance between the freshness of data and the load on the network and systems. Other parameters like scrapetimeout define how long Prometheus waits for a response from the target, whereas jobname is used to label the job for identification purposes.

Q384: In Prometheus, which of the following mechanisms can be used to aggregate time-series data to provide a summarized view of the metrics, such as calculating average CPU usage over a period?

A) Alertmanager

B) PromQL

C) Nodeexporter

D) Grafana

E) Blackboxexporter

F) Pushgateway

Answer: B

Explanation: Prometheus Query Language (PromQL) is a powerful query language used by Prometheus to select and aggregate time-series data. It allows you to perform operations like calculating averages, sums, or rates over a defined time window, providing essential insights into your metrics. PromQL supports various functions and operators to manipulate the collected data and create meaningful visualizations or alerts. While Alertmanager is used for managing alerts, Grafana is for visualization, and exporters are for collecting metrics, PromQL is specifically designed for querying and aggregating metrics data.

Q385: Which of the following statements is true regarding Prometheus's approach to data storage and retrieval?

A) Prometheus stores data as JSON files on disk.

B) Prometheus uses a push-based model to retrieve metrics.

C) Prometheus stores time-series data in a custom database on disk.

D) Prometheus only supports storing metrics in third-party databases.

E) Prometheus uses SNMP to store and retrieve metrics data.

F) Prometheus stores data in a NoSQL database.

Answer: C

Explanation: Prometheus is designed to store time-series data efficiently using its own custom database format on disk. It employs a pull-based model where it scrapes data from defined endpoints at specified intervals. This approach ensures that Prometheus can efficiently manage and retrieve large volumes of metrics data. The custom database is specifically optimized for time-series data, allowing for high-performance storage and retrieval operations. Prometheus does not rely on external databases for its core functionality, although integrations exist for exporting data to other systems.

Q386: In a situation where you need to monitor HTTP endpoints for availability and response time using Prometheus, which component would you use to achieve this?
A) Nodeexporter

B) Alertmanager

C) Blackboxexporter

D) Grafana

E) PromQL

F) Thanos

Answer: C

Explanation: The Blackboxexporter is a specialized Prometheus exporter designed to probe endpoints for availability and response time. It supports multiple protocols, including HTTP,

HTTPS, DNS, TCP, and ICMP, making it versatile for monitoring different types of endpoints. Blackboxexporter allows you to define probe configurations in Prometheus, which then scrapes results from the exporter. This capability is essential for ensuring that your application endpoints are accessible and perform within acceptable response times. While nodeexporter collects system-level metrics, Blackboxexporter is specifically tailored for endpoint monitoring.

Q387: True or False: Prometheus can only alert based on real-time metric evaluations and does not support alerting based on historical data patterns.

A) True

B) False

Answer: B

Explanation: Prometheus supports alerting based on both real-time metric evaluations and historical data patterns. Through the use of PromQL, Prometheus can evaluate metrics over time and trigger alerts based on predefined rules and conditions. This capability allows you to detect anomalies or trends that deviate from expected patterns, thus enabling proactive monitoring and response. By analyzing historical data, Prometheus can generate alerts for issues that develop gradually, such as increasing error rates or resource usage, rather than just real-time spikes or drops. This flexibility in alerting makes Prometheus a powerful tool for comprehensive monitoring strategies.

Q388: A startup company has just migrated its infrastructure to the cloud and is leveraging cloud-init for initial server configuration. They require each new instance to automatically configure a specific partition scheme, resize the root partition, and mount an additional data volume. Additionally, they need to ensure that the primary user account is set up with SSH key authentication for secure access. The company's DevOps team also wants to automate the installation of essential software packages from the distribution's repository as part of the instance initialization. Which cloud-init configuration file snippet accomplishes these tasks?   ---

A) Configures the partition scheme, resizes the root partition, mounts the data volume, sets up user accounts, and installs packages.

B) Only resizes the root partition and mounts the data volume, but does not configure user accounts or install packages.

C) Configures user accounts and installs packages but fails to resize or mount any partitions.

D) Focuses solely on installing packages without addressing any partition or user account configurations.

E) Partially configures the partition scheme but does not include user account setup or package installation.

F) Only sets up SSH key authentication without touching partition configurations or package installations.

Answer: A

Explanation: In cloud-init, the configuration is usually defined in YAML syntax within a configuration file or included in the user data when launching the instance. The correct configuration to achieve all the tasks mentioned would involve several sections. The disksetup and fssetup modules allow defining and formatting partitions. For resizing the root partition, the growpart module is used. Mounting additional volumes is managed by the mounts module. User accounts, including SSH key setup, are handled in the users section of cloud-init configuration. Finally, package installation is facilitated by the packageupdate and packageupgrade directives, where necessary packages can be listed under packages. This comprehensive approach ensures all requirements are met during the initialization process.

Q389: To configure a new server instance with cloud-init, a DevOps engineer needs to ensure that the /dev/sdb device is formatted with the ext4 filesystem and mounted on /data. Which cloud-init configuration module should be used to achieve this?   ---

A) disksetup

B) fssetup

C) mounts

D) growpart

E) bootcmd

F) runcmd

Answer: B

Explanation: The fssetup module in cloud-init is specifically designed to handle filesystem creation on block devices. It allows the user to define which device should be formatted and with which filesystem type, such as ext4 in this case. This configuration is crucial for setting up the initial filesystem on a new device and is separate from mounting, which is handled by the mounts module. The disksetup module, on the other hand, is used for partitioning tasks, and growpart is involved in resizing partitions. The bootcmd and runcmd sections are for executing commands but are not specific to filesystem setups.

Q390: A company needs to automate the creation of a user account with a specific username and authorized SSH key on all newly launched cloud instances. Which section of a cloud-init configuration file should be used to define this user account?   ---

A) writefiles

B) runcmd

C) users

D) mounts

E) packageupdate

F) bootcmd

Answer: C

Explanation: The users section of a cloud-init configuration is explicitly designed for managing user accounts on a system. This section allows the specification of user details such as username, groups, home directory, and SSH keys for secure access. By defining a user in the users section, the account is created during the instance's initialization, ensuring the automated setup of login credentials. The writefiles section is for creating files, and runcmd is for executing commands post-boot. mounts is unrelated to user configuration, while packageupdate and bootcmd are concerned with package management and boot time commands, respectively.

Q391: True or False: Cloud-init can be used to automate software installations from a distribution's repository during the instance's initialization process. ---
A) True

B) False

Answer: A

Explanation: Cloud-init is a versatile tool used to automate various configurations during the initialization of cloud instances, including the installation of software packages. This is achieved through configuration modules such as packageupdate, packageupgrade, and packages, which are specifically designed to update package indices, upgrade existing packages, and install new software from the distribution's repositories. By specifying the required packages in the cloud-init configuration, the software is automatically installed as part of the instance setup, ensuring a consistent and repeatable environment across multiple instances.

Q392: An organization is leveraging cloud-init to ensure that all new cloud instances have the latest security updates applied upon startup. Which cloud-init directive should be used to achieve this goal?

A) writefiles

B) runcmd

C) packageupdate

D) bootcmd

E) users

F) fssetup

Answer: C

Explanation: The packageupdate directive in cloud-init is used to update the package index files, ensuring that the system is aware of the latest available versions of packages. By including this directive in the cloud-init configuration, the system will automatically check for and apply the latest security updates when the instance starts. This is a critical step for maintaining system security in cloud environments. While runcmd and bootcmd can execute commands, they are not specifically tailored for package management. writefiles, users, and fssetup have different functionalities unrelated to package updates.

Q393: Your company is working on a large-scale software development project involving multiple teams spread across different geographical locations. The project is hosted on a Git repository, and one of the teams is responsible for a specific module that is frequently updated. To maintain a clean and manageable project structure, you decide to use Git submodules for this particular module. The team needs to ensure that they can pull the latest changes from the main repository as well as update the submodule to reflect any new changes. How should the team proceed to correctly update the main repository and the submodule, ensuring both are synchronized with the latest changes?

A) Use git submodule update --remote to update submodules and git pull to update the main repository.

B) Use git pull --recurse-submodules to update both the main repository and submodules.

C) Execute git fetch followed by git submodule sync for the submodules.

D) Perform git submodule update --init --recursive followed by git fetch.

E) Run git submodule foreach git pull to update submodules, then git pull for the main repository.

F) Use git clone --recursive to clone the repository along with its submodules.

Answer: B

Explanation: When working with Git repositories that include submodules, it is important to keep both the main repository and its submodules up to date with the latest changes. The git pull --recurse-submodules command is specifically designed for this purpose. It not only pulls changes from the main repository but also ensures that submodules are updated to their latest commits as specified by the superproject. This approach simplifies the process for developers, allowing them to synchronize both the main project and its submodules in a single command, avoiding potential inconsistencies or outdated code in the submodules.

Q394: In Git, when attempting to push changes to a remote repository, you encounter an error due to outdated local branches that haven't been synchronized with the remote branches. What command can be used to fetch and prune stale branches, ensuring that your local repository is synchronized with the remote repository's current state?

A) git prune

B) git remote update --prune

C) git fetch --prune

D) git pull --prune

E) git clean -fd

F) git gc --prune=now

Answer: C

Explanation: The git fetch --prune command is used to clean up stale references in your local repository. When branches on the remote repository are deleted, corresponding remote-tracking branches may remain in your local repository, leading to potential confusion and errors. By using git fetch with the --prune option, Git automatically removes these outdated references, ensuring that your local view of the remote repository is accurate and up-to-date. This is particularly useful when you need to maintain a clean branch structure and prevent errors during operations such as pushing or merging.

Q395: A DevOps team is tasked with managing a complex project that includes multiple third-party libraries. These libraries are stored as submodules in a Git repository. The team wants to ensure that whenever they clone the main repository, all necessary submodules are also cloned and initialized automatically. Which Git command should they use to achieve this?

A) git clone --recursive

B) git submodule update --init --recursive

C) git submodule add

D) git clone

E) git submodule init

F) git fetch --recurse-submodules

Answer: A

Explanation: To ensure that all submodules are cloned and initialized automatically when cloning a repository, the git clone --recursive command is the most effective choice. This command not only clones the main repository but also initializes and updates each submodule according to the configuration of the superproject. This approach streamlines the setup process for developers, ensuring that all dependencies and modules are ready for use immediately after the initial clone, without requiring additional manual steps to initialize submodules.

Q396: A company is developing a distributed application where different features are developed in isolated branches. To keep the development consistent and avoid integration issues, developers are required to frequently rebase their branches with the main branch. What is a common Git command sequence to accomplish a rebase operation from a feature branch onto the main branch?

A) git checkout main && git pull && git checkout feature && git rebase main

B) git checkout feature && git rebase main

C) git checkout main && git merge feature

D) git checkout feature && git fetch origin && git rebase origin/main

E) git fetch --all && git checkout feature && git merge main

F) git pull && git rebase main

Answer: D

Explanation: Rebasing a feature branch onto the main branch is a common practice to keep the feature branch up to date with the latest changes from the main branch. The correct sequence involves checking out the feature branch and then rebasing it onto the main branch. However, before doing this, it's crucial to ensure that the local representation of the main branch is current by fetching updates from the remote repository. Therefore, the sequence git checkout feature && git fetch origin && git rebase origin/main ensures that the feature branch is rebased onto the latest version of the main branch as it exists in the remote repository, helping to avoid conflicts and integration issues during the subsequent merge.

Q397: True or False: When working with Git submodules, the git submodule update command will automatically fetch and update the submodule to the latest commit on the default branch of the submodule's repository.
A) True

B) False

Answer: B

Explanation: The statement is false because the git submodule update command does not automatically fetch and update the submodule to the latest commit on the default branch. Instead, it updates the submodule to the commit specified in the superproject's configuration. Submodules are intended to point to specific commits rather than tracking branches or the latest commits, which provides a stable and consistent development environment. If you need to update a submodule to the latest commit on a branch, you would typically need to enter the submodule's directory and perform a git checkout or git pull to update it manually to the desired commit or branch.

Q398: You are working for a cloud service company that provides custom virtual machine images to various clients. The company wants to automate the deployment of these images using a configuration management system. You are tasked with creating Jinja2 templates that will generate configuration files based on the client's needs. The configurations should include different services and settings, which can vary depending on the client's subscription level. For example, clients with premium subscriptions get additional services enabled. How would you structure a Jinja2 template to conditionally include these premium services only for premium clients?

A) Use Jinja2's built-in {% include %} directive to always include all services and use comments to disable them for non-premium clients.

B) Use Jinja2's {% if %} directive to conditionally include services based on a subscription variable.

C) Always generate all service configurations and include a separate script to enable or disable them post-deployment.

D) Use Jinja2's {% for %} loop to iterate over a list of services, conditionally enabling them based on service level.

E) Create separate Jinja2 templates for each subscription level and select the appropriate one during deployment.

F) Use Jinja2 filters to manipulate service levels directly within the template.

Answer: B

Explanation: In this scenario, the most efficient way to handle conditional inclusion of services is by using the {% if %} directive. This allows the template to dynamically include or exclude sections based on the value of a variable, such as the client's subscription level. By defining a variable that indicates whether a client is premium or not, you can use {% if ispremium %} to include premium services only for those clients. This method is efficient, reduces redundancy, and ensures that the correct configurations are generated based on the client's subscription level. Using separate templates or post-deployment scripts, as suggested in other options, would increase complexity and maintenance overhead.

Q399: When using Jinja2 for templating within a Linux environment, which of the following Jinja2 filters could you use to convert a string to lowercase within a template?

A) upper

B) lower

C) capitalize

D) title

E) striptags

F) int

Answer: B

Explanation: The lower filter in Jinja2 is specifically used to convert a string to lowercase. This is particularly useful when you need to ensure that string comparisons are case-insensitive or when you need to standardize the format of strings within your templates. The upper filter, in contrast, converts strings to uppercase, and filters like capitalize or title change the string's capitalization in other ways. Knowing the appropriate filter to use is crucial for string manipulation tasks in Jinja2 templates.

Q400: True/False: In Jinja2, the {% for %} loop can be used to iterate over a dictionary's keys and values without any additional filters or directives.

A) True

B) False

Answer: A

Explanation: Jinja2's {% for %} loop is quite versatile and can indeed be used to iterate over both keys and values of a dictionary directly. When you loop over a dictionary using {% for key, value in mydict.items() %}, Jinja2 provides direct access to both the keys and the values. This makes it very straightforward to generate content dynamically based on dictionary data without needing additional filters or directives. This capability is particularly useful in generating configuration files or other structured data formats where key-value pairs dictate the configuration options.

www.ingramcontent.com/pod-product-compliance
Lightning Source LLC
LaVergne TN
LVHW051434050326
832903LV00030BD/3078